HOBBSY
A Life in Cricket

Robin Hobbs

First published in Great Britain by
VON KRUMM PUBLISHING
31 Highcroft Villas
Brighton BN1 5PS
www.vonkrummpublishing.co.uk

A CIP record of this book is available from the British Library.

Cover and all interior graphic design by Lottie Warren & Patrick Ferriday

Printed and Bound in King's Lynn by Biddles

ISBN 978-0-9567321-7-0

HOBBSY

A Life in Cricket

Rob Kelly

von Krumm publishing

Foreword

When I started my career, I was very fortunate to enter an Essex dressing room that was led by the legendary Tonker Taylor. He had nurtured some considerable Essex cricketing talent since his appointment as Essex captain in the late 1960s. His team contained not one spinner but three, all having different attributes and characters.

What a difference from today's modern game where you are lucky to see a lone spinner in most county sides up-and-down the country. More often than not, the said spin bowler owes his place in the XI to the fact that he is quite handy with the willow.

The Essex spin triplets were all brilliant specialists in my eyes. David Acfield, off-break bowler and a Cambridge Blue; his stock in trade was to bowl tight and give the batsman nothing – maidens bring pressure and pressure brings wickets. Ray East, left-arm orthodox, the joker in the pack; whereas Ackers was the 'Ernie Wise' straight man character, Easty was the 'Eric Morecambe' of county cricket – he would always be getting up to various shenanigans on the field interspersed with some skilful and underrated left-arm spin bowling. These two great characters would underpin Essex's first county championship title in 1979. To complete the trio was R. N. S. Hobbs who was the senior pro of the three.

I looked up to Rob as an Essex great, he was very helpful to me as a young player making my way in the game. In my book he played the game the right way; he enjoyed his cricket but gave 100 per cent on the field to the point where he represented his country at Test level between 1967 and 1971. Leg-spin bowling is a tough art to master and only the best survive in the testing atmosphere of county cricket. He was the last English leg spinner to take over 1000 first-class wickets in his career with a best of 8 for 63 at an average of 27.09. His first-class strike rate of 56.7 ranks with any spinner of his generation. I was very lucky, I learnt my batting skills against the turning ball by playing and practising against the East, Acfield, Hobbs triumvirate, three fantastic exponents of the art of spin.

I am honoured and delighted to write this foreword for Robin's book. I salute him, he is without doubt one of Essex's finest. He was one of the cricketers who set the foundations for the club's future success, and, more importantly, set the style of Essex cricket which remains today.

Graham Gooch – February 2018

Chapter One

The quicker he bowled it, the more I deposited him over the boundary.

IT WAS A cricket match to look forward to, the highlight of the summer. Robin Hobbs, now in his 16th season as a professional cricketer, was still as full of eager anticipation as he had been when he'd first begun following the sport as a schoolboy. Matches against touring Test sides were big events and in the summer of 1975 Essex would be hosting the Australians.

A few months earlier Australia, spearheaded by Dennis Lillee and Jeff Thomson, had blown England away 4-1 in the Ashes down under. Now, in the return series, they were leading 1-0 with one to play. The final Test at The Oval would begin just two days after the end of the Essex match. Lillee, McCosker and the Chappell brothers were rested but seven of the team that would go on to draw that final Test featured against Essex under the captaincy of Rod Marsh whose usual duties behind the stumps would be performed by reserve 'keeper Richie Robinson.

The match started on Saturday 23 August with the second and third days' play on the Monday and Tuesday. On Sunday Essex would be playing a John Player Sunday League match against Hampshire.

The crowd was larger than usual and there was a good atmosphere even though by this stage the tourists were winding down, having already played a World Cup, three Tests and several county matches since arriving in England at the end of May. Among the spectators at Chelmsford was 13-year-old Peter Smart, eager to watch the Australian side again after seeing them a few weeks earlier at Lord's in the second Test. It was Peter's first visit to the county ground with his father Colin, and he was fascinated by the green oasis in the centre of Chelmsford. The ground, which had been purchased by Essex only a few years earlier, was still largely underdeveloped, the only modern addition at that stage being the pavilion. Wooden benching, just a few rows high, stretched along the Hospital side of the ground, there was a mobile scoreboard and a selection of chairs of all shapes and sizes around the boundary completed the scene.

As Robin recalls, Marsh and the Australians wholeheartedly entered into the spirit of the occasion.

It was played in a real festival way; Marsh was bloody good as captain against us and played it in the proper spirit, but they were always going to win. It was

1

sponsored by a champagne company and two or three of the Aussies slept in the marquee, they never went back to the hotel. It was a fun event but the cricket was still fairly serious.

Having won the toss, the Australian openers Alan Turner and Bruce Laird justified Marsh's decision to bat first as they put on 103 for the first wicket before Robin trapped Turner lbw for 33. Laird went on to score 127 and Ross Edwards weighed in with 101 before the Australians declared on 365-6. In reply Essex lost both openers with only 23 on the scoreboard before Ken McEwan and Keith Fletcher saw them through to 75 for 2 at the close on day one. The following day Essex played, and lost to, Hampshire in the Sunday League at Chelmsford during which Fletcher was struck by a ball from Andy Roberts. Fletcher was unable to resume his innings against the Australians on Monday due to a badly bruised left shoulder and in his absence Robin would lead the side for the remainder of the match.

At the start of play on the second day, Graham Gooch joined Ken McEwan in Fletcher's place and the pair added 75 to the score before McEwan was bowled for 71. Gooch scored 68 before he was stumped off Ashley Mallett. Keith Boyce and Neil Smith put together a half-century stand but Robin only managed five before he was caught off the bowling of Jim Higgs. Once Boyce had been run out for an entertaining 79, Essex declared, eight wickets down and 27 runs behind the Australians who then began their second innings with the best opening partnership of the tour with Turner and Laird putting together 185. Essex, and their stand-in captain, were right up against it.

I led the side out on the last morning and I thought I don't fancy this. I'd bowled 30 odd overs in the first innings – David Acfield bowled about the same at the other end – two for 116 and so I thought I'd better bowl, show willing, I didn't want to. Doug Walters hit me all over Chelmsford, I bowled eleven overs for 73, I then managed to sneak myself off after that and put Stuart Turner on.

Walters went on to score 61 not out before the Australians declared four wickets down on 325, setting Essex a target of 353 to win.

Always likely to be a tall order the challenge was made near impossible by the continued absence of Fletcher plus the addition to the injury list of Brian Edmeades. Essex's slim hope of victory looked even less likely once Jeff Thomson and Max Walker had ripped the heart out of the innings reducing them to 109-5, effectively 109-7. With 244 runs needed to win and only three wickets in hand, Robin stubbed out his Embassy Regal, pulled on his gloves, picked up his trusty Gray Nicolls and headed out from the pavilion to join opening batsman Brian

Hardie in the middle. As Robin strolled out, Colin Smart turned to his son Peter suggesting it wouldn't be long now before Essex would be all out – any similarities Robin shared with Sir Jack Hobbs began and ended with the surname.

Robin played and missed the first couple of balls he faced and was lucky to survive the over.

Walker was bowling seamers at a bit quicker than medium pace. He was in the middle of an over when I went in to bat and Marsh signalled and said "Bring Walker's sweaters down he's only going to have another two balls". So Walker bowled these other two balls which I missed and then Marsh put the spinners on and he kept them on.

With Thomson – the scourge of England in the 1974/75 Ashes – out of the attack, Robin would be facing the off spin of Mallett and leg spin of Higgs. Brian Hardie recalls the pair of them agreeing it was a lost cause but that they would do their best to put on a show for the crowd. Having taken five balls before getting off the mark with a four, Robin played watchfully to reach 11 not out from 15 balls before freeing his arms. He'd decided to go down fighting and after hitting his first six off Mallett, which sailed over mid-wicket, he then struck four successive boundaries off Higgs, all sweetly racing off the bat. He brought up his fifty with a four: despite the circumspect start it had taken just 30 balls and 32 minutes.

"I was a bloody good square cutter." Richie Robinson seems to agree.

Having momentarily paused to acknowledge the crowd, Robin went on the assault again, launching Mallett for two sixes in a row over long-on. The bank-holiday crowd at Chelmsford was enjoying the fireworks as time and again Robin advanced down the wicket and launched the ball out of the ground. The crowd might have been enjoying it but one of the Australian bowlers wasn't entering into the spirit of it Robin remembers.

Ashley Mallett was bowling from the River End and he was tearing his hair out, but the quicker he bowled it the more I deposited him over the boundary. By contrast, Jim Higgs was treating it like a benefit game, he was at the Hayes Close End bowling gentle leg spinners. It was friendly at one end and not so friendly at the other.

Mallett's mood was not helped when he was hit for 27 off one over as the partnership grew. Robin's approach was generally to charge down the pitch and swing a cross bat towards long-on. It was highly effective. When Mallett and Higgs changed line or length, Robin was sufficiently quick to react with a square cut, a sweep or an improvised scoop into the mid-wicket area. He never offered a real chance and middled virtually everything. One huge pull was caught by the Essex number 10 – the next man in – John Lever, sitting ten rows back in the crowd. Lever, like everyone else, was enjoying the show.

'The ground's not very big but Hobbsy was a good timer of the ball and Mallett and Higgs took quite a seeing to. I think the game was done and dusted really but he just took them to the cleaners. Every time they pitched it up he thought I've got nothing to lose so he just smashed it, and it was very clean hitting, it wasn't a case of being dropped a few times here, there and everywhere, he just hit it out of the ground.'

Hardie remembers Marsh encouraging his spinners even though Robin was hitting them far and hard. 'I can remember him geeing them on, "Keep tossing it up Rowdy, you'll get him soon" – but it just became some of the cleanest hitting of a cricket ball I've ever seen.'

Robin smashed Higgs through extra-cover to the boundary and two more sixes followed off successive balls, one of them – a towering straight drive – cleared the sight-screen and a row of trees and broke a house window at the Hayes Close End. After another six and a missed stumping, Robin launched Mallett out of the ground and into the River Can which flows beside the ground and the ball was lost. Four sixes were struck off Mallett, all of them well clear of the fence at the River End of the ground, at least 80 yards from the wicket, and his longest hit finished up on the river bank 90 yards away. It was all too much for some elderly spectators basking in the August sunshine as two fainted and another was taken to hospital. Whilst some of the older spectators were struggling with all the excitement, 13-year-old Peter Smart was loving it: 'the ball was flying over our heads at the River End – straight into the river, I don't recall how many went in but at the time it seemed like every other ball.'

Neil Burns – who went on to become a professional cricketer playing over 200 first-class matches for Essex, Somerset and Leicestershire – was nine years old at the time and had gone to the game with his friends. Robin's innings was totally different to anything else the boys had witnessed at a cricket match. 'There was a degree of disbelief between me and my friends' says Burns – "Oh wow, there's a six. There's another one!" he remembers excitedly. 'It was almost like each one we saw was going to be the last and then there was another one.'

The atmosphere was electric and Hardie was enjoying it too having been reduced to the role of a virtual spectator: 'I was amazed to start with and then from when he was thirty-odd I hardly faced another ball' he says. Robin hadn't quite realised he'd scored his runs so quickly until he found himself on 96 and thoughts of the fastest hundred of the summer entered his mind. Garry Sobers had achieved the feat the previous season and Robin was now on the verge of matching one of cricket's greatest players. He waited as Higgs approached from the Hayes Close End to deliver the next ball; as it was released Robin picked it as being slightly short of a length and rocking back he connected sweetly, square cutting the ball to the boundary to reach his hundred. In the 45 balls it had taken he'd hit 7 sixes and 12 fours. In 12 minutes he'd blitzed his way from 50 to 100 in just 15 balls, an incredible sequence which ran: 6,6,1,4,6,6,0,6,1,2,1,0,6,1,4.

At that moment I felt euphoric, to get a hundred, I felt absolutely over the moon. It was like a dream, it still is really. Silly isn't it, I mean who would have imagined it? There was a decent crowd there that day and I shook my bat all around the ground to acknowledge them. It was one of those things, 45 minutes is a very short period of time and it all happened so quickly, it was like being in a bubble.

The euphoria of the moment was interrupted, and Robin was brought back down to earth by a brash Australian voice: "OK mate," growled Rod Marsh, "we've had a f***ing 'nough of you, you've had your fun now get out otherwise I'm going to bring Thomson on to bowl a few at you."

Marsh had kept Mallett and Higgs on but had grown tired of watching Robin dispatch his spinners to all corners of the ground. Jeff Thomson had been fielding at third-man throughout his innings and to Robin – not the bravest of batsmen – the prospect of facing one of the fastest bowlers of all time, wasn't a challenge to be relished and he wasted no time in taking Marsh's advice.

I promptly got out the next ball off Higgs. I skied it and Bruce Laird at long-on dived full length to take the catch and off I marched. I got out like a coward. I can say that I played against Australia when he was playing but I wasn't going to face Mr Thomson, sod that!

Robin left the field to a standing ovation and was mobbed by hundreds of schoolboys who ran on to the field to congratulate this most improbable century maker. The praise he received from Essex chairman Doug Insole was more reserved. "I got a right bollocking from Doug having holed out to long-on, he said to me 'Well played but you've let your mate down there.'"

The official Essex CCC scorebook entry – 44 minutes of mayhem; 7 sixes,12 fours and a strike rate of 217.39.

Brian Hardie had batted throughout the innings for his 88 not out but was denied a century when the last three wickets fell in a cluster. The sixth-wicket stand between Hardie and Robin had been worth 133 but once Robin had been dismissed, Higgs had next batsman John Lever caught by Thomson at mid-off for a duck and last man David Acfield headed out to the middle wondering how he could follow Robin's pyrotechnics. 'The general manager [Peter Edwards] actually asked me to try and block until tea', recalls Acfield, 'I said you're joking, aren't you? I cannot block after that!' Acfield hit a four and a six before, attempting another big hit, he was stumped as Mallett finally recorded a wicket and ended up with figures of one for 76 from his 7.4 overs.

Australia won by 98 runs and after the match Robin had to deal with the press, eager for the inside story of his century.

> At the lunch interval after the Australians declared the press were shouting out to me and David Acfield as we walked round the boundary – "Do you want to know your bowling figures?" "No thank you." I replied. After I got the hundred they were all clamouring at the door asking how did you plan your innings and all this rubbish. They'd changed their tune, now they all wanted personal interviews.

Ironically the speed of Robin's century eclipsed one scored in 58 minutes by his team-mate Keith Boyce on the same ground against Leicestershire in May. Boyce joked in *The Daily Express* 'I enjoyed it really. Robin's just set me a new target. I'll go for it against Northants tomorrow.'

Talking to the press about the hundred immediately after the game Robin remarked:

> I went out there determined to have a good slog and to entertain the crowd. I had no idea I was beating Boyce's time because I had no sense of time. The Australians played along with the spirit of the game.

A number of people suggested that the hundred was a mockery but Ashley Mallett was trying his hardest and Robin's innings was virtually chanceless with some clean, big hitting. As far as Robin is concerned it was a fairly genuine hundred, although the Australians were using spin bowlers they weren't tossing it up for him to score declaration runs, they were trying to get him out as David Acfield recalls.

> 'Jim Higgs, who certainly wasn't short of confidence at the time, came out with a comment to me at the bar the night before saying that he thought one-day cricket really was a joke and that he would get six for 20 every time he bowled in it. And I did ask him how he would play in it against a number nine batsman, therefore when Robin went down the wicket at him, he absolutely murdered him, hit him straight into the Hayes Close End at Chelmsford every ball. I've always said there

were two good, class spinners playing in that game, Robin actually hit them, they were trying and he hit them a very long way indeed. We couldn't believe it, he kept on going.'

Reflecting on his innings more than 40 years later, Robin gives an insight into his approach to batting:

> *I always thought I was a better batsman than I was. I tried to bat correctly, I was a bloody good square cutter and driver but anything above medium pace I wasn't very good at, but I was better than a slogger. I wasn't an out and out rabbit. I had a carefree approach; if it was there to be hit I'd have a go at it. Technically I wasn't correct so it was a matter of scoring from the most opportunities that I could before I lost my wicket. I wasn't a great defender, I took a lot more risks because I was a tail-ender, I had nothing to lose.*

This was how Robin played against the Australians, it seemed like the right occasion, and on that day it came off, much to the delight of the crowd. He'd wanted to entertain, and he certainly achieved that, his cavalier approach also left an indelible impression on some of the younger spectators that day. It was Robin's batting, not his bowling, which initially inspired Neil Burns and similarly Peter Smart credits Robin as a big influence in his love for the game.

> 'I will always remember that day and thank him for playing a large part in making me love the game – played in the right spirit for the benefit of the crowd. We were not used to rapidly-scored 100s and for a 13-year-old boy it was just amazing. Robin Hobbs became a hero to me – but not for the reasons he should have been. I know he was one of only a few great leg-break bowlers, and it certainly made me more interested in the leggies. Above all though, it showed that cricket could entertain and I was hooked.'

An amazing day for both Peter and Neil was capped by the Australians willingness to sign autographs immediately after the match ended and both vividly remember Ross Edwards pulling up a chair on the boundary, chatting happily and signing autographs for a line of boys which snaked around the outfield. Neil – having broken his wrist earlier in the summer – was able to get his plaster cast signed by Edwards and all the Australians and wore it with pride for the remainder of the summer.

In the evening there was a champagne reception held by the sponsors in one of the marquees. One of the biggest disappointments for Robin was that his dad Reg, who lived very close to Chelmsford, had gone home before he went in to bat. Robin's wife Isabel also had the misfortune to miss his innings but made it along to the reception where he received a crate of champagne as a reward from the sponsors. The next day Robin went down to Martin's newsagents in Ingatestone. Modesty prevented him from going in so Isabel went and bought all the papers which revelled in describing his whirlwind innings against the Australians. Any notion that he might get carried away by the sensational headlines was quickly dashed as Robin recalls his next visit to the crease following the hundred.

I was left out of the next game against Northants so I went and played for Chingford on the Saturday against Ilford. I was batting at number four and this little lad ran up to bowl. I played forward and it knocked middle stump out of the ground. I got nought, bowled first ball by a boy of 14! I'd gone from one extreme to another, what a leveller.

With only a handful of Championship matches left to play, Robin was in pole position to win the Lawrence Challenge Trophy and £250 for the fastest hundred of the summer. Neither Keith Boyce or anyone else that season was able to better his remarkable effort which had seen him score, at the time, the fifth-fastest century in first-class cricket with Percy Fender's all-time record of 35 minutes for Surrey v Northants in 1920 leading the way. A dinner was held in Robin's honour as winner of the Lawrence Trophy at Quaglino's in London on 22 April 1976 and the award was presented, quite fittingly, by Percy Fender.

Robin receives the Walter Lawrence Trophy from Percy Fender, the 1920 winner in 35 minutes.

It had been a remarkable achievement for the veteran leg spinner and, with added poignancy as, unbeknown to all at the time, it turned out to be Robin's last first-class appearance at home for Essex, the club he loved so much and had dreamed of playing for ever since he was a boy.

Chapter Two

The thought of being able to play cricket for 15-20 years; what a life that would be if you could succeed.

ROBIN NICHOLAS STUART Hobbs was born on 8 May 1942 in Chippenham, Wiltshire where his father, Reg, was stationed with the RAF. Robin was only four weeks old when he and his mother Betty had to move to Scotland to follow Reg who had been sent to a new posting in Dundee.

"My father's one love was flying", recalls Robin.

> *He qualified as a pilot and was a Flight Lieutenant during the Second World War. He flew Typhoons and Hurricanes and did a few raids into France blowing up so called Red Cross trains that were actually German trains under camouflage. Then he became a trainer and had numerous postings around the UK. The worst thing he ever did, he said to me many times, was coming out of the RAF. When the war finished I think a lot of them had had enough but he always regretted coming out because he loved flying aircraft.*

When Reg left the RAF the family settled in Essex and he resumed his pre-war occupation as a car salesman before buying and running a grocery shop in Dagenham. At that time the town was home to the Ford motor plant, the largest in Europe, producing models such as the Zephyr, Cortina and Anglia. At its peak it employed 40,000 workers; it was almost as if the whole of Dagenham worked there. Everything revolved around Ford and for miles around the glow from the plant's furnaces could be seen on the skyline 24 hours a day.

Robin enjoyed his early life and although rationing was still in place in the UK the family were never short of food, courtesy of Reg's shop.

> *I used to help in my dad's shop on Sundays. You were allowed to open from 9am until 1pm but in those days you were only allowed to sell certain items – not everything that was in the grocery shop – you could only sell things like perishables which were likely to go off. I used to enjoy serving when I was a kid, helping out the old boy.*

It was natural that Robin would have an inborn love for cricket as Reg had played for Chingford Cricket Club and his uncle Frank had been good enough to play for the Middlesex 2nd XI before the war. Throughout the years Robin's enthusiasm for the game has remained undiminished.

I've always read as much as I can and I've always been a bit of an anorak as far as cricket is concerned. When I was a boy I collected autographs, cigarette cards, anything to do with cricket. My dad gave me my first ever Wisden and I knew virtually every player's score on every page because I read it so often.

Like many boys in the 1940s and 1950s, Robin's favourite player was Denis Compton closely followed by Peter May. Summers revolved around cricket which still held mass appeal in the years immediately following the War, and there was always great excitement and anticipation when overseas teams arrived on tour as Robin fondly recalls.

In those days you had proper cricket tours. Every country that came to over here played all the counties at least once. They were four-month tours ending either playing against Arthur Gilligan's XI in Sussex or Tom Pearce's XI in Scarborough.

Whenever the opportunity arose, Robin would go and watch the tourists – it was the highlight of his summer.

I'd go with my dad occasionally but generally I used to go with a couple of mates after school. We'd get off the train at Leyton and go and watch the cricket at the county ground. Years ago tourist matches were watched by thousands, these days they jet touring sides in, play the games and jet them out. Before I became a professional, the only way you got to see what players looked like was if you went to a match. The opening pair for South Africa in the 1950s – Adcock and Heine, who were extremely quick bowlers – were only names to you. Nowadays modern players are on television, you can see cricket around the world every day of the week, you don't need to go and see them.

As well as watching games whenever he got the opportunity and reading all about it in books and magazines, Robin was keen to practise his bowling, which had always been leg spin.

I've always, ever since I can remember, been able to bowl leg breaks. I can remember living in Dagenham, going to Grafton School and bowling leg breaks at the age of seven or eight, it just came naturally to me. I used to practise my spinning action with an apple or orange from my dad's shop. Even up until 10 years ago when I was in my mid-sixties and still playing cricket, I'd sit in front of the television with an apple or an orange if I didn't have a cricket ball and spin it from hand to hand. I spent hours and hours as a boy bowling a ball against the wall of an outbuilding behind dad's shop, he had a lot of outbuildings, lots of walls which I could play my imaginary Test matches against. I had my scorebook and I had Willie Watson batting and Trevor Bailey bowling and I used to throw this ball against the wall and play it back and score runs – I'd spend all day on my own.

After spending hours round the back of his father's shop, Robin then graduated to practising his bowling in the nets.

I used to go down to Central Park in Dagenham, there was Nanny Goat Common and then there was the Dagenham Civic Centre and then the park. I used to go down there from the age of 12 to 14 years old with about 20 balls. They were good nets and the park-keeper used to let me bowl in them. That's what I did when I was that age, that was how I enjoyed myself.

Flight Lieutenant Reg Hobbs.

Without the distraction of television and computer games in the mid-1950s and no brothers or sisters to play with, Robin was content to spend much of his spare time honing his bowling. "I got as much enjoyment out of doing that and that's how I became a bowler, by spending hours just bowling." Robin's regime helped him develop a strong, repeatable action and good muscle memory which he retained in later life. "Even up until my late sixties, if you'd put a blindfold on me I could still pitch six cricket balls within an area the size of a newspaper because I'd done it so often. As a self-confessed cricket anorak, young Robin would keenly follow the fortunes of the English leg spinners of the day.

When I was a boy most county sides had a leg spinner in the side and I used to follow how England leg spinners like Eric Hollies, Doug Wright and Roly Jenkins were doing. I met Roly Jenkins when I was playing in the Birmingham League but he was the only leg spinner I got to meet from that era on a personal basis. I always picked up books or read snippets about the old leg spinners and how leg spin developed in South Africa with the googly bowlers in the early 1900s, Schwarz and Vogler and people like that.

Seeing that leg spinners could have successful first-class careers helped Robin to aspire to a life in cricket. "I never ever thought I'd play for England but I always wanted to be a professional cricketer, I thought I had the ability to do that."

When he wasn't practising or playing, Robin did have other interests outside cricket. Animals and birds always fascinated him and in his youth he built an aviary attached to the shop, where he kept a variety of tropical birds including a toucan. "He was a fine old boy, he lived for years in the garden and was very much king of all of the other birds. It was great fun, I enjoyed and still do enjoy wildlife." Another of his pets, and an inseparable companion,

Betty Hobbs and Robin.

was his Dalmatian dog – Currant Bun. Robin had reared him since he'd fallen down a flight of stairs as a pup which resulted in him having a limp. In the years which followed, Currant Bun would regularly be seen on various Essex cricket grounds, usually lying on the grass waiting for Robin to finish playing for the day. Towards the end of his life his back legs had started to become weak and Robin knew that he didn't have much longer to live when he had to go off to play at Worcestershire in the County Championship. "I knew that he wasn't going to live much longer when I went down to Worcester to play that game", Robin sadly recalls.

> *There used to be a red telephone box there and my dad phoned me during the match to tell me that he'd had to have him put down. He was a smashing dog, most loveable and I've still got photographs of him all round the house. He was such a dear dog and like everything else in life, animals break your heart and he broke my heart that day.*

Robin says that he wasn't very bright at school but he was bright enough to pass the 11-plus exam and make it in to the Raine's Foundation Grammar School for

Boys, Stepney, in September 1953. The family was still living in Dagenham at the time so Robin had to catch a bus each day to and from school.

There were two buses that used to leave Dagenham for Stepney – the A25 and the A23. If I got the A25 it meant walking three miles because that ended up at Stepney Green. The A23 used to go down Commercial Road so it stopped only a 100 yards from the school.

It was at Raine's that Robin met Basil Dowling, an English teacher and someone who was to have a massive influence on his development as a cricketer. Dowling was a New Zealander who moved to Britain in 1952 to begin a career in teaching, having previously been a Presbyterian minister and then a librarian. He was also a keen poet and had a number of his works published not only in Britain and New Zealand but also worldwide. He was also a cricket devotee, his nephew, Graham Dowling, was the New Zealand cricket captain from 1968 to 1972.

Raine's School cricket team. Robin is middle row third from right with Basil Dowling on the right.

With a shared love for the game there was an instant connection between teacher and pupil which Robin fondly recalls:

We were very lucky that Basil Dowling was not only a fine teacher but also a very fine cricket master; he was cricket mad. He was brilliant, if it hadn't have been for him I might not have become a professional.

Dowling organised cricket practice in the playground after school for two hours with the boys and for Robin this was heaven. It was unusual for a school like Raine's to have virtually a full fixture list but Dowling was quite prepared to spend his Saturdays during the summer with the lads sorting out the scoring and umpiring of games. By the time he was 13, Robin was in the first team and eventually went on to captain the school. His vice-captain, Tom Ford, was a good school friend and went on to become captain of Romford and Gidea Park Cricket Club in the 1970s, a highly successful side in Essex.

His time at Raine's was a key point in Robin's development.

> *That's where I started, with the encouragement Basil gave me, and because I had a fair amount of ability I thought that I could go further in the game. The last time I saw Basil I was playing at Arundel many years ago and he was there watching the game.*

Basil Dowling died in 2000 at the age of 90. Writing in the Old Raineian's Newsletter in 2002, Alan Russell, a fellow teacher at Raine's during the 1960s, paid tribute to him. 'I think he must have been one of those teachers who have a gift for encouraging individual pupils and cultivating in them seeds of talents, which they never knew they had. My guess is that hundreds, maybe thousands, of pupils remain grateful to him.' Robin certainly numbered amongst them.

> *Basil was very proud of what I achieved in the game and it was the encouragement he gave me which helped to set me on my way. He gave me the enthusiasm for the game – although I had it to a point – I needed someone like him who was prepared to spend all his time with you. He was a fantastic guy; he did everything for us at Raine's.*

Robin left school in the summer of 1958. His headmaster, Mr Goode, wrote that throughout his school career Robin maintained a moderate position in the 'B' form and that although he was not a brilliant boy he had made definite progress and sat for four subjects at GCE O Level. Even though Mr Goode only rated Robin as an average performer academically he couldn't fault his sporting prowess, noting that in cricket Robin had 'special ability' and that as school cricket captain 'he has shown considerable keenness and determination.'

In his final school year Robin began to play club cricket for Chadwell Heath. Home matches were played at St Chad's Park and it was here that he first displayed his potential as a serious leg spinner and began to attract some attention from the local press. "I've still got the press cutting from when I got eight wickets against a side called Guild Hall. I don't think they were very good but I did get headlines – 'Hobbs bowls out Guild Hall.'" His performances for Chadwell Heath during the summer of 1958 also singled him out for praise in the Essex CCC Annual stating that 'A very promising 15-year-old leg spinner, Robin Hobbs, came into prominence at the latter end of the season, taking 38 wickets…. This also included a hat-trick against Marconi.'

In the autumn of 1958 Robin entered the world of work as an insurance clerk with the Employers Liability Insurance Company on Bouverie Street in the City of London.

> *At the end of the month you used to go up to the top floor to get paid, you'd go into this room and you'd all sit there. This bloke used to get this great tin out and he used to go alphabetically through the names – "Abbot. Bartram. Hobbs."*
> *"Yes sir."*
> *"Come here boy."*
> *He was like bloody Fagin. He'd open this tin, full of brand new pound notes and ten bob notes it was. I used to get paid £22.50 a month.*

Working at Employers Liability also gave him the opportunity to play cricket for them and in one particular match Robin scored a century against another insurance company. This feat earned him a new bat under a scheme operated by the old London evening paper, *The Star,* and an opportunity of meeting a legendary Surrey and England batsman.

> *When I got into work the next day in Bouverie Street they said they were going to award me with a bat and took me straight up the road to Jack Hobbs' sports shop on Fleet Street. I met the great man and he let me pick a bat out; I was so overwhelmed at that age.*

A few years later, when Robin's career began to attract interest from the newspapers, journalists would inevitably make reference to the surname he shared with The Master.

In 1958 Reg Hobbs sold the shop in Dagenham and moved the family to Elm Park. His marriage to Betty was a bit rocky at the time and eventually Reg decided to leave her and moved into a flat in Walthamstow taking Robin with him. Robin didn't see much of his mum until many years later.

She was a good mum, I couldn't fault her. I never had any arguments with her. There were family arguments at times because money was tight in those days. My dad worked very hard and she wanted the better things out of life and he had to strive.

Robin was quite philosophical about his parents splitting up and although he didn't take sides he was happy to stay with Reg.

I was always dad's boy rather than mum's. I never found it traumatic, it was just one of those things which happened, I think it was very traumatic for my mum but that's the way it went unfortunately.

As a result of the split, Robin ending up having to leave Chadwell Heath and joined Reg's old side Chingford, which was to remain his club side for most of his career. The Essex captain at the time, Doug Insole, was at Chingford and the proud link between club and county continues with current Essex players, Dan Lawrence and Jamie Porter.

I actually played quite a number of games with my dad. Even when I went to Chingford as a 17-year-old he was still playing. We put on 200 runs together against Southgate in a B team fixture – I got a hundred and ran him out for 90. I've still got the press cutting – I ran out the old boy! I look back at those times and the times I played with my son Nick as days to be treasured. When I was 17 my dad would have been in his early forties but he was still active and played regularly on Sundays. He was a number four batter and quite a good fielder.

Another influential figure in Robin's upbringing and his development as a cricketer was his uncle Frank although he didn't get to see him that often during his childhood as Frank worked in Royston for Johnson Mattey – the gold and bullion company. Frank was a member at Essex and went to watch matches regularly when Robin turned professional.

"My uncle was a very good cricketer, far better than my dad" says Robin.

I've got photographs of him playing at Lord's against Ken Farnes – the great Essex fast bowler – in the Club Cricket Conference. Frank was a very good club cricketer; he played for Finchley and was a solid number-four batsman. During the 1930s he was highlighted as one of the best amateurs in the Middlesex and Surrey area. He played a few games for Middlesex seconds and then one night they went out on a binge in Hove and they moved a load of road signs and took them all back to their hotel. Poor old Frank, him and four others, got banned and never played for

Middlesex again. I remember him as a very sound brainy guy and a great listener. I used to discuss things with him far more than with my father.

Robin was fortunate to be nurtured through his early cricketing development and at Chingford he received great encouragement which held him in good stead during his career as a professional cricketer – something which he has never forgotten.

> *I owe a great deal to Ken Dowding, my captain during many of my years at Chingford and also to Cliff Crafer, who captained me in the 2nd XI. I was very lucky in 1959 to find the Chingford wicket thoroughly responsive to spin and managed, with help from the fielders and dear old Reg Rowlands as wicket-keeper, to take over 100 wickets on Saturdays and Sundays.*

Looking back, Robin considers those summer months in the late 1950s as really happy days. He lived for cricket and his biggest dread was of rain falling on a Friday and washing out the two days of playing he'd looked forward to all week.

As much as he loved his cricket, Robin, like all teenagers, sometimes engaged in a bit of mischief. "I weren't the nicest in those days, I got away with murder" he remembers with a hint of guilt. "If there was any trouble I was always in the front of it but never got the blame; I could do no wrong – 'It couldn't have been him', people would say – 'he's too nice a bloke!'"

Robin may not have got noticed for some of the pranks he was involved in but around this time he was getting noticed for his cricket. Reporting on Chingford's season in 1959 the *Essex County Cricket Club Annual* noted that 'A promising 16-year-old leg-break bowler was discovered in R. Hobbs who was promoted to the 1st XI during the latter part of the season.'

This new-found attention was something Robin was becoming aware of and thoroughly enjoyed.

> *There I was at 17 playing in top-class club cricket, I took 100 wickets and I thought I was the dog's bollocks. People were coming to see me play and I felt like the icing on the cake. I was occasionally getting a bit of coverage in the press and that's when Kent took an interest.*

Essex had seemed interested in taking Robin on at that stage but with eight spin bowlers already at the county, he felt his best option would be to approach Kent who had been without a quality spinner since Doug Wright had retired in 1957. Kent had advertised in the newspapers that they were holding trials and so on Wednesday 9 September 1959 Reg drove Robin down to Canterbury to attend a

Rockabilly rebel – Robin later traded the Buddy Holly
hairdo for a Beatles cut.

trial along with 100 other boys who all harboured the same dream of a career as
a professional cricketer. It was a bright sunny day and the boys all tried hard to
impress in the net sessions which were overseen by Les Ames, the former Kent
and England wicket-keeper-batsman and the county's secretary/manager. At the
end of the day Reg drove Robin back to Walthamstow and the pair of them
anxiously awaited news.

Within days of the trial, a letter, hand-signed by Ames, arrived addressed
to Robin. Ames wrote that he was 'favourably impressed' by Robin's bowling and
invited him to attend Kent's indoor cricket school at Eltham Swimming Baths
during the winter. Robin was elated and still has the letter.

*I think that at that age the thought of becoming a professional cricketer was utopia.
You didn't think about what the wages were going to be, just the thought of being
able to play cricket for 15-20 years; what a life that would be if you could succeed.*

Reg and Frank were both thrilled and encouraged him on this next step of his career – "If that's what you want to do Rob" they told him "go and do it, have a go."

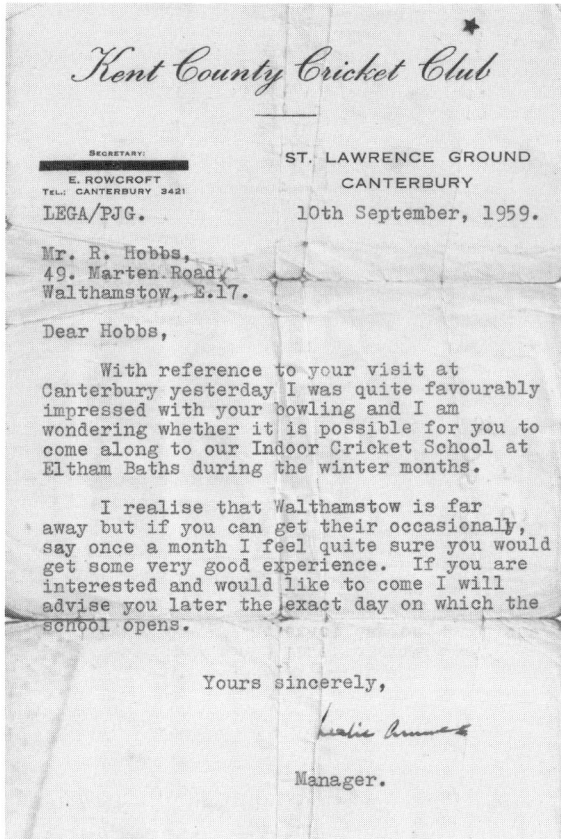

Kent County Cricket Club

SECRETARY:
E. ROWCROFT
TEL.: CANTERBURY 3421

ST. LAWRENCE GROUND
CANTERBURY

LEGA/PJG.

10th September, 1959.

Mr. R. Hobbs,
49. Marten Road,
Walthamstow, E.17.

Dear Hobbs,

     With reference to your visit at Canterbury yesterday I was quite favourably impressed with your bowling and I am wondering whether it is possible for you to come along to our Indoor Cricket School at Eltham Baths during the winter months.

     I realise that Walthamstow is far away but if you can get their occasionally, say once a month I feel quite sure you would get some very good experience. If you are interested and would like to come I will advise you later the exact day on which the school opens.

Yours sincerely,

Leslie Ames

Manager.

"Dear Hobbs" – an invitation from Les Ames and the opportunity to become a man of Kent.

Robin eagerly accepted Les Ames' invitation and during the winter of 1959/60 he pedalled his bicycle on a 13-mile journey via the Blackwall Tunnel to attend Kent's indoor cricket school. There was no real coaching at these sessions, just nets, but it gave Robin the opportunity to show what he could do with the ball. Afterwards he was spared having to cycle home as Reg would pick him and his bicycle up in his Austin A30 van. Robin was only able to make it along to about six of the sessions that winter but this wasn't a problem for Les Ames. In his invitation Ames had said that he realised Walthamstow was far away but even if Robin could only make it to nets occasionally it would be very good experience for him. Kent had seen enough and, having been impressed with Robin's skill and attitude, Ames asked Essex whether they could sign him. At the time, with Robin being an Essex boy, Kent were obliged to approach their county rivals before a signing could be made.

Former England allrounder Trevor Bailey was still playing for Essex at the time and combined his playing duties with the role of club secretary. Essex had missed the opportunity of signing the great Jack Hobbs and were now in danger of repeating the mistake with a promising young cricketer sharing the same surname. Trevor Bailey and Doug Insole, now in his final year as Essex captain, were not prepared to allow history to repeat itself. Despite the presence of two leg spinners in Bill Greensmith and Ronnie Carr, plus the availability of a third in the West Indian Dr Bertie Clarke, Essex decided to offer Robin a place on the playing staff.

Events had taken an interesting turn, Robin was happy that his home county had made a move for him but playing opportunities would not come easy.

Essex had shown no interest in signing me but when Kent did that's when Trevor Bailey stepped in. I think they probably thought we might as well sign him and pay him £5 a week just in case. It was ridiculous really because back then Essex were playing on green wickets and had plenty of spinners on the staff anyway.

It would be an achievement for Robin to break into the Essex second XI let alone the first team.

He had taken his first steps to becoming a professional cricketer but could things have turned out differently if he had signed for Kent? In later years Robin was selected for a couple of overseas tours managed by Les Ames giving him the opportunity to reflect with Ames on how he'd slipped out of Kent's grasp.

Les was such a nice man and he did remember when I showed him the letter he'd written to me back in 1959. Because of the set-up at Kent I don't suppose that I would have lasted more than two years, I'd have ended up on the scrap heap.

My third year at Essex was not very good and if I'd been with any other county I'd have got the sack. A friend of mine, David Baker, who was also a leg spinner, joined Kent just about the same time I joined Essex. Kent were desperate to get a spinner so they signed him up. He had a reasonable time in his first and second years but there was this certain person at Kent who either liked you or he didn't. He sacked David Baker and I'm sure if I'd have joined Kent he would have sacked me too. There were characters around in those days, much more than there are now, who were all important in county cricket and whose word went. If they didn't like you were out the door. I was very fortunate, I could have ended up like David Baker, gone and forgotten.

For the time being though Robin had achieved his ambition of becoming a professional cricketer. A greater challenge now lay ahead – how would he get from being ninth- to first-choice spinner at Essex?

Chapter Three

The outlook looked very bleak indeed for my getting into the first team.

IN 1960 BILL Greensmith was the first-choice leg spinner at Essex. Hailing from Middleborough, Greensmith had made his debut in 1947 at the age of just 16 but it had taken time to establish himself as a regular due to National Service and, more significantly, the presence of leg-break bowler Peter Smith in the first team. When Smith, with 1610 wickets to his name, retired at the end of the 1951 season, Greensmith was finally able to cement a place in the first team. Having only just joined the playing staff, 17 year old Robin was expected to serve a lengthy apprenticeship in the second XI and it was likely to be some time before he could hope to fulfil his ambition of playing for the county.

The second XI was captained by 45-year-old Arnold Quick, a fine striker of the ball for an amateur cricketer but someone who was never a regular at Essex due to commitments with his printing business in Clacton. Like many of his contemporaries, Quick had lost the best years of his playing career to the Second World War in which he served as an officer in the Royal Marines.

Quick was a handsome man, well turned out and his military manner could make some of the young professionals quiver in their footwear. One of his oft heard remarks was "Clean boots boys, clean boots." but, according to Robin, underneath, Quick had a real soft heart.

I played a lot of second-team cricket and got on so well with him in the end. We played one game up at Coalville against Leicestershire and they hadn't seen me bowl before and he said to me "I'm not going to bowl you in the first innings Hobbs."
"Right sir." I replied
"I'm not here for the second innings, I've got to go to Russia on the second day, I won't be in the country and I'll leave the captaincy with Roger Luckin. So I'm not going to bowl you in the first innings because you're our secret weapon."
Well, he'd flown off to Russia and the secret weapon let him down because I got one for 73 off 18 overs – they sorted me out.

Joining Robin on the Essex staff around the same time were Brian Edmeades and Keith Fletcher who were to become regular team-mates in later years. In his autobiography, Fletcher said that the new professionals were the lowest of the low. 'Class distinction was rife….The capped players had their own dressing-room and we were not allowed to enter unless they wanted us for an errand. Our room was shared with the second-team capped staff, and there were times when it seemed we were scarcely allowed to speak to them.'

Against this backdrop of segregation, which was to prevail in cricket for many years to come, Fletcher described the challenge which lay ahead for the young players. 'When I joined, there were thirty on the staff. A lad like me, however promising, had to wait his turn, and it was two years before I made any significant progress.'

To a large extent Robin and the other young professionals were learning on the job. There wasn't much opportunity, if any, for coaching or practice in the early 1960s, most of the time was spent on the field. Robin would be playing second-team games and Club & Ground games (a mixture of Essex playing staff and ground staff), sometimes as many as 30 times a season. Then there would be club games for Chingford on Saturdays and Sundays.

Strong friendships were formed during the long hours spent together in the field and club houses.

> *Lads like Terry Kent and Peter Lindsey – a great spinner and someone who I thought would go all the way to the top – we all got on well together, I was friends with them all. There was only one guy who was really not the nicest person and that was Peter Spicer who bullied a lot of the younger players and came to a very untimely death in a car accident in 1969. He was a chap with so much ability, a fine left-handed batsman he could bowl slow left arm or he could open by bowling swing, he was the only one you felt you should keep your distance from but the rest of them were all smashing lads.*

Most of the young players lived within five or six miles of each other in Walthamstow, Buckhurst Hill or Woodford Wells. Unless they were playing away with the second XI most nights they would get together for a few beers at various cricket clubs or pubs. Drink driving in the early 1960s was not a social taboo, it wasn't until November 1964 that the first advert warning of the dangers was aired.

> *You never worried about drink driving in those days. I wasn't a big drinker anyway, I'd have a couple of pints, quite happily over three or four hours, I always drove, never had any second thoughts about it at the time.*

Hours spent together driving to the various grounds around Essex and beyond were part and parcel of the job for Robin and his team-mates. Before Chelmsford became the permanent home of Essex they led a nomadic existence, playing games all around the county at grounds such as Clacton, Brentwood, Leyton and Southend. The players would generally pile in with whoever had a car in order to get to games and on occasion they might be one of the seven or eight who crammed into Frank Rist's estate car. Rist worked for next to nothing on the coaching staff and was a popular figure at the club. He'd been a professional footballer with Charlton and Colchester and had played 65 first-class games for Essex. Rist kept wicket in the tour match against Australia at Southend in 1948, a game in which the tourists racked up 721. "He was a lovely guy," recalls Robin, "he made the best cup of tea in the world, big pots of it he used to make. He was a great taxi driver taking us around to all the games. He wasn't a great coach but he was certainly a great guy."

Robin went on to make his second-XI debut on 16 May 1960 against Leicestershire at Oakham, but preparation for the game was far from ideal:

I was supposed to have been picked up along with Peter Lindsey from Epping. We waited there for three or four hours but Willie Dow – a quick bowler from Scotland – who was supposed to be giving us a lift, never showed up. He'd forgotten all about us so we had to find our own way there by train and eventually got to Oakham, after getting a taxi from Leicester Station, at three o'clock in the morning. The hotel the team were staying at was locked and Peter and I couldn't get in so we spent the rest of the night sleeping on two coffins in a churchyard; I thought, that's a good start to my second-team career.

Robin was out for a duck as Essex batted first and later scored 10 runs in his second innings. More importantly though he had his first experience of bowling for the county and recorded his first wicket, a stumping by John Taylor. Rather frustratingly Robin would have to wait four weeks before getting another second-XI game, ironically against Kent, the county which had tried to sign him only a few months previously. "To give you some idea of how strong competition was" recalls Robin,

During that season I took six for 39 against a very strong Kent second XI at Chelmsford and was left out of the next match to give other bowlers a chance. I was probably thinking at that stage that I should be playing in every second-team game. I can remember feeling pretty frustrated.

Although he'd only played half-a-dozen matches for the seconds in 1960, Robin had shown enough promise to impress his captain. In his review of the season, Arnold Quick noted that 'Hobbs for his age showed unusual promise and at this rate should develop into a very good cricketer within the next two to three years.'

However, reflecting on the situation at the time, Robin wasn't optimistic about furthering his career at Essex.

Looking back it seems quite extraordinary that Essex, whose attack was based on seamers, with Trevor Bailey, Roy Ralph, Ken Preston and Barry Knight, should ever have entertained having so many spinners on their staff. These included Peter Lindsey, Ronnie Carr , Terry Kent, Peter Spicer, David Daniels, Paddy Phelan, Bill Greensmith and Dr CB Clarke. The outlook looked very bleak indeed for my getting into the first team.

In spite of the frustrations of 1960, the breakthrough into the first team at Essex came quicker than expected as, all of a sudden, in 1961 there were fewer spinners on the staff with Clarke retiring and Carr having returned to his native South Africa.

Robin started the season in good form for the second XI. In the match against Kent at Braintree in May, the pitch was one of the best he'd seen, giving his leg breaks fine assistance as he took three for 64 in the first innings and seven for 78 in the second. Robin has proud memories of the wickets he took. "They had some bloody good players in those days; there was John Prodger, David Constant, Brian Luckhurst, Mike Denness and Tony Cant to name but a few." People were starting to take notice of the fresh-faced 19-year-old and in the next game he took five for 1 in a spell against Middlesex second XI and ended up with his photo on the front page of *The Times*.

Those two games were a pinnacle; it just showed the powers that be at Essex what Robin could do and so, despite wondering if he'd ever get in to the first team and in only his second season as a professional, he went on to make his first-class debut against Leicestershire on 31 May 1961 at Valentine's Park, Ilford.

According to Robin the wicket at Ilford was:

One of the greenest I can ever remember, I should never have played but I did and I was absolutely over the moon. To make my Essex debut was incredible. I never looked like bowling in the match because the seamers, Bailey and Knight, put the fear of god up Leicester – they knocked seven bells out of them they really did. It was a dangerous wicket, I was at cover watching these balls flying into people's heads and bodies.

The game was over in two-and-a-half days and unsurprisingly Robin didn't get a bowl. He did however get to bat and thoroughly enjoyed the experience – "I got 10 runs, I square cut Alan Wharton for two fours; I thought I'd got a hundred!" he remembers with a broad smile.

Despite his bit-part debut, Robin kept his place in the side for the next match against Gloucestershire at Stroud and went on to enjoy his first taste of success in county cricket. His maiden wicket was that of England player David Allen, caught behind by Brian Taylor for 24. Allen, an accomplished off spinner, had played seven times for England at that stage and would go on to play a further 32 Tests. He returned the favour in Essex's second innings, bowling Robin for two. Robin took two for 34 in Gloucestershire's first innings and two for 64 in the second and although Essex went on to lose the match by two wickets it was a significant moment in his fledgling career.

That game at Stroud made me. We lost the game by two wickets which we should never have done, David Allen got fifty but should have been lbw first ball. I got off to a good start, the ball turned square at Stroud as it always used to, I got my first four wickets in county cricket and felt that I'd really contributed to the game.

The next match was against Yorkshire at Harrogate and Robin recorded his best bowling figures to date of three for 31 including the wicket of Ken Taylor – bowled by a delivery all leg spinners, except maybe Shane Warne, dream of.

I bowled a ball that pitched leg and knocked Ken Taylor's off stump out of the ground. I couldn't believe that I'd bowled him; nor could he! You remember those things. It was only my third game, I remember the wickets I got at Stroud but when you bowl an England player with a magic ball that pitched leg and hit off you think, how did I do that?

We lost the game by an innings. Yorkshire had had two injuries; Don Wilson had broken his arm and Ray Illingworth was ill and so they brought in an off spinner called Alf Bainbridge and he got 12 wickets in the game, six in the first innings and six in the second. He only played five county games in his life, never played again and he got 12 wickets in the match.

Playing against Hampshire at Cowes on the Isle of Wight at the start of July, and in only his fifth appearance, Robin caught the eye of The Times cricket correspondent John Woodcock who reported that 'Hobbs, 19 and fresh faced, is included with an eye to the future. He spun the ball quite appreciably and was decently accurate. It was stimulating and encouraging to see Bailey giving him his head and relying on his spin to break down the Hampshire innings.' Reserved praise that would certainly catch the eye and re-introduce the name

'Hobbs' to a wider cricketing public.

Essex 1960
Standing: Harold Dalton (Masseur), Barry Knight, Roy Ralph, Geoff Smith,
Michael Bear, Alan Hurd, Les Savill, Robin Hobbs, Cecil Jenkinson (scorer)
Sitting: Brian Taylor, Ken Preston, Trevor Bailey, Bill Greensmith, Gordon Barker.

In addition to his Essex duties, Robin continued to play club cricket for Chingford whenever he could and notable performances included six for 41 against The Mote and five for 53 v North Middlesex. Whilst playing for Essex v Surrey at The Oval he skipped the rest day to come back and play for the Sunday A side, scoring 36 not out in the win against Old Libertians.

By the end of his first season in county cricket Robin had played 12 matches for Essex taking 23 wickets at a respectable average of 28.65. The experienced and senior-pro Bill Greensmith had taken 64 wickets at 26.15.

Writing in the 1962 *Essex Annual,* Trevor Bailey stated that

'Hobbs surprised everyone by his rapid advance. He was easily the most improved bowler in the Club, and although his figures in the 1st XI were not sensational, he certainly impressed everyone who saw him. At his best he looked to have great potential, and to be one of the most exciting newcomers that the County have had for a long time. He must, however, learn to relax and appreciate that few bowlers of his type reach their peak until comparitively late in their careers.'

28

Bailey was less reserved in his praise when writing personally to Robin in September 1961. He congratulated him on what he considered to be 'a quite outstanding season' before continuing:

'At the start of last summer I didn't expect you to be pressing for a place in the 1st XI, and if you continue to improve, there is no reason why this should not become permanent. Hoping that the winter job is going reasonably well, and will let you have details of our winter coaching arrangements in due course. With practice and hard work, I feel that you can, in addition to being a good bowler, turn yourself into a very useful run-getter for the county.'

Practice would have to wait. There would, however, be plenty of hard work for Robin over the coming months, but not in the cricket nets.

Robin still had to find employment for six months of the year. He'd left his job with Employers Liability to pursue his dream of becoming a professional cricketer but in those days it only paid for the summer months. During the winter he would need to find paid employment outside cricket.

A couple of winters were spent selling frozen food in Stepney and he also spent time working for the Hann Timber Company in Walthamstow after a friend from Chingford had got

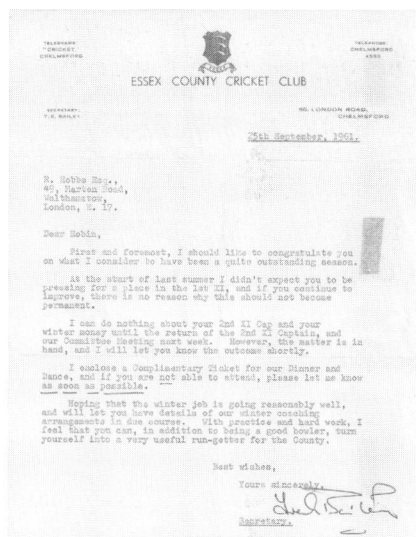

Congratulations from Trevor Bailey on Robin's fine start to his career at Essex.

him the job. Robin spent three months at one end of a lathe whilst at the other a workman shoved in timber at speed. It was hard physical work but it helped him keep fit during the off-season.

Another job, delivering paraffin around Walthamstow, also kept Robin fit. Reg Hobbs was by now the manager of Clapps, a Ford garage in Walthamstow, and in addition to selling and servicing Ford cars, Clapps had started a door-to-door service selling pink paraffin – a popular domestic heating fuel. In the 1960s portable paraffin heaters were commonplace, and were a cheap and effective, but often smelly, way of keeping a room warm. Clapps had sensed a business opportunity to supply fuel for thousands of heaters in Walthamstow and when the regular paraffin delivery man left, Reg asked if Robin would like the job. "I enjoyed it" remembers Robin.

I used to go round the blocks of flats in Walthamstow, hoicking five gallon drums of paraffin up four floors and never thought a thing about it, it kept me as fit as a fiddle in the winter.

There were three main brands of paraffin on sale in the 1960s; Esso Blue, Aladdin Pink and Regent Green. On Robin's pink paraffin round he was in competition with the Esso Blue man.

In those days people were very trustworthy. Everybody left their empty paraffin cans out overnight with a ten bob note underneath – you wouldn't do that now, you wouldn't leave the can out let alone the 10 bob! My first port of call on the round was Howard Road and if I got up there before the Esso Blue guy I'd fill up with pink paraffin and take the 10 bob and he'd do the same thing and fill up with Esso Blue if he got there before me. So there were certain roads I went to in Walthamstow and got double whammy and others I never got anything because he'd been there before me.

Robin drove a Bedford truck on the delivery round which held a 400-gallon tank with a tap at the rear which he would use to fill the five-gallon cans whilst out on the round. Health and safety, and environmental considerations were not major concerns.

We used to go up these hills without a top on the tank, probably 350 gallons of paraffin in there swilling around and you'd lose 30 gallons down places like Howard Road. You'd see this paraffin flowing down the road, the stuff was pissing out the back down into the main road but nobody cared a bit. You'd never get away with it now.

Filling the huge tank on the truck was a laborious and lengthy task each morning. Initially it had to be filled by hand from a main tank at Clapps garage before Reg Hobbs hit upon an idea to speed up the process which nearly ended in disaster for the residents of London E17.

My father got this great idea; he got a petrol pump in there to pump the paraffin into the tank on the truck. That was all very well but he forgot to clear the pump out and so what went in the first time to the 400 gallon tank was not only paraffin but segments of petrol too. We were on national radio, all this stuff we'd sold during the day – "Please do not light your paraffin heaters!" I had to go back out and get the whole bloody lot or else half of Walthamstow could have gone up in smoke!

Robin did two winters of delivering paraffin,1962 and the harsh winter of 1963. With temperatures so cold that the sea froze in places, it was one of the coldest winters on record and became known as the Big Freeze with the whole country lying almost paralysed for three months.

Having broken into the Essex side in 1961, Robin could have been forgiven for thinking that he'd arrived as a first-teamer but come the start of the 1962 season Bill Greensmith was still there and, more significantly, Jim Laker the veteran former England off spinner came out of retirement to play for the county on special registration.

For Robin this meant a season of second-XI cricket and throughout the summer he was ever-present in 16 games. At cricket grounds from Motspur Park to Wanstead, Robin toiled away for 428 overs and was rewarded with 55 wickets at an average of 23.33. In the review of the season, the *Essex Handbook* stated that 'Robin Hobbs, despite his lack of first eleven games, continued to improve. He was our most successful wicket taker, and in a number of games his batting proved most useful.' The review also picked out his 'grand slam' against Surrey seconds at The Oval in June 1962 when Robin achieved a 'hurricane' score of 91 not out batting at number nine in Essex's second innings. "I just went in and played a few shots and got away with it" says Robin modestly.

> *Geoff Arnold, who was playing for Surrey, still talks about it funnily enough whenever I see him, he remembers me smacking it around the park, more by luck than judgement. He doesn't talk about games when we went on tour to Pakistan or anything like that; whenever he sees me he always says "Christ, Hobbsy; that bloody innings you played in that second-team match!"*

Among Robin's regular team-mates that season were Keith Fletcher, Brian Edmeades and Graham Saville; the side also included Geoff Hurst who, four years later, would achieve footballing immortality by scoring a hat-trick in the 1966 World Cup final at Wembley. Hurst, an aggressive batsman, also kept wicket occasionally and at Brightlingsea in June, he stumped Somerset's Terry Barwell off Robin's bowling.

Hurst went on to make one first-class appearance for Essex that season but things could have been very different, as he explained to The Daily Mail in an interview in 2014. 'There wasn't a decision to choose between the two sports.

It's just that the football took off at a senior level quicker than the cricket. Had I played more games for Essex in the first team than I did, I may have ended up choosing cricket. I never officially made that decision.' "Geoff was a good player" recalls Robin.

He never really forced himself into being a top professional cricketer, but football just took over and he went with football at that time which was obviously the right decision as far as he was concerned. Most of the West Ham boys played decent cricket in that era – Bobby Moore, Brian Dear, Alan Sealey and Ronnie Boyce, they were all good cricketers.

Robin continued playing for Chingford and throughout the season put in some superb individual performances including a century against Loughton and a number of five-wicket hauls. He also played plenty of games for the Essex Club and Ground team and according to the *Essex Handbook* impressed in all areas of the game. In his batting he demonstrated that he possessed 'an excellent eye' and, when bowling, frequently demonstrated his potential to become 'a top class leg spinner'. His fielding also warranted special mention – 'Hobbs brought off several brilliant catches.' This aspect of his game was consistent even when his bowling form briefly deserted him or the wickets were against him. It kept him in the game at all times, a positive benefit for himself and any side he played for.

Robin had not played any first-team games during 1962; by the end of the season Bill Greensmith was still the first-choice Essex leg spinner having taken 77 wickets. Surprisingly Robin wasn't overly disheartened.

I wasn't too frustrated mainly because I didn't think that in my first season in 1961 that I'd play 12 games. I went from playing second-team cricket in 1960, about six or seven games, straight into the first team which was unusual. I knew Bill was coming to the end of his career, he was going to retire before too long and then I'd be a regular choice.

Nineteen sixty-three was a notable year for the UK. It was the year of the Profumo affair, the launch of *Dr Who* on the BBC and the rise of Beatlemania. The country was moving into a new, modern era which was also reflected in English cricket with the distinction between amateurs ('Gentlemen') and professionals ('Players') being abolished before the start of the season. The year also marked the introduction of the Gillette Cup, a 65-over one-day knockout competition which was a response to strong calls being made since the mid-1950s for brighter cricket to be played with the added bonus of being a potential money earner. It would also prove to be the start of a brighter future for Robin whose promise had not gone unnoticed. His season began with the honour of selection by MCC for the second match of the season at Lord's against Surrey.

In hindsight it seems a baffling choice considering he had played no first-class cricket the previous season but the line between Chelmsford and Lord's was clearly an open one.

MCC in those days played at least two matches at the start of the season against county sides and it was a great feather in the cap of any player to be selected and represent them in a three-day match against the County Championship-winning side from the previous year.

No play was possible for the first two days due to rain. On the third, Surrey won the toss and elected to field. Robin was batting at number nine and found himself joining his county captain, Trevor Bailey, in the middle with the score at 86-7. Awaiting him with ball in hand was the hostile fast bowler Peter Loader.

I was facing at the Nursery End and Loader ran up and bowled and unfortunately I went and hit the ball straight for six which was a silly thing to do because he didn't like that. He went absolutely ape, he gave me a right amount of verbal, swearing and shouting which was really uncalled for, I was only a young kid but he didn't liked being plonked into the seats. Trevor walked down the wicket and said "That was a rather stupid thing to do old boy." It was a very silly thing to do because the next ball Loader bowled nearly took my bloody head off. He was a nasty bit of work, he wasn't liked around the counties because he did throw the ball as well which didn't help.

Robin didn't hang around for much longer before he was inevitably bowled by the fiery Loader. "I was a poor player of quick bowling and once I'd got to double figures I was happy. It was time to go before I got knocked over, literally."

Essex were slow to catch on to the attraction of the Gillette Cup in its inaugural season and were knocked out in the first round, losing by 81 runs away at Lancashire. Robin didn't bowl as Lancashire were bowled out for 213 from 59.2 overs. In reply Essex limped to 132 all out from 45.1 overs.

Some of the Essex players viewed the new competition as an unwanted intrusion and it didn't help that in an effort to save money the county arranged for them to stay with various members of the Lancashire committee rather than book into a hotel. Robin remembers that nobody really had much interest in it at the time:

The Gillette Cup became big stuff in the end but that first year people just thought it's another game of cricket. We didn't even bother practising much before the game, just went out and played, got knocked out and came home.

Robin continued playing club cricket for Chingford whenever he could and put in a number of star performances in the first half of the 1963 season including six for 25 against The Mote and seven for 18 against Mill Hill.

I played cricket whenever I could, every opportunity. I played in a game when I was an Essex first-XI player. You tended to have Sunday off and people didn't ask you what you were doing, you played Saturday, Monday, Tuesday and whatever you did on a Sunday was up to you. I played for the Chinghoppers, an offshoot of Chingford, down at Maidstone. I went into bat at number four because I thought I could bat, and this bowler who was on the Kent ground staff hit me right on the end of the elbow, it really gave me a nasty whack. The next day I turned up for Essex and I could hardly walk I was hurting so much and I got the biggest bollocking of all time having not told them I was playing cricket on the Sunday.

Bill Greensmith had been granted a benefit in 1963, and in a tribute to him in the *Essex Annual* that year the club talked of him hopefully playing on for many more years to come. Unfortunately for him he lost his place in the side early in the season through ill-health and when he did reappear it seemed that his bowling form had totally deserted him and he finished the season with a solitary Championship wicket. This gave Robin more first-team opportunities and a chance to stake his claim but he couldn't quite manage to nail down a regular place in the side. "It was a very wet summer and I was in and out of the first team and averaged over 40 with the ball. I was most disappointed."

The conditions did seem to be against Robin as the review of the season in the *Essex Handbook* concurred:

'In a summer when "green" wickets were more numerous than ever before the life of a leg spinner was bound to be difficult so that it is not really surprising that Robin Hobbs was not able to hold his place. He always bowled steadily, but temporarily lost the ability to turn his leg break sufficiently and in consequence was unable to produce the figures.'

This was a constant theme of Robin's career. On green wickets the seamers held sway with the spinners providing respite between spells and on drying wickets it was the turn of the finger spinners. Only later in the summer could the leg spinner really hope to find the occasional perfect fit when dry, hard and dusty conditions prevailed.

Although his final analysis for the season of 32 wickets at 42.65 may not have been impressive statistically, Robin was learning and making progress. He appeared at the end of season Scarborough Festival, including representing the Young England side, and, more importantly, Robin was chosen for the MCC tour to East Africa in 1963 under the captaincy of MJK Smith.

The furthest Robin had been until then, he jokes, "was Clacton or Southend on holiday". For a young Essex lad in the early 1960s, a tour to Kenya and Tanganyika would be like flying to the moon.

MCC XI v Yorkshire at Scarborough, August 1963. From left: Gordon Barker, Brian Bolus, Tony Lewis, Keith Andrew, Colin Milburn, Trevor Bailey, Keith Fletcher, Keith Gillhouley, David Larter, Barry Knight, Robin Hobbs.

Chapter Four

The driver just got the thing going in time before the elephant reached us.

THE MCC TOUR party to East Africa flew out from London Airport on a Comet aircraft on 29 September 1963 and after refuelling in Beirut arrived in Nairobi, Kenya, the following day. The itinerary for the five-week tour included matches against Kenya, Tanganyika and Uganda. The squad consisted of a blend of experienced players and those, like Robin, on tour for the first time. Willie Watson, the former England and Leicestershire batsman, was the manager, and the side was captained by Warwickshire's Mike Smith, the seasoned players included Micky Stewart of Surrey, Warwickshire's Tom Cartwright and Peter Parfitt from Middlesex – one of *Wisden's* five cricketers of the year in 1962.

Robin had received a letter from MCC four months earlier 'anxious to know' whether he would be available to go on the tour if selected. The news in the letter got better stating that there would be a fee for the tour of £80, a £30 kit allowance and £7 per week to cover individual expenses such as tobacco and drinks. The choice between getting paid to play cricket for five weeks in East Africa or delivering pink paraffin on the streets of Walthamstow wasn't a tough one.

Upon arrival in Nairobi, he and three of the other young players – Richard Langridge, Colin Milburn and Jeff Jones – were placed in accommodation with a local couple who looked after them well. Robin felt spoilt by the whole experience; they were staying in a lovely house and had the use of a Mercedes which they would use to drive round to the local hospital to meet the nurses who worked there.

Robin recalls at one stage of the tour being billeted with a local couple who kept pet mongooses.

> *These two people we stayed with used to go off to work and we used to go off to cricket and Peter Parfitt's party trick before we left was to throw four ping pong balls in the mongooses' run. When the couple came back from work these mongooses were absolutely knackered, they were lying on their backs still trying to crack these bloody ping pong balls thinking they were eggs.*

The cricket in East Africa was to be played on artificial wickets, either coir or jute matting laid on concrete, and for five of the six MCC bowlers it would be their first experience of playing on such surfaces. Robin was to find them helpful to his bowling and the extra tennis ball-like bounce was extravagant, almost chest-high at times. This was a huge asset to a wrist spinner and one usually absent on soft English turf although it did require a bit more air to take full advantage and drive the batsman onto the back foot. At the very least Robin was furthering his education and adaptability by learning to bowl on unfamiliar wickets.

MCC in East Africa, 1963. Standing: Robin Hobbs, Richard Langridge, Jeff Jones, David Larter, Tom Cartwright, Peter Parfitt. Sitting: Laurie Johnson, Micky Stewart, Willie Watson, Mike Smith, John Mortimore, Colin Milburn.

Robin performed steadily enough in the first two tour matches played in Nairobi but it was after flying on to Dar es Salaam for a two-day match against Tanganyika that his tour really took off. On a wicket offering some assistance he claimed 6 for 21 as the home side were dismissed for 84 in their first innings.

Playing conditions in Dar es Salaam weren't easy, even for Peter Parfitt – with experience of touring India, Pakistan and Australia – let alone youngsters like Robin and Colin Milburn on their first overseas tour. 'It was the warmest place I've ever played cricket', recalls Parfitt, 'I was 12th man and I'm pretty certain that Colin Milburn had to come off because he couldn't stick the heat.'

From the intense heat of Dar es Salaam the MCC side flew on to Mombasa for a match against an Invitation XI and Robin added a further five wickets to his tally. On something of a roll now he followed this up by claiming the best bowling figures of the tour as the side returned to Nairobi to play Kenya at the Suleman Virjee Indian Gymkana ground. The home side were dismissed for 118 as Tom Cartwright and David Larter shared nine wickets between them.

Unorthodox batting in a 50 against Kenya at Nairobi, October 1963. The matting wicket suited Robin's bowling as well.

At the end of the second day though, MCC had themselves struggled for runs and their score stood at 158-6, a lead of only 40. Robin led a charmed life with the bat but after being dropped on seven, and again on 10, he decided it was his day and began to hit out happily at the Kenyan bowlers. A drive off the bowling of Don Pringle (father of Essex allrounder Derek) brought up Robin's 50 before he was clean bowled by the same bowler two balls later. Thanks mainly to Robin, and fellow tail-ender Larter with 34, MCC had a first-innings lead of 131.

A more determined effort from Kenya in the second innings saw them at one stage reach 121-1 before Robin made the breakthrough as Gursaran Singh was stumped by wicket-keeper Laurie Johnson. Three further stumpings by the Hobbs-Johnson combination followed as Kenya were bowled out for 247 and Robin could reflect contentedly on figures of seven for 73.

Peter Parfitt felt that Robin benefitted from having a top quality wicket-keeper.

'Hobbsy was unlucky in that he played his county cricket with Tonker [Taylor] behind the stumps. Plenty of people used to say that Tonker was "a good goal-keeper" and called him "iron gloves" whereas Laurie Johnson was a fantastic wicket-keeper, really high-class, and so Robin would have benefitted from that.'

In between the busy playing schedule there were opportunities to view the wonderful landscape of East Africa and Robin and his team-mates took advantage of every opportunity which came their way. On one occasion one of the locals asked the young MCC players if they wanted to go to Kilimanjaro, explaining that he and his friend had a couple of Chipmunk planes and would fly them up from Nairobi where they would land at the base of Mount Kilimanjaro and embark on a safari. Robin was eager for the experience.

We got in these two vehicles and they drove us round this place and there were wild animals everywhere. At one point our driver started to wheel spin; I was sitting in the back of this Land Rover with Jeff Jones and this huge elephant came charging towards us. The driver just got the thing going in time before it reached us.

As if that experience hadn't been nerve-wracking enough they then had to face the flight back to Nairobi.

We flew back in these planes and it starting pissing it down. This bloody plane was going from side to side, the rain was lashing down and I was shitting myself but it was an experience, it was a great, great trip.

Meeting local dignitaries before play; Robin flanked by Milburn and Langridge as Cartwright shakes hands.

The players enjoyed the hospitality of their various hosts throughout the tour, some taking advantage of it quite literally.

"We were in Uganda overlooking the Kampala golf course", remembers Robin.

> It was a beautiful golf course and we were staying with these two people in their home. She was a very stunning lady and obviously one of the lads and her eyes crossed because he said to me one evening;
> "You've got a day off tomorrow Hobbsy, you're playing golf."
> "Playing golf?"
> "Yeah", he said, "With the old man."
> "Eh?" I replied, slow to catch on.
> He said again "You're playing golf tomorrow down there with the old man, 18 holes while I'm up here."
> So off I went and this bloke looked at me after about three holes and he said;
> "Do you play much?"
> "No, not a lot these days"
> "I didn't think so, the way you're hacking around here."
> I kept looking up at this house thinking "You dirty bastard." But that's what it was like on tour, things like that went on.

Towards the end of the tour the MCC party moved on to Uganda, staying in a game park at Murchison Falls near the tip of Lake Albert. They were housed two or three to a rondavel, traditional circular African huts with conical thatched roofs, dotted around the park; another new experience for the young cricketers, totally alien to their lives back in the UK. Little wonder Robin likened it to going to the moon. On arrival Jeff Jones enquired about how they were going to get to dinner? There was a main hall for dining but between it and the rondavels would be elephants roaming wild.

> You couldn't get outside for elephants, there'd be one outside the door ripping the top off the rondavel. We were having dinner one night and the guy at the place said the elephants would all come back in a bit, they know when the food is being chucked out and they'll all come past the front door. We all thought he was joking. We went out there to look, Mike Smith had his wife with him, and sure as eggs are eggs a whole herd came stampeding past the hotel. Mike Smith ditched his wife and ran for cover!

At the end of the 1963 English cricket season Robin had been disappointed by his modest bowling average of 32 wickets at 42.65. By the close of this five-week tour he was the leading wicket taker with 46 wickets at 18.17. He had also impressed in the field, and whether at cover or cover-point he stood out, delighting the crowds with his catching and throwing. "In terms of the cricket the whole tour was a fantastic experience," he recalls, "Mike Smith was a terrific captain and Willie Watson was a magic manager."

Peter Parfitt also remembers it as a lovely tour and says that Robin fitted in well. 'They were good blokes on the tour. Plenty of jokers, people like Laurie Johnson and Hobbsy was a joker too, good looking bloke, 21 years old on tour, he had a fantastic time.' It was not the last time that Robin would be remembered for being a 'good tourist'. A happy-go-lucky nature both on and off the field, superb and enthusiastic fielding and being prepared to bowl wherever and whenever required ensured his popularity with both management and fellow players. The tour was more than just about the cricket for the young buck from Dagenham. To see the wildlife and the game parks which were largely untouched by tourism at that time was a privilege for Robin and Africa had found a special place in his heart.

He returned to England brimming with confidence and his performances on the tour resulted in newspaper talk of him potentially moving on to greater things. *The Walthamstow Guardian* stated that 'The cricketing world now lies at the feet of Hobbs….. With experience, Hobbs could reach the very top.'

No sooner had Robin returned home than the offer of a place on another overseas tour arrived, this time to Jamaica in January 1964 with the International Cavaliers Cricket Club. He was aware that Trevor Bailey was organising the tour and following his East African success he received a phone call from his county captain asking if he fancied coming along. Without a moment's hesitation he accepted, the paraffin round could wait.

The Cavaliers were an *ad hoc* team of famous players whose aim was to encourage local cricket in the countries they visited. They were usually made up of Test players whose countries were not touring at the time or who weren't required for Test duty. The team heading for Jamaica was a who's-who of England Test cricketers past and present. Denis Compton was captain and alongside him he had three old comrades in arms from the England side of the 1950s – Trevor Bailey, Jim Laker and Godfrey Evans. Current Test players included the England captain himself, Ted Dexter, supported by Fred Trueman, Tom Graveney, Peter Richardson and John Murray. Hampshire captain Colin Ingelby-Mackenzie was included too, with Robin and fellow leg spinner Alan Castell, also from Hampshire, very much the babes of the team who would be expected to do more than their fair share of fielding to compensate for the lack of mobility of the veterans.

Laughing Cavaliers leaving for Jamaica, January 1964. From the top
down (left to right): Peter Richardson, Tom Graveney, Denis Compton,
Roy Marshall, Jim Laker, Ted Dexter, Fred Trueman, Godfrey Evans,
Colin Ingleby-Mackenzie, Alan Castell, John Murray, Ken Palmer,
Reg Hayter, Trevor Bailey, Robin Hobbs.

After a 24-hour flight via New York the Cavaliers arrived in Jamaica and
the tour began with two warm-up games, the first of which was played at Jarrett
Park, Montego Bay, against the Combined Parishes. Thousands of fans packed
into the ground eager to see some of the greats of English cricket although they
would have to wait as, having won the toss, Compton decided to bowl first on a
wicket displaying some life.

Robin was in the thick of the action in the field taking two catches
including one to dismiss the Parishes captain, George Batts. Batts had swung

a delivery from Alan Castell high over square-leg and a six looked certain until Robin, racing to gain ground, leapt full stretch, and to the crowd's amazement pulled off a stunning catch. Referring to his bowling, the Jamaican newspaper, *The Gleaner*, reported that 'Hobbs, flighting them nicely and on a better length than Castell, kept the batsman guessing.' Robin took 4 for 57 in a satisfactory victory and there was time before moving off to Kingston – and the first-class games against Jamaica – for the tourists to spend some time at Fred Perry's hotel in Runaway Bay.

To some extent it was a social tour more than anything for some of the old stagers, they played the matches but they were more interested in going to the horse races. Britain's most famous jockey Lester Piggott was in Jamaica at the same time and, as Ingleby-Mackenzie was a good friend of his, the Cavaliers took time to socialise with him and pick up racing tips. Unfortunately for those who did enjoy a flutter, odds-on favourite Piggott never rode a winner while they were there.

All three matches against Jamaica were played at Sabina Park, Kingston with the side skippered by the recently retired West Indies captain, Sir Frank Worrell. The Jamaican team also included Test players Easton McMorris, Alf Valentine and Lester King; all of whom had been members of the West Indies party which had toured England in 1963.

Most of the Cavaliers hadn't played since the end of the English season in September, and, at 45 years of age, Denis Compton hadn't played a serious match since retiring from first-class cricket in 1958 but he rolled back the years with 103 in the first match. For Robin, to be in the same team and witness a century by his boyhood hero was an unbelievable thrill. Robin took 2 for 50 in Jamaica's first innings but both he and Castell were expensive as Jamaica went in search of quick runs in their second innings. Declarations by both sides had set up an exciting finish. Robin, batting at number 10, went in needing to score three runs off the last two balls to win the match but couldn't connect and the game ended in a draw.

Being in the company of so many great cricketers was an incredibly positive experience for Robin. They were impressed by his bowling which gave him great confidence and taking this into the second match of the series he found his groove taking 5 for 69 including the prize wicket of Worrell, caught behind by Godfrey Evans for 38. The local newspaper reports singled out Robin, praising his exceptional bowling and the manner in which he varied his flight. The sports editor of *The Gleaner* was particularly impressed: 'This youngster, I am confident, will play for England' he wrote and continued stating that 'He showed his ability on a hard true wicket yesterday in a manner which has won him my highest praise. It seems incredible that the youngster has had only two seasons of first-class cricket. With the experience he will gain on this tour Hobbs should serve England well in the future.'

Robin's recent experience in East Africa had been ideal preparation and, just as he had been able to do there, he was now able to adapt to the harder wickets in Jamaica with their extravagant bounce. He bowled more slowly than in England and got wickets through bounce as much as spin. The Cavaliers won the second match by four wickets having scored 377 in the fourth innings of the match, largely thanks to Dexter's brilliant 176 and 108 not out by Graveney.

By the time of the final match of the series at Sabina Park the Cavaliers as a team had found their form and won comfortably. Robin's excellent run continued with 4 for 73 in Jamaica's first innings and 4 for 65 in the second as the Cavaliers finished the tour with a five-wicket win in under three days. Over the course of the three first-class matches Robin had taken 16 wickets at an average of 23.81.

According to Robin, the Cavaliers tour and the preceding tour to East Africa were the making of him as a professional cricketer. As satisfied as he was with his own development he did spare time to think of a fellow cricketer who hadn't enjoyed a great tour, expressing a 'there but for the grace of God' sentiment. Alan Castell was a good player but in contrast to Robin he'd had a terrible tour, losing his form to such an extent that he eventually gave up leg spin and turned to bowling medium pace. "We were both about the same age and great mates," remembers Robin "and although we were in competition, so to speak, I did feel sorry for him because I'd had such a good tour."

Robin's performances earned him high praise back home. In his review of the tour for *Playfair Cricket Monthly*, Rex Alston wrote:

'After Dexter the man of the tour was 21-year-old Hobbs. He has been carefully nursed, coached and encouraged by his county captain Bailey, and England has in him her best leg-break prospect since DVP Wright. He has an easy action, an admirable temperament, and good control for one so young, and he really spun the ball on the hard wickets.'

For a young player making his way in the game to be mentioned alongside Ted Dexter as one of the successes of the tour was an incredible fillip. John Arlott, writing in *The Cricketer*, also gave Robin a glowing report.

'The most impressive bowling performance was that of Robin Hobbs, the young Essex leg-spinner. He turned the ball more widely than anyone else on either side; remarkably for one who spins the ball so much, he barely bowled one bad ball in twenty and from time to time surprised even his friends with the googly – which he did not bowl last summer. He took some heavy punishment without losing length or the courage to put the ball up to the bat, and no Jamaican batsman was ever truly his master. Given even slightly sympathetic pitches, Hobbs could be the surprise of the next English cricket season: he is half as good again as he was last August. Hobbs rounded off his cricket with some fine fielding in the deep: a running, leaping catch on the leg boundary from Batts' powerful hook at Montego Bay, was a staggering effort.'

Trevor Bailey was fulsome in his praise for his young Essex charge stating that the outstanding feature of the tour as far as English cricket was concerned was the bowling of Robin Hobbs. Both Bailey and Jim Laker, as his county colleagues, had known about Robin's potential but according to Bailey everyone else was amazed by his success. How had a player who'd only enjoyed a moderate English season manage to bowl so well in Jamaica? According to Bailey the answer lay in the Sabina Park pitch which 'transforms cricket into a very different game from that played in England. On such wickets the best attacking bowlers are undoubtedly the wrist spinner and the really fast bowler. However, to do well the wrist spinner must have the ability to keep a good length, to bowl to his field, and to impart sufficient spin to be able on occasions to clip the edge of a defensive straight bat.' Bailey continued. 'The greater pace of the West Indian pitches not only gave him a larger margin of error, but what was more important meant that he could afford to toss the odd delivery higher in the air than in England.' Turning his attention to Robin's potential at international level, Bailey made a confident prediction.

'If I were picking a team to go to the West Indies or Australia next winter Robin Hobbs would be in my party now, even if he fails to make any impact at home this summer. The South African pitches [the destination for the 1964/65 MCC tour] are slightly slower, but I still fancy him when I remember the devastation Johnny Wardle caused with his chinamen and googlies on the last tour. It is an interesting thought that if we had been sending an MCC team to the West Indies this winter, Robin Hobbs would not have been considered, because our selectors are unwilling to gamble on "horses for courses."'

One might expect a county captain to talk up local prospects but Bailey was clearly proud of his young protégé. Perhaps the greatest thrill for Robin though was the nod of approval he received from his boyhood idol Denis Compton who wrote, 'The development of a young leg-break bowler who, I feel certain, will be a key man of English touring teams for the next few years has been the most gratifying feature of the tour of Jamaica by my team of county cricketers.' Compton also noted that former West Indies captain Sir Frank Worrell shared his optimism about Robin's future and spoke in glowing terms of him.

Compton was particularly impressed by the speed in which Robin had adapted to the hard wickets. 'He has all the attributes of a top-class bowler. He genuinely spins his leg breaks, bowls top-spinners and has a good googly which he uses intelligently.' Words of caution were issued too, echoing those of Bailey, as Compton, perhaps reluctant not to heap too much pressure on the 21-year-old's shoulders, warned that 'This does not mean that Hobbs is certain to have a great record in English county cricket this summer. He needs hard wickets where the slow ball bounces, such as those in the West Indies, Australia, and, to a lesser degree, South Africa.' In the three serious matches Robin had played for the Cavaliers, Compton had clearly seen enough to suggest that 'When it comes to selecting the side to go to South Africa next winter, I hope the selectors give Hobbs a chance.'

On returning to the UK at the end of January 1964 Robin was back selling paraffin during the week and off to the greyhounds at Walthamstow Stadium on a Saturday night. At least he had the ringing endorsements of some of the most influential voices in English cricket for company. He'd enjoyed spending eight successful weeks away during the hard English winter and for him the new cricket season couldn't come soon enough.

Chapter Five

Above any caps I got, hearing that I'd been picked to go to South Africa was the proudest moment I had in cricket bar none.

AFTER TWO SUCCESSFUL winter tours, and with lavish praise still ringing in his ears, Robin was brimming with confidence and raring to go at the start of the 1964 season. Bill Greensmith had retired giving Robin had the opportunity to nail down a spot in the Essex team and, perhaps, harbour greater ambitions that others had already expressed. This was to be his breakthrough year as a professional and he got off to the perfect start in one of the traditional curtain raisers to the season at Lord's after being selected to represent MCC versus Surrey; a showpiece game, watched by MCC President, Gubby Allen, and the chairman of the England cricket selectors, Walter Robins. It was a game Robin still has fond memories of.

> *Although it was played early in the season, MCC versus Surrey was a match which all the hierarchy attended; I remember Walter Robins coming into the dressing room after the match and shaking me by the hand and saying "Well bowled young man." I've still got a photo of me bowling in the game with an Essex second team sweater on. I got ten wickets in the match which at that time, with no other cricket being played, got a full page in the papers. I was a young leg spinner against a good county with people like Ken Barrington and John Edrich. It was tremendous.*

Having recorded his career-best match figures with five for 75 in Surrey's first innings and five for 68 in the second, the plaudits for Robin's bowling continued.

Writing in *The Daily Express*, former Australian great, Keith Miller, declared that Robin 'tied Surrey batsmen in all sorts of knots…. he sends down leg-breaks and top-spinners astonishingly accurately for a bowler of his type.' Miller was also impressed by Robin's temperament after Barrington had been dropped off his bowling by Doug Slade in the covers. Barrington proceeded to thump 14 runs off slow left-armer Slade who was bowling the next over but when Barrington tried to hand out the same treatment to Robin he was 'unable to ruffle the little spinner.' *The Times'* cricket correspondent John Woodcock was similarly impressed by Robin's controlled bowling. As Surrey pursued a victory target of 193 Woodcock noted that whilst Barrington took every scoring opportunity he could he was 'forced to show reluctant respect for Hobbs' and was subsequently caught at backward short-leg by John Price off Robin's bowling for 23. It was a notable scalp as Barrington would go on to top the batting averages that season.

Bowling for MCC against Surrey at Lord's, May 1964. The umpire is Len Muncer.

Kenny Barrington was a pretty selfish player but you need players like that, he went out there with the Union Jack on his back every time he played for England. He played balls on their merit so if you bowled a decent ball he played it properly not like now when it would disappear out of the park, they played differently in those days and if you were bowling to someone like him and he's not scoring off you it gives you loads of confidence.

Robin was given the responsibility of bowling the final over with Surrey requiring seven runs to win with five wickets in hand. David Gibson departed to the third ball of the over and with one run needed and going for the winner, Ron Tindall could only succeed in picking out Brian Bolus at square-leg who took the catch to seal a thrilling draw with the scores level. Bolus's catch had also secured Robin's second five-wicket haul, giving him ten in a match for the first time. He had chosen a good occasion as well; influential pressmen couldn't fail but notice that three England batsmen, Barrington, Stewart and Edrich, were among Robin's victims. Perhaps even more impressive was his ability to immediately adapt to English wickets after his spells on the harder surfaces in East Africa and the West Indies. He felt that he now understood better the mechanics of bowling and as a result was a better bowler on all surfaces. His stock was rising at a considerable rate.

Robin celebrated his 22nd birthday in Hull on 8 May as Essex succumbed to Yorkshire on final day of their opening fixture of the County Championship. In reply to Essex's first-innings score of 206, Yorkshire had been bowled out for 167. Robin removed both openers; John Hampshire caught by Trevor Bailey at mid-wicket and Geoffrey Boycott – mistiming a drive – was caught by Brian Edmeades at mid-off. When Brian Close came in and took 12 runs off an over, Bailey temporarily removed Robin from the attack, bringing him back once Close had been dismissed by Paddy Phelan. Bailey was protective towards his young protégé and shielded Robin at times during his early Essex career. This instinct was soon to cause some controversy for Bailey.

Robin was the first name on many people's lips as potential new blood in the England Test side to compete against Australia in the five-match Ashes series to be played that summer. Following his 10 wickets against Surrey, many observers were now clamouring for his inclusion in the MCC side to play against Australia at Lord's at the end of May. The fixture was less than two weeks before the first Test at Trent Bridge and, as such, was regarded as a Test trial.

'Play Hobbs' was John Clarke's headline in *The Evening Standard* suggesting that the young leg spinner needed to be blooded in the atmosphere of a big game before potentially being thrown into the Ashes series or the forthcoming winter tour to South Africa. Brian Scovell in *The Daily Sketch* was also of the opinion that Robin needed to be given a chance to prove himself for a second time. So confident was Scovell of Robin being selected that he accepted a bet with

Robin Hobbs, aged 22.

Richie Benaud at odds of 10-1 against! The odds may have seemed generous but the wily Benaud collected and Robin missed out. EW Swanton, writing in *The Daily Telegraph* with inside information, made clear his feelings on the matter. 'Essex wrong to deny Hobbs Test-trial chance' he wrote and went as far as describing Robin's omission as a 'sinister absence'. When Swanton enquired of England's chairman of selectors, Walter Robins, as to why Robin hadn't been chosen the response was that Essex had specifically asked that he not be considered as they did not think that he was ready. Swanton considered that in making this decision Essex were 'thoroughly and utterly wrong' and felt it reflected very badly on their former captain – and current England selector – Doug Insole.

Trevor Bailey felt compelled to defend Essex's decision. Writing in *The Cricketer* he stated: 'Nobody is more interested in the development of Robin Hobbs than myself' before reasoning that the apprenticeship of a leg-breakbowler in England is long and hard with few reaching their peak before they are 30. According to Bailey the main reason why he wasn't in favour of Robin playing for MCC was not that he wasn't ready but that he felt Robin wasn't bowling well at that stage of the season. In Bailey's words: 'Had he been collared on the easy-paced Lord's wicket it might have done him a great deal of harm.'

Up to the point that the MCC team was announced Robin had only made a modest start to the County Championship. In three games he had bowled 74 overs and only taken four wickets at an average of 53.5. Matches against Cambridge and Oxford Universities respectively had seen a better return – seven wickets at 30.71 – but against inferior opposition. It had only been a couple of weeks since Robin had taken 10 wickets for MCC against Surrey so it would have been understandable if it had been a disappointment that Bailey had stood in his way. Not so, according to Robin even though he disagrees with Bailey's assessment of his form at the time.

I think at the time, although I knew I was bowling well, I was quite happy not to be

50

selected. Trevor looked after me and if he thought that playing against them was a backwards step and that I might get collared then fair enough, that was fine by me as a young kid, I fully appreciated that and I had no problems. I wouldn't say I was disappointed not to play, I was possibly quite relieved when I think back, I'd really come a long way in a fairly short space of time. They're talking about playing Test cricket – in 1961 I'd hardly played a first-class game.

In his piece Bailey concluded by saying that he considered Robin to be a better bowler overseas than in England due to the difference in nature of pitches. 'This will probably always be the case', wrote Bailey, 'but in time I believe that he will also be a match winner in England. He is not at the moment.' The Lord's match at the start of the season seemed to have been largely forgotten.

Being chosen for MCC would be no guarantee of inclusion in the Test side for the 1964 Ashes. Worcestershire's slow left-armer Doug Slade, who had played alongside Robin in the Surrey game, was selected but never played Test cricket. Of the 11 selected only four – Ted Dexter, John Edrich, Jim Parks and John Price – went on to play for England against Australia that summer. Although he wasn't overly disappointed not to be selected, Robin was slightly aggrieved to miss out on the £30 match fee. "Trevor said to me, 'Don't worry Robin, we'll reimburse you for the £30' – I never got it!" There's no doubt that Bailey's insistence forced MCC's hand and equally little doubt that Bailey's motives were laudable. He wished to protect a young prospect and, incidentally, an Essex asset. There was time enough for Robin to make his international mark if he was good enough. As it turned out, the match was played on an unsuitable wicket and Australia won comfortably. In retrospect Bailey had almost certainly done his young team-mate a considerable favour.

Although personally the 1964 season was the breakthrough year for Robin, for his county it was a very disappointing year. Essex finished 10th in the Championship, winning seven and losing 11 matches. The season had started with the defeat against Yorkshire at Hull and had stuttered until the first win was achieved against Hampshire at Southampton in early June. It was a close run thing though, completed by five wickets with only 10 minutes to spare. A target of 201 runs in 138 minutes had been set – the kind of challenge Essex enjoyed. Robin demonstrated his value as a quick run getter in the lower order by blasting 21 runs in an innings lasting less than 10 minutes. Nineteen of his runs came off four successive deliveries from the Hampshire opening bowler Derek Shackleton.

I was promoted up the order. Trevor said put your pads on and go have a good slog against Shackleton, you might turn the game for us. And I did, I actually did turn the game, it was drifting towards a draw and suddenly bang, bang, bang, bang and we won the game. To go in and get those runs off one of the most economical bowlers in the country, you come off having got 20 in an over you feel like a million dollars. Not many people hit Shackleton for that many runs in an over.

This was no idle boast. Shackleton's 1428 overs in Championship games that summer show a economy-rate of just 2.02.

Writing in *The Sunday Times* about the drawn Surrey versus Essex match at The Oval in June, Ian Peebles described Robin as 'the best prospect among the leg-break bowlers this country has seen since the war.' Peebles – briefly a much heralded and capped leg-break bowler in the 1930s – continued enthusiastically on a subject which he openly admitted was close to his heart. 'Hobbs has very good control, and already a nice selection of parabolas and changes of pace. His talents are capable of much further expansion. His googly does not appear to be very vicious at the moment, but this could well be amongst the developments envisaged.'

Robin has always maintained that the googly is overrated, stating that all of Shane Warne's 40 wickets during the 2005 Ashes were taken with legbreaks, and ironically that Ian Peebles ended up losing his leg break because he bowled too many googlies early in his career. At this stage Robin was happy enough to master his stock delivery.

It's hard enough bowling leg breaks and if you are a good leg spinner you'll get people out anyway. The googly were certainly over-rated as far as I was concerned because I didn't have confidence, I didn't have the confidence in bowling it well regularly. I was more content to be economical, the last thing I wanted to do was to bowl three decent overs of leg spin going for one run and then in the fourth over bowling a googly and getting hit for four.

Wins against Gloucestershire and Middlesex followed and Essex, unbeaten during June, began to entertain thoughts of finishing near the top of the table. Unfortunately these ambitions foundered as they then embarked on a disastrous run of form in July losing six out of their next seven games, defeat against eventual County Champions Worcestershire was only avoided due to rain.

A new month brought about a change in fortunes and August 1964 was most certainly a good month for Robin. It got off to the best possible start when his name was announced as one of the 11 chosen to tour South Africa with

MCC, a further five names would be announced later that month. Essex were starting the first day of their Championship fixture against Warwickshire on the day of the announcement. "There was a little red telephone box outside the ground," recalls Robin, "and I phoned my dad up to say that I'd been selected to go to South Africa. It was mind-boggling to me."

On the second day of the match Robin remembers walking out to bat and receiving a tremendous ovation from the Warwickshire crowd and describes it as the highlight of his career.

It was my proudest moment ever in cricket, being selected on the Saturday and going out to bat on the Monday. Above any caps I got, hearing that I'd been picked to go to South Africa was the proudest moment I had in cricket bar none.

Marylebone Cricket Club,
Lord's Ground,
London, N.W.8

1st August, 1964.

Dear Robin,

I am directed by the M.C.C. Committee to invite you to join the M.C.C. team, which will tour South Africa next winter.

The team will fly from London Airport on October 15th, 1964 and will return on February 15th, 1965. The Committee have agreed that the players' salary for the tour will be £700, plus a kit allowance of £125 and an allowance of £7 per week throughout the tour for incidental expenses. Furthermore, M.C.C. may consider a reward up to a maximum of £150 for discipline and contribution to team spirit on and off the field.

I shall be sending you the Notes and Instructions for the tour together with the contract and copies of the itinerary in the near future.

I should be grateful if you would confirm your acceptance of this invitation as soon as possible.

Yours sincerely,

Secretary, M.C.C.

R.N.S. Hobbs, Esq.

"My proudest moment in cricket."

Flushed with confidence, Robin and Brian Taylor put on a 50-run partnership for the ninth wicket which was to make the occasion even more memorable. Writing in *The Evening Standard*, John Clarke considered it 'refreshing to see an MCC party emplaning for distant parts with two leg-spinners among them' – allrounder Bob Barber being the other. Clarke pointed out that Robin was the only player without any Test experience in the 11 named and that he'd 'been through lean times lately'. In spite of that Clarke saw it as a positive move and felt that South African pitches would provide Robin with better hunting grounds than any in England.

Ian Wooldridge, writing in *The Daily Mail*, seemed equally pleased with the selection of Robin and in his view it indicated that English cricket was at last ready and willing to give a new generation a chance. He also wrote that Robin's inclusion, in the words of a selector, was 'a considerable gamble.' Earlier in the season Essex did not believe that Robin was ready for consideration for a Test place against Australia but that view had clearly changed as, according to Wooldridge, Trevor Bailey was among the nine selectors who picked him to tour, presumably remembering his words earlier in the season concerning the suitability of pitches outside England. Wooldridge concluded that 'The choice is

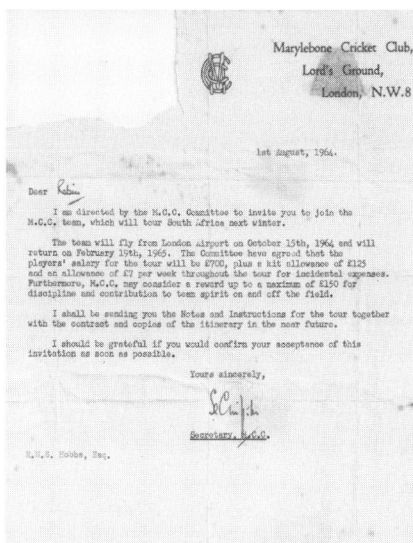

a brave one, but I trust that their bravery will not end there.'

Looking back more than 50 years later Robin still matter-of-factly considers that he was very lucky to be chosen for the tour because, in his opinion, he hardly warranted a place.

I was at The Oval recently and saw Roger Harman who was in my era a left-arm spinner for Surrey. The year that I got selected for South Africa, Roger Harman bowled over 1000 overs and took well over 100 wickets. I hadn't seen him for years and he quietly had a word with me and he thought he should have gone to South Africa in my place and he had every reason to say that, but I think it helped my case having Doug Insole around.

That said, England had lost a dull series to Australia and the bowling attack was looking less than sparkling. Fred Titmus had managed just 10 wickets in the five Tests and Norman Gifford and David Allen had fared no better when included. Robin would provide some variety and might possibly prosper on South African pitches where the traditional English virtues of finger spin and fast medium swing could fall on stony ground.

Essex began to climb up the County Championship table and it coincided with their young leg spinner beginning to find more reward for his bowling. This was hardly a surprise as the harder wickets enabled him to exploit his experiences abroad the previous winter. In the drawn match against Somerset at Weston-super-Mare a couple of important milestones were reached. Robin achieved his first five-wicket return in an innings in County Championship matches with figures of six for 73 in Somerset's first-innings total of 298 for 9 declared. His sixth wicket took him to 50 first-class wickets for the season. In spite of his developing prowess as a bowler, Robin credits the poor state of the wicket playing a part in that first five-for.

Weston-Super-Mare was a poor wicket, you'd never play on it now. Groundsmanship was never as precise as it is now, a lot of the county wickets that we played on were OK but not flat like they are these days and as the season went on the wickets got worse. If you went to some of the outgrounds they dusted up towards the end of the season, they'd been played on once or twice and invariably it turned more than they would now where they play on a perfect wickets in County Cricket. In the old days, especially if you played at Ilford or outgrounds like that, you were playing on park wickets. Fred Titmus used to say he didn't get a great deal of wickets during the early part of the season but come late July/August it was benefit time, he picked up 50 or 60 wickets in that time each year.

MCC President's XI v Australians, Lord's, August 1964. Standing: Mike Griffith, Keith Fletcher, Robin Hobbs, Geoff Arnold, Roger Harman, Colin Milburn. Sitting: Geoffrey Boycott, David Brown, Mike Brearley (Captain), Gubby Allen (MCC President), Richard Hutton, David Green.

Although arguably he'd been unfortunate not to be chosen for MCC versus Australia in May, Robin did find himself selected to play for MCC President's XI against Australia at Lord's in August. He wasn't used much during the Australian's first innings, only bowling 2.5 overs, but enough to dismiss his opposite number – leg spinner Rex Sellers – who top scored for the tourists with 36 out of a total of 162. In the MCC reply Robin scored 21 before he was lbw to Alan Connolly. A slender lead of 31 was achieved when MCC declared on 193-9 and the young side were instantly buoyed by the dismissal of Australian captain Bobby Simpson for a duck. Any hopes of pulling off a famous victory were dashed however by Bill Lawry and Barry Jarman who put together a stand of 186. Once the partnership was broken the MCC bowlers were able to establish some control. Left-hander Lawry was neatly caught at slip by Keith Fletcher off a rare googly bowled by Robin and the wickets of Ian Redpath and John Martin followed as he finished with figures of 3 for 83 from 21 overs. The Australians declared setting MCC a target of 228 in 2 ½ hours which looked within their reach as openers Geoffrey Boycott and Mike Brearley scored at five runs an over in an opening stand of 121. However, once they were both out in quick succession the run chase fell away and it fell to Robin and Richard Hutton to bat out the last half hour with MCC six wickets down. Robin was dismissed for 15 as the draw was all but achieved. He emerged with credit from his first encounter with the Australians and was left to ponder on what might have been had he had the opportunity to face them at the same ground three months earlier that summer.

The following day Robin went straight into playing another three-day fixture against the Australians, this time for his county at Southend. It would be the highlight of the season for Essex as they went on to beat the tourists by six wickets. It was a special occasion, even more so for Robin and team-mate Paddy Phelan, both of whom were awarded their county caps during the match. The win for Essex erased the memories of the massive defeat inflicted on them at the same ground by Don Bradman's Invincibles in 1948. Captained by Trevor Bailey, who had played in the 1948 fixture, Essex won the toss and enjoyed a fine opening day thanks to third-wicket partnership of 184 between Gordon Barker, who made 123, and Keith Fletcher, who scored 125. Essex declared on 425 for 6 and then proceeded to dismiss the tourists for 218. Among the early wickets to fall was that of Norm O'Neill who'd been burdened with the tag of 'the new Bradman' from early on in his career.

> It was a bit grey when the Australians were batting. Ken Preston bowled to Norm O'Neill who was my boyhood hero, I met him towards the end of his life in Sydney. O'Neill picked it up, it came down to me at fine-leg and I just about hung on to it in this grey sky on the boundary.

Paddy Phelan was the pick of the bowlers taking five for 94 with his off breaks. Robin was used sparingly, bowling only nine of the 73.2 overs and taking one for 18. His one success however was a prize wicket, and it took a perfect ball. "I bowled [left hander] Bob Cowper with an absolute blinder. He played forward and it pitched outside the off-stump and knocked his middle stump out." Cowper top scored for the tourists with 39 in the first innings, less than two years later he became the first Australian to score a triple hundred on home soil before prematurely giving up Test cricket at the age of 28.

Essex had achieved a first innings lead of 207 and Trevor Bailey had no hesitation in inviting the Australians to follow on – the only occasion in

1964 that they had been put in such as a position and the first time this had happened to any Australian team since Northamptonshire had done the same to Bill Woodfull's side in 1930. Aware that the wicket at Southend was liable to deteriorate, Bailey sensed an opportunity to gain revenge for 1948. Not surprisingly there was stiffer resistance from the Australians second time around but Phelan and Robin were the mainstays of the Essex attack, working their way through the Australian batting order, who – despite half-centuries from three of their batsmen – were dismissed for 313. Phelan's second-innings haul of five for 154 gave him an overall match analysis of 10 for 248. Robin provided excellent support, his three for 73 from 26.4 overs included the wickets Wally Grout, Graham McKenzie and Alan Connolly.

I got the tail out again. I can't remember any chances going down, I bowled adequately, they were probably my just desserts and the main one being Cowper, he was worth ten of Connolly, Cowper was a prize wicket.

Essex's victory target was 107 which they reached, four wickets down, much to the delight of their supporters and the many holidaymakers who'd been attracted by the prospect of witnessing a rare win against the Australians.

They were captained by Brian Booth and it was the game before the final Test at The Oval...and they treated it like a proper game, they tried bloody hard but it turned square and they were beaten soundly. Our spinners bowled better than their spinners.

Among the Australian spinners was Rex Sellers, who played a solitary Test match later that year against India in Calcutta, taking 0 for 17 from five overs. Robin had some sympathy for a fellow leg-break bowler.

They have a funny attitude the Australians, Rex Sellers wasn't a bad leg spinner but they never believed in sweepers. He bowled short quite a lot but they never had a man out square and he got hit a lot down there whereas we put a sweeper out, give the batsman one. No, they didn't believe in that the Australians and he went for quite a lot of runs.

At the end of the game Trevor Bailey, who lived at Westcliff, held a monumental party in a marquee in his garden for both sides who chatted, swopped stories and drank long into the night.

Robin had started the season with 10 wickets for MCC versus Surrey and he neatly bookended his county season with another 10 wickets in the final Championship match against Leicestershire at Grace Road. Having won the toss Essex chose to bat first on the concrete-like wicket and reached 382-9 at close of play on day one. When play resumed on the second day Trevor Bailey declared hoping that Robin and the other Essex bowlers would cause Leicestershire problems on a surface showing end-of-season wear. Leicestershire looked like following on at one stage having slipped to 157-7 but were saved by an unbelievable eighth-wicket partnership of 164 by Maurice Hallam and Terry Spencer. Leicestershire were eventually dismissed for 338, Robin taking 6 for 100 from 34 overs.

Essex, with a lead of 44, set off in pursuit of quick runs in order for Bailey to give his bowlers enough time to dismiss Leicestershire second time around. They declared on 215-8 which included a fine quick fifty from Keith Fletcher and set a target of scoring 260 with just under three hours remaining in the match.

Leicestershire went about the task with considerable skill and at one stage were in a commanding position. Brian Booth and Clive Inman shared a stand of 148 for the third wicket in just under 90 minutes and had taken the score to 210 and only 50 more runs were required with wickets in hand. A typical piece of brilliance in the field by Robin changed the game. Collecting the ball he sent in a throw from 30 yards which hit the stumps, narrowly running out Inman for 93. This galvanized the Essex side who regrouped and set about defending their total although there was a slight delay before play could continue as in the melee of the run-out the ball had unfortunately ricocheted and injured Brian Taylor.

It actually hit the top of the stumps and knocked four of Tonker's teeth out and he carried on keeping wicket, he didn't go off. That was Tonker all over, hard as bloody iron he was. Took no prisoners on the field and he was fearless when he batted.

When play resumed, Robin's subtle bowling then accounted for Hallam and Spencer before Bailey swiftly removed Jack van Geloven, Steve Greensword and Ray Julian, all clean bowled. With 10 minutes remaining in the match, Leicestershire were 19 runs short of victory with one wicket left. Tom Thompson seemed unperturbed by the situation and raised the hopes of the home side as he lifted Robin for a big six. Thompson attempted a repeat of the stroke, and for a second or two, it looked as if his blow would clear the boundary, but John Wilcox coolly got under the ball, and held the catch above his head to seal a thrilling 12-run victory for Essex.

Essex's season may have finished but Robin still had two further games to play at the Scarborough Festival and headed straight up to the North Yorkshire coast from Leicester in his Ford Thames van which he used to carry the Essex kit. Sharing the journey was Leicestershire player Jack van Geloven who ran a pub in Scarborough during the winter.

Jacky was a good bloke, he liked a drink, and he was called Scamp, don't ask me why. I took him up to Scarborough and I've had to stop on the Doncaster bypass in a row of traffic. I'm in the inside lane, there's a Rolls Royce on my right-hand side and I see this great big lorry bearing down on me, it hit me straight up the arse, pushed poor Jacky through the windscreen. My little van was wrecked and the lorry driver got out and said "I'm sorry mate the brakes failed and it was either you or the roller." We had to leave my van there, someone else had to take us and when we got there his wife opened the door and there he was covered in plasters, looked like he'd been in the ring with Henry Cooper.

In spite of the shock of the accident Robin was still looking forward to the festival. It was very much a social affair providing a slightly light-hearted end to the summer and it attracted many of the top players who generally approached it in a fun, free-spirited nature with the emphasis on entertaining the large crowds. Tom Pearce, the former Essex captain, picked a side to play there each year – Tom Pearce's XI – and whilst the Essex connection aided his selection, Robin's demeanour and attitude towards the game were equally important.

Because I was the type of bowler that lobbed it up a little bit and wasn't frightened to go for a few runs, I was included. I probably played 10 years running there. County cricket had finished, so there were no other matches, the only cricket on was the Scarborough Festival and the ground was full, I mean they used to get 10 to 12 thousand a day there, it was brilliant when it was packed. The tourists played there, World XI sides played, bloody good cricketers played in those matches and the spectators, the Yorkshire old lads, they came along in their droves to watch them, it was terrific stuff.

On arrival in Scarborough the players generally used to have to find their own accommodation and weren't paid until the end of their involvement in the festival so had to fund themselves as Robin recalls.

They had a secretary called Nash. I used to go up to his office and he opened up a big tin and paid you in cash, £90 for three matches, 30 quid a game, that's what you got and you generally came home with 45 quid. You never bought a drink, there was the Mayor's cocktail party with free drinks.

Along with others including Ted Dexter, Colin Milburn and Trevor Bailey; Robin had also been selected to play for an England XI versus Sir Frank Worrell's XI. It was a chance to pit his wits once again against Worrell and Lester King. Several prominent West Indies players were also in Worrell's XI including Garry Sobers, Basil Butcher, Seymour Nurse, Rohan Kanhai, Deryck Murray, Wes Hall and Lance Gibbs. On the final day of the game, the England XI had been set a target of 238 in three hours to win. They were seemingly well set on 140 for 3 needing 98 more runs in 80 minutes when a sea fret rolled in the during the tea interval reducing visibility to less than 50 yards. Unfortunately it failed to lift and the game finished as a draw. Robin had once again acquitted himself well in a representative game taking four for 80 from 28.2 overs in the second innings including the wicket of Worrell, bowled by a top spinner for one.

Robin's final first-class appearance of the 1964 English season was for Tom Pearce's XI versus the Australians, the third time he had faced the tourists that summer. Australia had won a rather turgid Ashes series but still had a number of tour fixtures to fulfil. For Martin Douglas, eight years old at the time, it was his first time at a cricket match and he attributes much of his lifelong love of the game to watching Robin that day.

'An end of season festival at Scarborough was to be cherished and the crowds turned up from Yorkshire and beyond to watch the Australian tourists towards the end of their tour. The festival cricket was supposed to be competitive but fun and on the first day of the game the Aussies scored freely at around five an over to record a score of 400. In 1964 this was thrilling stuff. The Yorkshire crowd was mostly men and boys. The men wearing suits and ties and mostly smoking. The boys in shorts and quilted anoraks clutching autograph books; I was one of them on the busy popular terrace.'

Robin was happy to provide entertainment and play to the crowd by lobbing his leg spinners high for the batsmen who'd either hit boundaries or get out. For young lads like Martin watching in the stands it was great fun. One incident during the match against the Australians is one of Martin's earliest cricketing memories although it involved Robin's fielding rather than his bowling.

'During the afternoon Robin was fielding at mid-wicket in front of the popular terrace. In between balls he would engage with spectators and have a bit of fun like non-serious fieldsmen do. This was really good natured and the crowd took him up as their "man". His Essex colleague Barry Knight was bowling short balls to the Australian 'keeper Barry Jarman and encouraging him to hook. Jarman top edged high into the air and sent the ball towards the rapidly retreating Robin who was about to catch the ball when his feet tangled and he fell backwards onto the turf. He took the catch on the way down and then milked it by lying prostrate on his back with his arms in a crucifix position. I would like to recall team-mates rushing to congratulate him, but it wasn't that serious and in my mind's eye they were all creased with laughter. I, on the other hand, only saw this as a miracle catch.

For the next decade or so I spent many happy days following cricketers around Scarborough with my autograph book and so on many occasions got close to Robin. His autograph had little currency because he would sign whenever asked. You could judge a player's character in the way he responded. Trueman never signed and was rude and surly, Boycott in a prearranged and orderly way, but Robin whenever and wherever. My recollection is of him in an MCC sweater, cigarette in left hand chatting to whichever passer by wanted to say hello, whilst keeping lots of small boys happy by autographing away. I think he must have been happy to have been a cricketer.'

The Australians won the match comfortably by seven wickets, Robin picked up a couple including a stumping by stand-in 'keeper Brian Close, deputizing for Keith Andrew who'd dislocated a finger. More important than the result or the wickets though was Robin's *joie de vivre* which clearly inspired young lads like Martin Douglas. 'That day he taught me that cricket could be fun and joyful and he helped to ignite a lifetime's passion.'

The frivolity usually extended into the evening as Robin recalls.

We always had a good drink in the evenings. There was a renowned hotel before it burned down called the Balmoral where everybody ended up at nine or ten o'clock and stayed up until about three o'clock where people like Phil Sharpe and Don Wilson used to sing with a piano going along.

It wasn't uncommon for the players to emerge on to the field the following day still fairly inebriated and the fun continued until the end of the festival which also signalled the end of the cricket season.

They were great days. I used to come back after Scarborough driving through Pickering down the A1, it was mid-September and you knew then when the fields were all cut that it was truly the end of the season and you had to get a job or be lucky enough to go on a tour.

Looking back on his career, Robin considers that he had a reasonable season in 1964. It was though, without doubt, his breakthrough year as a professional cricketer. It all seemed to come right for him that year beginning with the confidence he'd gained from the winter tour to East Africa and Jamaica. He'd enjoyed his first full season with Essex, taking 59 Championship wickets at an average of 29.9. His success in the representative games had seen him take a total of 81 first-class wickets for the season at a decent average of 28.91. The season had been capped off with selection for the 1964/65 MCC tour of South Africa and so Robin, at the age of 22, had reached the England squad where only five years earlier he had been playing for the Chingford 3rd XI. It was a source of great pride for the Essex club side and Robin still found time to turn out (not for the thirds) when he could although he was unable to play a full part in one of their end-of-season matches. In the Chingford Sunday A game at Northampton Exiles on 20 September the *Palmers Green Gazette* reported that he declined an invitation to bowl as he was still feeling the effects of his travel inoculations; an occupational hazard now for Robin as a touring cricketer.

Chapter Six

They took me as a good fielder and for experience – whether it was the right experience I'm not sure.

THE MCC TEAM departed from London Airport in two separate planes on 15 October 1964 and was the first to fly to South Africa rather than take the more leisurely journey by boat. Ten of the party, including the captain and manager, flew via Nairobi while the other nine took a westerly route arriving in Salisbury, Rhodesia, the following day.

Having decided not to lead England abroad again, Ted Dexter instead chose to stand for Parliament representing the Conservative Party in the constituency of Cardiff South-East in the 1964 General Election. Polling day was the same Thursday as the MCC team flew out and Dexter may well have regretted not being with them. His attempt to become an MP was unsuccessful, losing by 7841 votes to the future Labour Prime Minister James Callaghan. Parliament's loss was MCC's gain and Dexter was now free to join up with the team, arriving in Salisbury one week into the tour on 23 October.

Colin Cowdrey had initially indicated that he was unable to tour for family reasons and so with both him and Dexter out of the frame the MCC selectors turned to another amateur, MJK Smith, who had been a great success as captain the previous winter in India. Smith was a popular choice among the players. Geoffrey Boycott referred to him as 'a superb captain....If he lacked anything tactically compared to Close and Illingworth, he more than compensated for that in terms of his personality and attitude.' Wicket-keeper John Murray also welcomed Smith's appointment as captain reflecting that 'MJK would come out to dinner with you in the evening and have a laugh and a joke. I can't remember Colin or Dexter ever doing that. They were both rotten captains.'

For Robin it was an opportunity to be reunited with the man who had captained the MCC team to East Africa in 1963, the tour which had been instrumental in kick-starting his career. Like Boycott and Murray, Robin greatly respected Smith's captaincy.

We had a great team spirit because Mike Smith was such a good leader. He was so short sighted that he used to field at short-leg. He'd be there with his cap on and his horn-rimmed glasses, he was such a fearless fielder and you admired him for that, there was the skipper fielding in that terrible position, the worst place he could.

I remember on that tour he went for a haircut in Kimberley, forgot to take his glasses and came back looking like a bloody hedgehog. He pissed himself laughing when he put his glasses on and saw himself, he was completely bald, they'd cut all his hair off. He was one of those guys you couldn't help liking. Although he was one of the boys you still held him on a pedestal. Mike would mix with the players totally but you knew who was boss the next day although he wasn't ever one of those guys who wagged his finger. If there was a situation where he'd get drunk with you, he'd have a laugh but the next day you knew exactly on what side you stood and you treated him with great respect. He was good fun but he was also a damn good captain, most players would have walked through fire for him.

They weren't to know it at the time but they were to be the last MCC team to tour South Africa for 30 years and it wasn't until 1995 that normal Test tours could resume. John Arlott, who had previously voiced his distaste for the South African government's policy of apartheid, refused to tour as did *The Daily Telegraph's* EW Swanton.

The players had been told by MCC to focus on the cricket, something which most of them – Robin included – were, by and large, happy to do. "As a young man," recalls Robin,

It came as a bit of a shock to see the public lavatories, the trains and the buses were 'Whites Only' and 'Coloureds Only'. Being in another country I accepted it for what it was but it was obviously wrong. Mike Brearley was so anti-apartheid that he visited people in the townships, although he probably wasn't allowed to, to find out more about apartheid. I remember the beach at Durban with big signs up saying 'Whites Only' and then along the beaches where they didn't have the shark nets they had signs saying 'Coloureds Only'. Unbelievable – you had shark nets up for the whites but down the road it didn't matter. But that was their attitude, life was that cheap.

Mike Smith led the team not only to a 1-0 Test-series win but they also went undefeated through all 19 tour matches. It was quite an achievement particularly in view of the fact that MCC's pace attack was lightweight compared to South Africa's. Fred Trueman, despite having claimed his 300th Test wicket during the summer, wasn't selected. In the opinion of many, none more so than himself, he should have been included.

We were so short of bowling, when you look at that seam attack. I mean John Price
– who was a decent bowler, Ian Thomson who was medium pace but managed
to keep going through the whole tour, Cartwright and Dexter – that wasn't a Test
attack. Fred Trueman, over a hundred wickets that season but they wouldn't take
him because he was too disruptive. He was livid, he should have gone on that tour.

Robin played in five of the eight tour matches before the Test series started, bowling well enough in the match against Western Province at Cape Town to impress Harold Butler of *The Cape Times*. In his match report Butler wrote that Robin 'has come right back into form in the last two matches and if his present progress is maintained, he should be back in the Test line very soon.' The Daily Mirror expressed similar sentiments writing that 'Off his showing here Hobbs might yet find a place in one of the later Tests.' Robin's bowling was all the more impressive as, during one over, he only had eight fielders; the other two were busy adjusting the sightscreen for Fred Titmus's next over. Peter Parfitt remembers Robin bowling well in the Western Province match and he took slip catches off him to dismiss their number-three batsman Lynton Morby-Smith in both innings. The second innings dismissal was particularly impressive as Parfitt dived full length to his left and as he emerged with the ball in his hand he remembers Robin's delight in exclaiming "Parfers, I wish you were in the Essex side!"

Norman Crookes, South African Colts, bamboozled
and bowled. Peter Parfitt is at slip, John Murray is the 'keeper.

Robin wasn't selected for the first Test in Durban, England preferring to go with the twin off-spin attack of Titmus and Allen, with the occasional leg spin of Barber and Barrington to call upon if required. Peter Parfitt believes that England had two world-class off spinners at their disposal in Titmus and Allen and as such they were always going to get priority. Ironically Parfitt recalled England using two leg spinners in tandem – Roly Jenkins and Doug Wright – for three of the five Tests in the 1948/49 series in South Africa. Jenkins had replaced another leg spinner in Eric Hollies when the latter withdrew from the squad before the start of the tour. Another wrist spinner, Johnny Wardle, had been the most successful bowler on the 1956/57 tour.

John Murray, reserve wicket-keeper to Jim Parks, agrees with Parfitt's views. 'Robin really had very little opportunity, unless there were two or three injuries he was never going to get into the Test team, he was only there as a guy to play in the up-country games almost.' His fielding prowess ensured that he would play at least some part in the Test series.

'I didn't get in the side until the last Test and so I was the unelected senior pro of all the boys who didn't play. We all went to the game before start of play and then I used to organise the boys depending on whether we were batting or bowling. Robin was an obvious 12th man, he was a great fielder. He quickly agreed to anything I said. I told him, "When we're in the field you're here, whether it's one day, two days or three days, you're here when we're in the field. When we're batting you can be where you like." He was a terrific fielder, quick, bloody quick, he was always in the covers or somewhere like that. He was a bloody good catcher if he got in close to the wicket, his reactions were so quick.'

Robin watched from the boundary as England won the opening Test of the series comfortably, scoring 485 for five declared with Ken Barrington and Jim Parks both hitting centuries, before bowling out the South Africans cheaply twice to win by an innings and 104 runs. "In actual fact," according to Robin, "we got about 25 or 26 wickets because the umpiring was so terrible."

Ken Barrington scored another century in the second Test at Johannesburg and Dexter hit a magnificent 172 in England's first innings total of 531. "Peter Pollock was their opening bowler and he was really quick but Dexter hit him all over the Wanderers in bad light," remembers Robin, "it was one of the greatest knocks I've ever seen."

Robin felt the England team had their backs to the wall in the three remaining Tests. The South Africans had worked out the spin bowling of Fred Titmus and Allen by the third Test, and injuries to John Price and Bob Barber amongst others also took their toll. England held on to win the series 1-0 helped in no small part by Geoffrey Boycott's match saving 76 not out in England's second-innings total of 153 for six in the fourth Test. Boycott also made a significant contribution in the fifth at Port Elizabeth with 117 in England's first-innings total of 435. The unadventurous tactics of the home side hardly helped their cause in the days before Eddie Barlow's belief and the genius of Graeme Pollock and Mike Procter made them almost unbeatable.

Mike Brearley, Robin, Ian Thomson and David Brown. Of the four, only Thomson featured in the Test series.

As the tour party moved from hotel to hotel the players each shared a room with a team-mate. There was a fair amount of swapping around and at various points throughout the tour Robin found himself with David Brown, Mike Brearley and generally other players who weren't involved in the Test matches. He did also at one stage find himself rooming with Geoffrey Boycott, and without the responsibility of playing in the Tests Robin was able to let his hair down more often than his room-mate.

I was 12th man and was never going to play a Test in South Africa for all the tea in China. I used to come back at four o'clock in the morning a bit worse for wear after a good night out and he'd go bloody mad.

"I've got to play cricket tomorrow and you've woken me up you drunken bastard"
Boycott would yell.

"Oh Geoffrey, shut up and go back to sleep" I'd shout.

"I need my sleep!" he'd yell back.

He hated me for that but we got on alright. It was probably the wrong thing to do but there I was, I was only 12th man, it didn't matter unless I had to go on and field yet he was having to get ready for a Test match. I can understand that now.

Boycott's behaviour on the tour was viewed by many of his England colleagues as self-centred and curt. He often didn't want to socialize, preferring his own company. He could be incredibly rude to hotel staff and members of the public; if he'd had a bad day then there was no reason why the rest of the world shouldn't have one too. After one game in particular a crowd of children had gathered outside the ground to collect autographs, Boycott told them to clear off before heading straight for his car, leaving team-mates to do the signing.

Robin remembers this aspect of Boycott's character well.

It was his first tour and for Mike Brearley, David Brown and myself – all youngsters, Boycott was really out of order. In the first few games he never raised his cap or his bat to the crowd and refused to sign autographs. The manager, Donald Carr, Mike Smith, and senior players like Barrington and Dexter took him to one side and said you can't do that, you've got to change your ways otherwise you're going to end up in trouble. And he did change.

Like so many others, although Robin was often annoyed with Boycott the person, he couldn't help but admire Boycott the batsman.

He was such an independent, selfish batsman but he made himself into a great player – he was the last one to leave the nets, he'd bat in the nets all day. He wasn't a good cricketer when he started but he made himself into a great player purely through hard work.

Even though he didn't play in the Test series Robin represented MCC in most of the tour games. He was more than happy to be there, away from the English winter and the paraffin round but at times wondered why he'd been selected as there were already two players capable of bowling leg spin in the side although neither Barrington nor Barber bowled much in the Tests. Of the 7686 balls bowled by England only 3.4 per cent were bowled by the leggies. By comparison, off-spinners Titmus and Allen delivered 44.2 per cent.

Despite a Test blank, overall Robin was the fifth most used bowler of the tour, bowling 316 overs and taking 27 wickets at an average of 29.48 and with a very respectable economy rate of 2.52 runs per over.

Robin felt lucky to be there and was going to enjoy the experience. Being on tour for four months allowed for more time to explore the country in between matches on an itinerary which took the players all over South Africa. Playing matches in Rhodesia, Bloemfontein and East London gave him the opportunity of visiting places he would never have otherwise been to.

Playing against Griqualand West in Kimberley afforded the opportunity to visit The Big Hole, reckoned to be the largest hand-dug excavation in the world and which had been mined intensively for diamonds from 1871-1914. An awesome sight and in the 1960s, before health and safety concerns, you could stand on the side and peer straight down the 500 feet drop to the water which filled the bottom of it. "I had a pretty good throw in those days," remembers Robin, "and I actually threw a stone into the middle of the water, you could see it land. I was very proud."

A visit to a South African gold mine, Robin is just right of centre.

The tour gave the England players the chance to try water skiing which a number of them caught the bug for and became quite good at, Robin included – much to his surprise. He even became a fine one-ski water skier. With no cricket scheduled for most of the Sundays they were free to indulge in their new found hobby. *The Times* cricket correspondent John Woodcock and other journalists would sometimes accompany the players on their jaunts. Woodcock had arthritic hips and had real difficulty in trying to push himself upright on the water skis. Abortive attempt after abortive attempt followed and then, just near the end of the tour, Woodcock managed to get on his skis. He was delighted. Following a successful circuit of the water he lifted one hand off the handle to give the jubilant spectators a victory wave, lost his balance and slammed into the water.

Woodcock was a firm favourite among the players and was on good, jovial terms with them. There was a greater level of socialising between the players and journalists in those days; according to Woodcock it was almost like an extended family. Writing in *The Times* about the MCC tour match in Cape Town against the South African Invitation XI, Woodcock – with his tongue perhaps firmly in his cheek – suggested that Robin's score of 36 in a last-wicket partnership of 62 with Tom Cartwright was one of the finest he had seen on the whole tour, with some fine late cuts.

The Invitation XI was a near Test-strength side and included rising star Barry Richards and Graeme Pollock who, in his second innings score of 91, hit one of Robin's deliveries out of the ground, over the railway line and into the neighbouring Newlands brewery. Robin had hoped he could avoid being selected for the game. "I was just sorry to be picked", he says ruefully:

> *I knew I was going to have to play, I didn't want to but I had to. It was the game before the last Test at Port Elizabeth and when I saw the line-up with Pollock and the likes in the side I thought 'Christ almighty I'm going to get some bloody hammer here' and I did, I got one for 114! There was no way I could avoid it unless I cried off injured and there was no way I could do that, they'd have known I was pulling the wool but I didn't really fancy it. I averaged 29 with the ball on tour, if I hadn't have played in that game it would have been more like 24.*

Earlier in the match, during the Invitation XI's first innings, Robin turned the tables on Colin Bland. One of the greatest fielders in the history of the game, Bland, batting at three and already on 116, turned a ball to square-leg and set off for a run but Dennis Gamsy rightly refused the call. Bland turned on his heels but he was too late as Robin, moving at speed from mid-wicket, executed a perfect pick-up and throw to hit the stumps with Bland's bat inches short.

As with the tours to East Africa and Jamaica the South Africa tour helped Robin to mature, not only as a cricketer but also as a person. The senior professionals had made Robin feel welcome and he made some firm friends; Peter Parfitt and David Allen were both party animals whose company Robin particularly enjoyed. There were numerous parties throughout the tour as the MCC players criss-crossed South Africa. Each member of the tour party was issued a card with an itinerary of the tour printed on it and for the single guys both sides of the card would have the phone numbers of women they'd met all over South Africa.

Whilst there were plenty of opportunities for socialising outside of the tour party, Saturday nights were reserved for team gatherings. One of the players would be designated as chairman for the evening and would then appoint two others to serve drinks. The drink and food flowed and a lot of home truths were imparted. They were good get-togethers and helped sustain the team spirit and morale – very important as the players were living out of each other's pockets for four months. One team meeting turned out to be a bit awkward though:

The chairman used to designate what you wore for the team meeting in the evening, so he could say you'd wear swimming trunks and tie, or you wore socks and just your underpants. Bob Barber was going out after one particular team meeting and, refusing to conform, he was dressed in his tuxedo and bow tie whereas everyone else turned up in what they had been told to wear. Whoever was chairman on the night had ordered these beautiful prawns in a basin and somebody threw a load of them at Bob and his tuxedo. I thought he was going to kill somebody. Bob was as strong as an ox and didn't have a great sense of humour; he was someone you didn't tangle with.

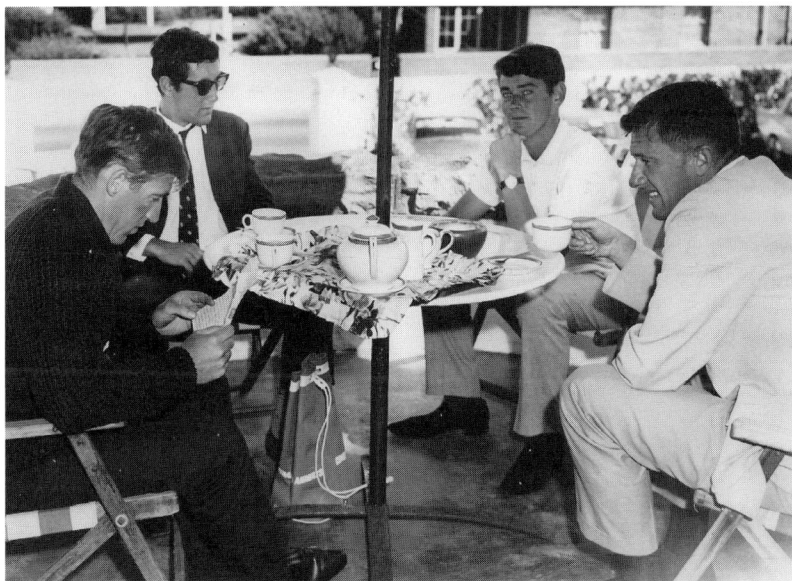

Tea and letters from home. Peter Parfitt, Mike Brearley, Robin (plus winkle pickers) and Ian Thomson.

The success of the tour both on and off the field was in no small part due to the excellent leadership of Mike Smith, tour manager Donald Carr and the team spirit they engendered. Carr had only recently retired from playing for Derbyshire and as such perhaps still considered himself at times to be one of the boys. At a function the night before the first Test at Durban, Carr had encouraged Bob Barber to drink a whole bottle of scotch which he duly did before going on to score 74 the next day.

Robin remembers sneaking back to the team hotel in the early hours after a night out, turning a corner and coming face to face with the tour manager. Fearing the worst and that he'd be losing some of his good behaviour bonus, Robin braced himself but Carr looked at him, simply nodded, and said "Hobbsy, I haven't seen you and you haven't seen me."

Socialising with the opposition was also a feature in those days and allowed Robin to get to know players like Colin Bland quite well.

Blandy was a lovely guy. We used to go to these parties and the South Africans were obviously told not to drink because there was a Test match coming up and he used to have a Coke bottle, a big pint bottle that was full of cane spirit, drank like a fish he did.

Robin also became friendly with Glen Hall, a fellow leg spinner, who played one Test for South Africa. Hall had some success with the ball against MCC in consecutive tour games for South African Universities and North-Eastern Transvaal. He was selected for the third Test at Cape Town and he got his one and only Test wicket, bowling Peter Parfitt for 44. He became a very firm friend of Robin and they used to write to each other for several years before the letters suddenly dropped off. Hall had become a pharmacist and married a former Miss South Africa. After the couple divorced, Hall unfortunately became a recluse, fell into depression and tragically took his own life in 1987 at the age of 49. It was through Glen that Robin came to meet his future wife, Isabel Abrahamse, a school teacher from Pretoria.

We were travelling back to Pretoria and we had a couple of days off so I phoned Glen and asked him if he could organise a party on the day we got back and it happened to be the 16th December, the day they called Dingaan's day which became the Day of the Covenant. There's a big statue in Pretoria, it was to do with when the Zulu uprisings were suppressed. So Glen organised a party at a house and four or five of us went along and that was the first time I met Isabel. It wasn't love at first sight, which seems a terrible thing to say, but we got on well and then later on things went from strength to strength.

After the tour, in his appraisal for *Playfair Cricket Monthly*, Basil Easterbrook wrote:

'MCC have sent more powerful teams from Lord's than this one but never one more superior in terms of corporate effort on the playing pitch and harmony in the pavilion. I'm still convinced that Hobbs has a lot of cricket in him, he did not enjoy the best of luck either with his bowling or the extent to which he was used. One of the mild criticisms I will make of M.J.K. Smith was his typical England captain's reluctance to use his leg-spinners more. There were times when a big score was inevitable and nothing much would have been lost and perhaps a deal to gained by greater trust in wrist spin than Smith was prepared to show.'

Robin had been convinced from the moment he was selected for the squad that he wouldn't get to play a Test in South Africa particularly as Ken Barrington and Bob Barber, both in the side as batsmen, could bowl leg breaks.

It was totally unexpected; I didn't think I'd get picked to go to South Africa. I was very lucky to go but right from the start they didn't need me really, they should never have taken me, they had Barrington and Barber bowling leg breaks, what the hell did they want me for? I'd been selected as the main leg-break bowler and there was one tour game we played where Kenny Barrington got five for 29 and I got one for 32, that really griped. I'm supposed to be the main spinner and he'd gone and got five.

Did it do me any good, the tour of South Africa? I had a great time, 5 ½ months out there was a fantastic time, but did it improve my cricket? Not really. They took me as a good fielder and for experience – whether it was the right experience I'm not sure.

It was certainly an experience; one which lasted longer for Robin and John Price who both stayed on in South Africa to take a holiday after the official tour had ended in Port Elizabeth. The two players shared a road trip down the Garden Route to Cape Town in a brand new Volkswagen Passat, which they had agreed to deliver on behalf of a VW dealer who told them there was no rush and to enjoy the trip. So Robin and Price did as they were told and took a leisurely month to complete the 600-mile journey, stopping off at lovely little places along the way they were looked after brilliantly by locals who would then phone ahead on to the next person who would then put them up for a couple of nights.

On arrival in Cape Town they met up with David Brown who'd also stayed on for a holiday. The plan was always that the three of them would return to England, along with all the MCC cricket kit, aboard the Royal Mail Ship *Edinburgh Castle* but as Price was carrying an injury the MCC insisted that he flew back on his own.

When me and David Brown were bringing the bags back from the tour at Cape Town we had a four-berth cabin with just the two of us in which was good. There was a knock at the door I opened it and there was Isabel with a bunch of flowers and I said to her "Sorry, you're not in the right cabin here love, you must be somewhere else". She said "I'm Isabel" I said "Isabel? Oh Christ, yes, Isabel! Sorry Is, it's been a long trip I didn't recognise you." I probably hadn't seen her for 2 ½ months. That went down well didn't it!

Despite the *faux pas*, it was the most fabulous end to the tour, the cruise lasted a fortnight stopping off along the way at Walvis Bay in Namibia and Las Palmas in the Canary Islands before arriving in Southampton where they were greeted by Donald Carr. During the tour Robin had hardly spent a penny. The basic tour fee for each player was £700 plus a kit allowance of £125 and £7 per week for incidental expenses. On top of that there was a bonus of £150 for good behaviour. Robin received around £1000 for four months work, equivalent to approximately £13,500 in 2018, and to him it was a fortune. He wasn't sure if he had a future at international level but after his experience in South Africa he knew that being on tour was preferable to selling paraffin in the winter and he was determined to get on as many tours as he could.

Chapter Seven

It was an extraordinary tour, a real eye opener.

ROBIN HAD RETURNED from South Africa midway through Essex's pre-season training and it was back to normality as a county cricketer; there was no more sponsorship or special treatment although there was one spin-off as Robin was paid £100 to advertise cricket gear in a promotional brochure.

Before they had their own training facility at Chelmsford, Essex's pre-season work took place at the Old Blues rugby ground in Fairlop. Training in those days was not quite to the same level of professionalism and intensity recognised in modern cricket. There were a couple of nets at Fairlop but there was minimal coaching. "I've never been coached in my life" says Robin. Ray East similarly remembers receiving precious little by way of coaching from the Essex staff. 'Frank Rist was a lovable character but did not believe in some of the more scientific theories about instruction.' It's very much an opinion shared by Robin who remembers that Rist was very good at making tea – "gallons of it."

Aside from net practice there was little attention paid to fitness training. There weren't any runs or strength-and-conditioning training but there was a lot of football played. Games were usually between the capped and uncapped players and matches lasted as long as it took for the capped players to win. Trevor Bailey, very much now in the autumn of his career, had a novel way of regaining his fitness before the start of the season. He would wear a blue plastic suit, the kind worn by fishermen and sailors, and by bowling repeatedly in the nets would sweat off the weight he'd put on during the off-season.

Nineteen sixty-five was to be a disappointing season for Essex as they languished near the bottom of the Championship table for most of the summer. Points were hard to come by; a situation not helped by a wet summer which saw 17 out of 28 of their matches finish as draws. The conditions were far from ideal for a leg spinner, the pitches at Essex stayed green and Robin did very well to take 75 first-class wickets at 23.36.

As in 1964, Robin was selected to represent MCC for one of the traditional fixtures at Lord's which acted as a curtain raiser to the new season. The MCC side was captained by Colin Cowdrey and, as well as Robin, included other young and up-and-coming players Keith Fletcher, Colin Milburn, Alan Knott and Derek Underwood. Surrey included 18-year-old off spinner Pat Pocock in their side, the first time that Robin had come up against him in a first-class match and a player who would become a great friend over the years. Unfortunately the rain, as with many games that season, intervened and Robin only got the opportunity to bowl one over.

A full game was possible for Essex's traditional first match of the season at Fenners against Cambridge University in early May. In cold and miserable conditions, Cambridge won the toss and put Essex into bat. Essex scored 226 in their first innings, ground out off 118 overs. Robin was one of only two Essex players not to fall to the off breaks of Modern Languages student – and latter day writer and Guyanese politician – Rupert Roopnaraine, who recorded his best bowling figures in first-class cricket of eight for 88. Robin wasn't required to bowl as the University side collapsed to 37 all out in their first innings with Trevor Bailey taking five wickets for three runs. "Trevor did like to look after himself figure wise", Robin recalls, "In those Cambridge University games at Fenners you couldn't get the ball out of his hand."

Essex went on to win the match by nine wickets and Robin remembers that Bailey, himself a Cambridge graduate, was anxious to soften the humiliation inflicted on his old university. "He took the whole Cambridge side out for dinner that night at the Hawks' Club to celebrate. He didn't take the Essex players out!" says Robin with a wry smile.

Essex v Worcestershire, Brentwood, May 1965. Standing: Eddie Presland, Rodney Cass, Brian Edmeades, Geoff Smith, Barry Knight, Paddy Phelan, John Wilcox, Robin Hobbs. Sitting: Michael Bear, Trevor Bailey, Gordon Barker, Brian Taylor.

Essex's first Championship match of the 1965 season was against the title holders at Worcester with the first-day's play commencing on Robin's 23rd birthday. Under the popular and influential captaincy of Don Kenyon, Worcestershire would go on to retain the title but it was Essex who had the upper hand, needing just 21 runs for victory with four wickets in hand, when stumps were drawn. On a well-grassed pitch Robin went wicketless, only bowling a total of nine overs in the match. In a strange quirk of the fixture list the next meeting of the two sides commenced the very next day at Brentwood and would see Essex go one better and Robin's fortunes improve in a match which he describes as one of the most enjoyable he'd ever played in.

Brentwood was one of the many home venues scattered around the county, it was a lovely ground which Robin remembers fondly and all the nicer for the beautiful warm weather which lasted throughout the three days of the game. The beauty of the ground wasn't quite matched by the quality of the pitches. With Essex still leading a nomadic existence on pitches prepared by local groundsmen, the players never knew quite what to expect. On winning the toss, Trevor Bailey chose to bat and Essex, despite wobbling at one stage at 154-6, managed to post a decent first-innings score of 302 thanks largely to a seventh wicket partnership of 139 between Bailey and John Wilcox.

Rural county cricket at Brentwood in 1965. Robin bowling to Doug Slade, Basil D'Oliveira is the relaxed non-striker.

Having bowled Essex out there was time for Worcestershire to face two overs before close of play on the first day. Barry Knight immediately trapped

Don Kenyon lbw in the first over and much to the surprise of everyone, himself included, Trevor Bailey threw the ball to Robin and asked him to open the bowling from the other end. Martin Horton, Worcestershire's other experienced opening batsman, was on strike. Robin hadn't entirely been looking forward to bowling against Worcestershire's powerful batting line-up and maybe it was a touch of nerves which contributed to him dropping a delivery short in his first over. Horton, keen to get off the mark and assert himself on the young leg spinner, shaped to pull the ball but missed it and was bowled for a duck.

Resuming the following morning, night-watchman Doug Slade attempted to drive a delivery from Robin's second over but only succeeded in skying a catch to Knight. Operating in tandem with off spinner Paddy Phelan on a pitch offering assistance, Robin went on to take five for 46 from 25 overs including the wickets of Basil D'Oliveira and Ron Headley. Essex had a lead of 167 but sensing that the pitch would get worse the longer the game went on, Bailey decided against enforcing the follow-on. The Essex second-innings was declared on 170-6 and Worcestershire were set a target of 338. At one point Essex seemed to be heading for a comfortable win as Worcestershire slumped to 146-6 on the final day. A brilliant century by D'Oliveira got the Essex supporters' nerves jumping but his dismissal for 163 – lbw to Knight – signalled the end and Worcestershire were all out for 289 and Essex had beaten the champions by 48 runs.

Robin had done the damage in the first innings with his five for 46 but went wicket-less in the second from 37 overs; the bowling honours going to Phelan with seven for 80. "I remember saying to Paddy afterwards what an unfair game cricket was. How can you get nought for 95 after taking five for 46? It seems crazy, but that's cricket for you, isn't it."

Despite his 10 wickets in the match, Phelan retired from professional cricket in 1965.

He knew he was going to leave at the end of the season. Trevor asked him to attend the last home match against Middlesex at Leyton and Paddy said "I'll come to Leyton but I'm playing, I'm not coming as 12th man." He played and he got six for 72 but he never really fulfilled his promise and he left and got a proper job in civil engineering.

Impressive match figures of nine for 68 from Robin weren't quite enough to secure a win for Essex in their Championship clash against Kent at Maidstone in early July and yet another game finished as a draw. The final match of the season saw a resounding win for Essex against Glamorgan at Llanelli and the victory enabled them to drag themselves off the foot of the table. Essex trailed by 72 runs after the first innings, but Robin with six for 30 and Barry Knight with four for

36 bowled the hosts out for 113. Robin had played a major role as Essex went on to win by five wickets. Along with his six for 64 in Glamorgan's first innings he had secured his best bowling analysis to date taking 12 for 94 in the match; it was only Essex's fourth win of the season but enough for them to avoid the wooden spoon as they finished six points above bottom club Nottinghamshire.

Despite having toured with MCC during the winter Robin wasn't called up by England for any of the Test matches that summer. In the three Tests against New Zealand followed by a further three against South Africa, the bulk of the spin bowling was done by Fred Titmus who played in all six matches. There was back-up from the part-time leg breaks of Bob Barber and Ray Illingworth played a solitary Test. Robin had proved on more than one occasion that he could be a match-winner at county level but finger spin and part-time wrist spin were still deemed more than sufficient in international cricket.

Although not featuring in the Test match stakes, Robin did get to play against South Africa in their tour match against Essex in early July which gave him the chance to catch up with one or two of the players he'd met and become friendly with a few months earlier on tour.

Fine weather and a good crowd greeted the tourists at the Castle Park ground in Colchester. Although he only took one wicket in the match, Robin played a key role in securing a draw as he and Paddy Phelan batted out the final overs with Essex nine wickets down. The game didn't pass by without a bit of controversy which revolved around the South African batsman Ali Bacher, who later became the country's captain and the leading light in the post-apartheid reintegration process. Bacher had struggled for runs in his first full tour and when he clearly edged a catch which was caught behind by Brian Taylor, he chose not to walk. Years later the incident was recalled in his official biography where Bacher stated that he 'broke his bat' on a delivery by the leg spinner Robin Hobbs. Bacher, desperate for runs, stood his ground and waited for umpire Syd Buller to make a decision. Rated as one of the best in England, Buller gave it not out and Bacher took the view that if the top umpire in England wasn't prepared to uphold Robin's appeal then he was happy to abide by the decision.

Robin, in his own words, "went ape shit" but Bacher batted on, scoring 59 before he was again caught behind by Taylor, this time off the bowling of Knight. Robin did enjoy the satisfaction of dismissing Bacher for 28 in the second innings but despite being livid at him for not walking in the first innings he didn't give him a send-off, it wasn't the done thing at the time.

One of the strangest matches that season was at Clacton in August as Essex took on Warwickshire. On the final day Essex were set 203 to win in just under four hours and had started their innings reasonably well when, with his opening bowler Webster unable to bowl, Warwickshire's captain, Alan Smith, took off his wicket-keeping pads to have a bowl. Unbelievably Smith took a hat-trick with the 11th, 12th and 13th balls of his spell and went on to record figures of four for 36 from 21 overs. Essex had collapsed to 136-9 when Robin joined Brian Edmeades in the middle but fortunately the last-wicket pair batted out the final 15 minutes to draw the match.

Although he wasn't selected for England during the summer, Robin was still very much in the thoughts of the selectors and he was picked for the MCC side to play against Yorkshire at the Scarborough Festival in September. In his final first-class outing of 1965, Robin took four for 107 in Yorkshire's first innings including the wickets of Ray Illingworth and Brian Close.

Robin was still living in Walthamstow in Avon Road with his dad, aunt and grandparents but by this point Isabel had moved to England to take a teaching position and was living in Notting Hill so he was spending quite a bit of time there with her. Robin hadn't been selected for the 1965/66 tour to Australia, the selectors again favouring finger and part-time leg spin, and instead found employment over the winter with H.L Puckle and Co, insurance brokers in London.

The year of football's World Cup was a poor one for Essex as once again they finished near the bottom of the Championship. It marked the end of an era with Trevor Bailey playing his last season as captain and fellow allrounder Barry Knight would depart acrimoniously before the start of the following season. The club was in a parlous financial state and were fortunate to secure a £15,000 interest-free loan from the Warwickshire County Cricket Supporters Association which they would use to help purchase the cricket ground at Chelmsford. Essex were still leading a nomadic existence playing festival weeks at eight different grounds around the county and establishing a permanent base was the first step to securing a brighter and successful future.

An unintended benefit of the county's predicament was that the reduction in playing staff to reduce the wage bill meant a core group of younger players were able to develop their talents more fully. As long as they kept themselves fit, and free of serious injury, then their places in the team were secure. Younger players making their first-team debuts included off spinner David Acfield and Barbadian allrounder Keith Boyce. Having made one first-team appearance in 1965, left-arm spinner Ray East would also go on and begin to establish himself as a regular. For Robin, now Essex's senior spinner, 1966 saw him produce another solid season for the county, bowling 648 overs and taking 73 wickets at 24.6. Together with the other first-class games he played that year his final analysis for the season was 88 first-class wickets at 25.77.

Robin was once again in the minds of the MCC selectors and was picked to represent MCC versus Yorkshire at Lord's at the beginning of the season. In a drawn encounter with the eventual winners of that season's County Championship, Robin's only wicket was Geoffrey Boycott, caught by John Mortimore for 68.

David Acfield and Keith Boyce were the standout performers in the Cambridge University match at Brentwood in June. Acfield, who would later represent Great Britain in fencing at the 1968 and 1972 Olympics, was a Cambridge undergraduate at the time and was playing for the University against his county side. He went on to take six for 69 in Essex's first-innings total of 284 and Robin was his fifth victim, falling for an entertaining 40, as Acfield achieved his first ever five-wicket return in first-class cricket. Robin went on to become good friends with Acfield but recalls that at the time there was some resentment towards the student amateur.

We felt at the time that because Trevor Bailey was a Cambridge man and David Acfield was a Cambridge man that Trevor was determined to get David into the Essex side. Trevor was pushing him so hard we didn't really want him in our set-up. We were professional and he was an amateur who couldn't turn pro because of his fencing. There was a little bit of resentment, not nasty but kind of hushed, and it took a bit of time before he was accepted but as history shows he was a great bowler for Essex. We became very good friends even though we're totally different characters.

Acfield's bowling efforts were over-shadowed by Keith Boyce who terrorised the Cambridge students with his pace bowling on an untrustworthy surface taking nine for 61 in the first innings and four for 47 in the second. Boyce had been discovered by Trevor Bailey during a Cavaliers tour to the Caribbean in 1965 and was signed up even though the Barbadian would first have to serve a two-year qualifying period before he could play county cricket. Boyce has been acclaimed as arguably the most thrilling allrounder ever to play for Essex and Robin recalls well his former team-mate's exciting all-round talent as if he was Learie Constantine reincarnated.

While he was qualifying to play for Essex he was playing for Walthamstow and he was the scourge of club cricket. Can you imagine a guy, bowling at nearly 100 mph, hitting the ball as hard as anyone has done in county cricket and fielding like a panther in any position, playing for a club side. He just devoured club after club after club. He was a fantastic athlete, when you think of the IPL nowadays, Ben

Stokes is worth £1.4 million this guy would have been topped that, he was that good. He was a fantastic athlete and a fantastic cricketer. Essex were so lucky to get him, he gave such tremendous service. He fielded anywhere, used to throw the ball in mid-air and it would come like a tracer bullet. A terrific cricketer!

Brian Taylor used to bowl him into the ground. On occasions, he'd bowl him for 15-over spells which were too long but Boycie would bowl and bowl and bowl and I never ever saw him chuck it in, he always gave 100%. I never saw him bowl off a short run, he ran in all day on pitches he should never have been bowling on.

'How did it get there?' Robin deceives Ernie Clifton and Peter Parfitt, Middlesex v Essex, 1966.

Robin had a fine season in 1966 with the ball taking five-wickets in an innings five times, the first of which came against Middlesex at Lord's in July. In a match eventually abandoned due to heavy rain, Robin bowled exceptionally well in Middlesex's first innings, sending down 22.3 overs and taking six for 31 including the wickets of Test players Eric Russell and Fred Titmus. Only a few days later Robin would go on to record his best bowling performance in first-class cricket in the match against Glamorgan at St Helen's in Swansea. This match was played under the experimental rule change whereby the first innings of the first 12 matches played by each county were restricted to 65 overs. It was a move to encourage brighter cricketer but the rule was scrapped after just one season.

Batting first, Essex scored 169-7 from their 65 overs and Glamorgan looked set to pass this having been well set at 50-1 but then Robin proceeded to tear through the Welsh county's batting to record career-best figures of eight for 63.

I can remember that it turned square at Swansea, and because it was the 65-over rule, towards the end of their first innings they had a slog and I got wickets that way. In that spell I think I got three players out for nought in the middle order, genuine balls, leg spinners that were caught at slip, and then the last three all had a slog and got out caught.

Robin took another five-wicket haul in Glamorgan's second innings (5-101) giving him an overall match analysis of 13 for 164. He was given the responsibility of bowling the last over of the match and when it came down to the last ball the scores were level. Glamorgan – eight wickets down – needed just one run to win, and Don Shepherd swung Robin's last delivery away but couldn't clear the field and Barry Knight was able to take the catch to secure a thrilling draw with the scores level.

Further success followed with five for 63 against Nottinghamshire at Trent Bridge in mid-August as Essex narrowly failed to force a win with the opposition nine wickets down before time was called. Essex were likewise unable to press home their advantage in the drawn match against Hampshire at Portsmouth a few days later. Once again the opposition were nine wickets down but Essex couldn't finish them off as the Hampshire last-wicket pair batted for over an hour to hold off Trevor Bailey's side who tried seven different bowlers in a vain attempt to take the last wicket. Robin had very nearly swung it for Essex with five for 65 including three caught-and-bowled dismissals.

In the process of taking one of three chances offered to him, Robin had damaged one of his fingers. "David Turner hit the ball back at me and it smashed my finger. He was one of the most difficult blokes to bowl to, he was a little guy, he stood in the crease and was a good cutter and puller, I never got the right length to him." With such a small playing staff Robin was needed to play in the next match – the penultimate game of the season against reigning champions Worcestershire even though, due to his injury, he wouldn't be able to bowl. As it was, only four of the Essex players were 100 per cent fit as injuries, niggles and end-of-season wear and tear began to take its toll.

It was a hard slog for the walking wounded as Worcestershire piled on the runs. "I was probably pleased I'd hurt my finger" – the fourth-wicket partnership of 271 between Tom Graveney and Basil D'Oliveira saw Worcestershire eventually declare on 405-6 much to the relief of a weary Robin. "I fielded third-man both ends, with my finger strapped up, and I never bowled a ball. We had nobody else." Essex were 122-7 with Robin still to bat when, after a number of interruptions due to rain, the game was eventually abandoned as a draw.

Earlier in the summer rain had also provided a welcome intrusion, interrupting Essex's three-day match against Surrey at The Oval. Play started on 30 July 1966, a big day in English sporting history as the World Cup final between England and West Germany was kicking off at 3pm over the river at Wembley. Nobody wanted to miss it, even the umpires.

It rained at 1.15pm and we never went back on so we watched the final live on TV. I think it drizzled most of the afternoon and we decided there wouldn't be any more play, funny that!

For Robin and the Essex players there was the added attraction of watching their former team-mate, Geoff Hurst, playing up front for England. Up until two years earlier he'd still been playing second XI cricket for Essex and now there he was just a few miles away, the first player to score a hat-trick in a World Cup final.

Robin's season concluded with two representative matches at the Scarborough Festival in September. Playing for an England XI, he took four second-innings wickets, including the South African trio of Graeme Pollock, Peter Pollock and Colin Bland, against a Rest of the World XI in a five-wicket victory. Robin was never afraid to go for runs at Scarborough and for a number of years was probably the first name on the team sheet for the people who ran the festival. He was an entertainer and would continue to toss the ball up regardless of the stick that might be meted out by the batsmen.

The England XI were led by Brian Close, who had recently captained England to a consolation win against West Indies in the final Test of the summer and had also led his county to the Championship. Yorkshire would once again be captained by Close in Robin's next match, representing MCC against the newly crowned champions. For Robin it would be a perfect end to the season and a match in which he undoubtedly caught the eye of the current England captain.

MCC scored 252-9 declared in their first innings of which Robin contributed 29 not out in an unbroken last-wicket stand worth 65 with Fred Rumsey. Buoyed with confidence from his batting exploits, Robin bowled attackingly taking five for 56, including the wicket of Close for eight, as Yorkshire collapsed to 117 all out. MCC, under the captaincy of Derbyshire's Derek Morgan, declared on 107-2 in their second innings setting the champions a target of 243 to win. With licence to attack once more, Robin tossed the ball up and was rewarded with his second five-wicket haul of the match taking five for 113 including, once again, the wicket of Close. Robin dismissed Close eight times in first-class cricket, six of which were at Scarborough over the years. "I got him out at Scarborough a few times," recalls Robin, "but not that often when he played for Yorkshire or Somerset; at Scarborough when it was a bit fancy free, he'd whack it up in the air."

As the curtain fell on the 1966 season Robin knew that he had another winter tour to look forward to, having been selected as part of the MCC England under-25 squad to tour Pakistan for six weeks beginning in January 1967. Without a senior England tour that winter it would give the England selectors an opportunity to assess the next generation of Test players.

Doug Insole, chairman of the England selectors, was quoted in *The Daily Express* about the challenge which lay ahead for some of the country's brightest young talent.

'Obviously we are looking to these players to provide us with Test material in the not too distant future. These are the pick of the under-25s in England. Everybody we invited to tour accepted. The aim is to give them experience of playing in an atmosphere of international cricket.'

Three of the 14-man squad were front-line spinners and in essence Robin was competing with off spinner Pat Pocock and left armer Derek Underwood to be ready to make the step up to the full England side during the summer of 1967, should a spot become available. Also in the squad, and on his first MCC tour, was 20-year-old Kent wicket-keeper Alan Knott who'd been looking forward to the challenge of keeping on sub-continental pitches and to Robin's bowling.

'It was very exciting to keep to a leg spinner on that tour. I'd been fortunate enough to keep to three leg spinners from when I was young – Ted Fillary and David Baker at Kent – and then I was very lucky to go on a Cavaliers tour to the West Indies in 1965 with a chap called Gamini Goonesena. I kept to those three and that got me the badge of honour of keeping to leg spin, and gave me the preparation to keep to Robin. That was the first time I ever kept to him on that under-25 tour.'

Under the captaincy of Mike Brearley the under-25s won four and drew four of the eight games; Robin finished with 27 wickets at 25 apiece compared with Pocock's 31 at 20 and Underwood's 13 at 31. Seven of Robin's wickets were stumpings by the nimble glove-work of Knott; had Robin signed for Kent instead of Essex the Hobbs/Knott combination could have a potent one. Knott may not have been the finished article in 1967 but he wasn't far off it and just as Robin had benefitted from Laurie Johnson's presence behind the stumps on the East Africa tour in 1963 he now had another top-class keeper backing him up who was eager and relishing the experience.

'Once you get to read the leg spinner's bowling it's wonderful to keep to them, you're in the game so much more with a leg spinner, there's always the chance of a stumping. I got three in the match at Lahore which, unless a leg spinner is in the side, is very rare.'

Robin's excellent fielding also caught the eye as team-mate Pocock well remembers:

'I think one of his talents as a cricketer certainly was that he was a great fielder at a time when you only had about four or five good fielders in the side so if you were good your skills shone a bit more. I remember a tour match once where Hobbsy was 12th man and he came on three times and got a run-out each time; he was brilliant.'

Alan Knott was similarly impressed by Robin presence and energy in the field.

'He was definitely one of the most naturally athletic people you could ever meet I don't think he trained or exercised much but he was naturally gifted. He could throw just by flicking the wrist, everything came from the wrist at tremendous,speed; amazing, he must go down as one of the great fielders.'

The tour did much to enhance Robin's prospects at international level. Peter Smith, who covered the tour for *Playfair Cricket Monthly,* wrote that on the bowling front Pocock and Robin 'were made to bear the brunt of the attack and confirmed the high promise they have shown in England.' Rex Alston, writing in the same magazine, commented that a number of the players enhanced their reputations and that 'to become a genuine international cricketer requires adaptability to all conditions and the experience gained on this tour should in the long run pay dividends.' He continued stating that 'leg spinner Hobbs has shown that he can spin the ball in South Africa and the West Indies as well as Pakistan'

For Robin it was a fantastic tour.

We were a good young team. Brearley was brilliant, he let you set your own fields but if he wanted to change it he did, but he was a very astute captain, a very nice

*guy. Pat and I did the majority of the bowling because Derek Underwood, poor soul,
for the first three or four games never looked like getting a wicket. They had some
bloody good players the Pakistan side. I think we played virtually every day for six
weeks bar two and Alan Knott was playing every game, keeping wicket in that heat.*

MCC Under-25s v Pakistan Under-25s at Lahore. Standing: Keith Fletcher,
Geoff Arnold, Pat Pocock, Mike Bissex, Alan Ormrod, Dennis Amiss, Alan Knott.
Sitting:Robin Hobbs, David Brown, Mike Brearley, Derek Underwood.

Robin nearly missed the first game after going down with stomach problems
but recovered in time – with help from tour manager Les Ames who produced
vast quantities of tablets and pills – to face Southern Zone in Hyderabad. At one
stage or another during the tour just about all the players were struck down with
illness.

*We were travelling around and staying in some really poor places, really poor hotels,
guest houses really. You had fried eggs most of the time because you didn't trust the
food. There was a time on that tour, certainly, when I was on the loo for two days,
you don't think anything else wants to come out.*

*It was a great bunch of lads out there – Neil Abberley, Dennis Amiss, David
Brown, Alan Knott, Richard Hutton and Tony Windows – all the same age, we had
to make our own fun and activity and you got to know them so well that we all*

became good friends.

In the fourth match of the tour, played against North Zone at Peshawar, Robin took six for 39 as the home side were bundled out for just 126, this in reply to 514-4 declared which included a mammoth 312 not out in a day from skipper Mike Brearley. Robin was not as effective in the second innings and his bowling was hampered by a cut to his right hand. In a quest to limit the possibility of further stomach problems he'd turned to tinned food and cut himself opening a tin of bully beef. Underwood hadn't had a successful tour with his bowling and with Robin off the field he now had to suffer the ignominy of watching part-time leg-break bowler Keith Fletcher ending up with four for 50. At that stage Fletcher had only taken three first-class wickets in his career. Underwood's unhappy experience ensured that Robin and Pocock were very much the next cabs on the rank for any spin-bowling spots which might become vacant in the full England side. The tour had received good coverage back home in the press and a lot of people had taken notice of the performances.

"A great bunch of lads" – MCC Under-25 tour to Pakistan.

Although it had been a full-on five weeks, and despite the dodgy hotels, stomach troubles, sapping heat, slow wickets and, at times, strange umpiring decisions, Robin enjoyed a great tour. He'd also been able to spend time getting to know the tour manager Les Ames, who had unsuccessfully tried to sign him for Kent seven years earlier. It was the first of a number of tours Robin went on to Pakistan and he developed a fondness for the country, the sights and the people.

We were very lucky, we had a fine manager in Les Ames, he was brilliant, just brilliant! It was an extraordinary tour, a real eye opener and gave us the experience of going up the Khyber Pass and seeing the Himalayas.

The tour had been a major boost to Robin's confidence; he'd greatly enhanced his reputation as a serious leg spinner and could look forward to the 1967 season and the strong possibility of a Test debut against the touring India or Pakistan sides.

Chapter Eight

I was over the moon; me, I thought, playing for England, goodness me.

NINETEEN SIXTY-SEVEN may well have been the summer of love in London and San Francisco but there wasn't much of it on show early in the year when the successor to Trevor Bailey as Essex captain was chosen. Many had expected either Barry Knight or Gordon Barker, vice-captain to Bailey, to be appointed but both would be overlooked.

> *I only found out in recent years that Doug Insole wouldn't have Barry Knight as captain at any price. Trevor Bailey was a great Barry Knight fan but Doug didn't think Barry was the right person to lead Essex because of his flamboyant lifestyle. You couldn't help but like him, he was a showman and a real woman's man, he had all manner of women around him, Petula Clark used to come to the county games. He liked the glamour and the high life, the cars and the suits. He was a nice bloke but he got involved with some of the wrong people.*
>
> *At the time we all thought Knighty should have been captain but on reflection he probably wasn't the right man. Gordon Barker wouldn't have been the right man either although he was bright cricket-wise, I don't think he would have handled it too well. Knight got the hump, understandably so, and went off to join Leicestershire.*

The Essex committee opted instead for wicket-keeper Brian 'Tonker' Taylor and despite any tactical nous he may have lacked he was very much the right man at the right time; they needed somebody solid who'd have a positive influence over the younger players. Tonker's recollections of this period in Essex's history illustrate his belief that backing the youngsters at the club was crucial to its future.

> 'I had always been upset when we played Yorkshire and Surrey as we found it difficult to compete against them, so when I was appointed captain I was determined to overcome that. We had no money, but experience in Gordon Barker, Trevor Bailey and Michael Bear plus nine youngsters in the field – Fletcher, East, Hobbs, Boyce, Lever, Acfield etc. The committee offered to bring in a couple of players released from other counties but I said there was only one way we could go and that was up with what we had. I wanted to get those youngsters

into our way of playing and thinking so that we could move forward. You had to be patient, though; I bullied the young players into believing in themselves.'

Robin had been nurtured under Bailey's leadership and in Tonker he was again fortunate to have a captain who was equally appreciative and supportive of his bowling. It seemed strange that Tonker should have had this approach according to Robin.

Tonker was brought up mainly with a four-pronged seam attack at Essex in Bailey, Preston, Ralph and Knight; he was a good wicket-keeper standing back but he had very limited experience standing up to spinners. It was odd then that when he took over the captaincy he really pressed for three spinners to play. If I'd had been a captain who wasn't very keen to keep to spinners I'd have had another seamer in the side. He dropped a lot of catches and missed quite a few stumpings – it didn't bother him. It made him look a bit stupid but if he'd have said "Bugger that I'm not having Hobbsy in the side we'll have another seamer" life would have been easier for him.

Robin was also fortunate that Tonker had his favourites and he was very much one of his blue-eyed boys. In Tonker's eyes he could do nothing wrong even when he was in the wrong. The upshot was that Robin could expect plenty of bowling and this remained absolutely crucial to both form and development.

The only way is practice; practice, playing and bowling in the middle. Those days will never happen again. 700 overs in a season was regular as far as I was concerned. If you bowl 700 overs chances are you're going to get 80 wickets, you're going to get one in nine, that was certainly the case if you look through my record but now they play so little county cricket [Crane bowled 193.1 overs in the County Championship in 2017]. I don't think you'll ever see another leg-break bowler playing for England in more than half-a-dozen Test matches in his career. You won't find a young leg spinner who'll be a regular county player, you'll have these guys like Parkinson and Crane, there's no place for them which is sad, I was very lucky to play when I did.

By this point in his career Robin had become a regular selection for MCC matches staged at Lord's at the start of the season as well as those at Scarborough at the close of it. It was a very wet summer that year, particularly in May, and much play was lost to rain in the MCC versus Surrey fixture but Robin got off to a good start with four for 80 including the prize wicket of Ken Barrington, stumped by John Murray. Robin was also selected for MCC versus India at Lord's in May – pretty much a Test trial – and bowled tidily enough in the first innings without reward. The match was cut short due to rain but in the second innings,

Robin bowled 12 overs for 14 runs and picked up the wicket of Surti, stumped by Murray. Brian Close was captaining the MCC side and was impressed by Robin's bowling which constantly threatened Ramesh Saxena and also tied up the Indian number four, Chandrakant Borde.

That summer, England would be playing three Tests each against India and Pakistan. Both teams were still in their relative infancy as far as Test cricket was concerned and whilst overall they were considered to be less of a threat than Australia, South Africa or West Indies, they did still possess a number of very talented players. Importantly for Robin, the batsmen from both sides were well used to facing spin bowling and, should he be selected, would not offer easy wickets.

Prior to the announcement of the team for the first Test against India at Headingley starting on 8 June, Robin caught the eye with a timely five-for in Northamptonshire's first innings in the County Championship fixture at Wantage Road.

Having had a successful time on the under-25 tour to Pakistan earlier in the year Robin was definitely one of the next spinners in waiting. He had an inkling that he might be in line for a Test debut although having seen the press link his name with a possible home Test call-up as far back as 1964 he wasn't taking anything for granted. Whilst he'd always felt that he had it in him to make it as a professional cricketer Robin had never harboured any serious ambitions of playing for England.

Although he may not have been entirely convinced of his worth as a Test cricketer there were others quite happy to talk up Robin's prospects. Writing in *The Daily Express*, Denis Compton, again, made a plea to the England selectors to give Robin a Test chance that summer and also looked even further ahead with one eye on the tour to the Caribbean in the winter.

'I believe he would be a great success in the West Indies. I took him there with the International Cavaliers in 1963/4 and he bowled magnificently on wickets where the extra bounce made him a menace to batsmen.

The late Sir Frank Worrell told me at the time "England have a natural in this youngster. He should be given all possible encouragement. He could become a Test match winner." Now is the time to blood Hobbs. He has served a thorough apprenticeship. All he wants is encouragement.'

Robin found out that he'd been selected for England a week before the first Test of the summer when a typed letter from MCC arrived, inviting him to report to the England captain at Headingley no later than 3pm the day before the match commenced.

A number of newspapers made capital of the surname Robin shared with Sir Jack, something he'd been used to ever since signing for Essex. 'Famous England name returns to Test cricket' heralded Crawford White in *The Daily Express*.

Robin's quotes in the press at the time reveal the extent of his surprise at being selected.

> *I'm delighted. I only hope I can justify my selection. I've never played at Leeds before so let's hope it's a lucky ground for me. I was surprised I was picked, even though I have been playing well this season, but I am really looking forward to my first game for England.*

Despite his modesty at being selected Robin was confident enough to predict the outcome of the Test: "I think we will win mainly because the Indians are so short of match practice owing to the atrocious weather last month."

News of Robin's selection was well received by a number of journalists, particularly John Woodcock when he announced 'Hobbs in England 12 for Leeds' in *The Times* on 5 June before analysing Robin's chances of making the team.

> 'When Thursday comes, either a batsman will stand down, or Hobbs if the pitch looks particularly green. If Hobbs plays he will be the first specialist leg spinner to be in an England side since Greenhough in 1960, and only the second since the days of Hollies, Jenkins and Wright. Leg-spin bowling, unlike bowling at medium pace, calls for more craft and touch than industry: it is associated with sunshine and freedom of expression, and many of the best things in cricket. For having been chosen, Hobbs may pass a word of thanks to Brian Taylor, his new county captain, who has given him every opportunity, even in the persistent floods rather than the darling buds of May.'

Dennis Amiss was the unlucky batsman from the 12 to stand down and Brian Close went on to inform Robin that not only would he be making his Test debut, he'd also play in all three matches of the series.

> *We had dinner the night before the game when Closey told me I'd be playing and it made me feel at ease. It was different from the 1970s and 1980s when people came in for one Test and were dropped. The number of people who only played one Test and never felt secure or had a run in the side. Nowadays when a guy gets picked for England, they get a good run in the side. It was very unusual though in those days, if you look through the sides, the established players like Barrington and Parks stayed*

in but the fringe players were in and out.

John Murray, who kept wicket for England during the series against India, agrees that selection decisions in those days could be unsettling for a player.

'Funny things used to happen in those days. Somebody might be given two matches, probably a captain or a chairman of selectors would have said to somebody you'll get a couple of matches but there was always some other people willing and ready to get in if you didn't perform. You didn't get that many chances. I think that helped Robin then, being told by Closey that whatever happens you're in.'

Robin already held a great deal of respect for Close due to his achievements with Yorkshire and now even more so. "Brian was one of those people who was larger than life," says Robin.

He fielded in the most incredible positions, a remarkable man. He was one of those chaps in county cricket who was never out genuinely, there was a fly on the sightscreen or somebody was at fault, he always made excuses but in the nicest possible way.

He was a true Yorkshireman and was feared in the Yorkshire side. Fred Trueman was scared out of his life of him. He once chased him over the Parks at Oxford, he'd had a row with him in the dressing room, Closey went for him and Trueman had to run across the Parks with nothing on at all to get away from him. You didn't meddle with Closey but he was a good bloke. He led his Yorkshire side like Surridge led the Surrey side in the late '50s. He had a hard job with that Yorkshire side, there were a lot of different characters, all looking after themselves but he got a terrific team spirit going.

He was a bloody good captain to play under because he said to me you'll be in for the three Tests against India come what may. There's not many captains I believe who'd say that and keep their word. I had a great deal of time for Closey, he led from the front, like in 1914 he'd be one of the first over the top and you'd follow, he was one of those guys.

The first Test started on Thursday 8 June 1967 and before the match Robin was welcomed into the England team, the 435th player to represent England in Test matches, an immensely proud moment.

I got presented with my cap and my sweaters, short and long sleeve, by Doug Insole in the Headingley dressing room in front of the rest of the players on the first morning of the Test: "Congratulations Robin on being selected for England, here's your cap and your sweater." I was over the moon; me, I thought, playing for England, goodness me.

First Test. England v India at Headingley, June 1967. Standing: John Edrich, Robin Hobbs, John Snow, Ken Higgs, Basil D'Oliveira, Geoffrey Boycott. Sitting: John Murray, Ken Barrington, Brian Close, Tom Graveney, Ray Illingworth.

Robin's debut was memorable as it happened to correspond with one of the most controversial selection incidents in English Test history and one which still rankles with Geoffrey Boycott more than 50 years later. On winning the toss England elected to bat and by the close of play on day one were 281-3 with Boycott undefeated on 106.

Boycott had spent the whole day making his century and was accused in some quarters of being selfish and treating his innings as virtually a private net. The English cricket authorities – under pressure to produce brighter cricket for a public which had begun to lose interest in the game – were exasperated and chairman of selectors Doug Insole tore a strip off him at the close of play on the first day. "I suppose you've got to think you're bloody unlucky," Robin recalls.

Boycott was told at the close of play what the hell was he doing spending all that time getting a hundred by Doug Insole and warned that if he didn't get a move on the next day he'd be dropped. I mean, being dropped after scored 246 not out and the side winning, he's a bit unlucky isn't he. I'd feel the same about Mr Insole as Boycott does if I'd have done that. I think that most people had a quiet snigger, people like D'Oliveira and Graveney. He never made friends very easily did Geoffrey, most people knew that he was an oddball. Don't get me wrong, I wouldn't say that people didn't have time for him. He didn't play cricket like most of the others played cricket, it was all centred around Geoffrey, it really was. But that's not to decry him. When he first came on the scene he was a very ordinary fielder and a very ordinary batsman but he made himself into what he became and you've got to take your hat off to him.

At the time, and ever since, Boycott protested he had been out of form and was batting his way back but the selectors refused to accept this as an excuse and he was subsequently dropped for the next Test. He had, after all, been warned at the end of the first day.

'Boycott plods to dreary Test century' was the headline in *The Times* the following morning. The message from all quarters was that Boycott needed to move up a number of gears, which he did as he progressed to an unbeaten 246, his second hundred being scored at a considerably faster rate than his first although an overall run-rate of 44 was hardly brighter cricket.

England declared on 550-4 and the Indian reply got off to a steady enough start as the openers Saxena and Engineer saw off the opening spell from Snow and Higgs but then fell away disastrously after Saxena was bowled by D'Oliveira for nine with the score on 39. It signalled a collapse and by the close of play on day two India had slumped to 86-6, 466 runs behind on first innings.

Resuming the innings on the third day, Guha was bowled by Snow without adding to his overnight score and the injured Surti, accompanied by Wadekar as his runner, joined Pataudi and there seemed to be more fight once the pair came together. They inched the score past the 100 mark and began to build a partnership which had reached 59 before Robin made the breakthrough in the last over before lunch. Surti drove a full toss hard to Robin's right and he confidently took the catch to record his first Test wicket as the Indian allrounder was dismissed for 22 – "I was thinking how lucky I was to get a caught and bowled off a full toss". Denis Compton wrote in *The Daily Express* that it was a well-deserved first wicket and 'ironical that it was one of the few bad deliveries in a most impressive spell.'

It may have been a bad delivery which handed Robin his first Test wicket but leg spinners perhaps more than most deserve these 'perks' as John Woodcock calls them.

Players generally seemed more restrained and less excitable in those days, and the fact that England were overwhelming favourites meant that wickets taken and runs scored against India were expected and almost taken for granted. Even so there was often a lack of joy in some of the England players at the success of their team-mates as Robin recalls.

I think in those days you came into the side and you looked around that dressing-room with Boycott, Graveney, Barrington etc., they all looked after themselves, they were interested in number one, it wasn't the team it was number one. There weren't many words of encouragement from other members of the side, they said good luck and things like that but their priority was number one.

First Test wicket – Rusi Surti caught and bowled for 22, Headingley 1967.

Following Surti's dismissal, India's score stood at 151-8 and after the annoyance of that fifty partnership England were looking to wrap up the innings as quickly as possible with the aim of inviting the tourists to follow on.

Bishan Bedi, batting at 10, also required the services of a runner. He limped out to the middle, took guard, and settled to face Robin. The leg spinner bound in off his six-pace approach and bowled to Bedi who was beaten by the delivery, rapped on the pad, and given out lbw by umpire Charlie Elliott. Runners, wickets, it was all happening out in the middle and Robin suddenly found himself with the chance of taking a hat-trick in his first Test match. Bedi was out to the last ball of the over so Robin didn't have the opportunity to bowl at the last man, Chandrasekhar, straightaway and would have to wait for the possibility of completing the hat-trick. There was a hush in the crowd as Robin bounded in to deliver the first ball of his next over but disappointment followed as the ball passed harmlessly down the leg side and the chance to write his name in the history books had gone.

"I got him out three times in that series, thank God he played." Umpire Charlie Elliott sends Bishan Bedi on his way.

Towards the end of the over Pataudi was dropped by John Edrich on the long-on boundary but it wasn't too costly; the end of the Indian innings only being delayed by five minutes. Fast running out of partners to keep him company, Pataudi decided to hit out and was the last man to fall for 64, mis-hitting a drive and being caught by Barrington at deep extra-cover off Robin's bowling, as the Indian first innings closed on 164. Robin had bowled 22.2 overs and had a decent return of three for 45. In typically understated fashion he is almost dismissive of his achievements at international level.

I got three for 45 and Keith Miller wrote an article in The Express which I've still got – 'What a find this guy is, he'll be a regular in the England side for years.' A load of rubbish really, I mean the wickets I got – Pataudi was caught at deep extra-cover, a bloke with one eye – smashed it he did, thank Christ he did only have one eye. Bishan Bedi, who couldn't bat was lbw – I got him out three times in that series, thank God he played – and I caught Surti off a full toss.

The Indian captain may have only had one eye but he was still a highly accomplished batsman, scoring six centuries and 17 fifties in his 46 Test matches at an average of 34.91. Left-handed allrounder Rusi Surti, who had earned the dubious but flattering nickname of 'the poor man's Garry Sobers', finished his 26-match Test career with a batting average of 28.70. Of the three only Bishan Bedi could be described as genuine rabbit.

The opportunity for Robin to add to his tally came quickly as India were invited to follow on 386 runs behind. The tourists were determined to make a better fist of it second time round but with the first wicket falling with the score on five India were in real danger of losing the Test within three days. Farokh Engineer was joined by Wadekar and together they entertained the Headingley crowd with a fine partnership of 168 before Close caught and bowled Engineer for 87. Wadekar and the new batsman took the score to 198-2 at the close.

As Robin recalls, the pitch turned a little bit but was pretty flat in the second innings and on the fourth day the Indians advanced their score. Wadekar fell nine runs short of his century, Singh made 73 and shared in a partnership of 134 with Pataudi who went on to score 148 before being bowled by Illingworth and departing with the score on 506-9. England were now looking to take the last Indian wicket as quickly as possible and Robin was brought back on to bowl having so far gone wicketless.

Bedi, in a last flourish of defiance, hit Robin for four and seemed to enjoy it so much that he tried to repeat the stroke but only succeeded in picking out John Snow at deep mid-on who had no trouble taking the catch to finally earn some reward for Robin's efforts as he ended the innings with one for 100 from 45.2 overs. India were all out for 510 which left England with the task of scoring 125 which they achieved relatively comfortably as they won the match by six wickets. Boycott's batting skills were not required this time.

Writing in *The Cricketer,* John Woodcock stated that 'Hobbs…was not out of his element although he will find few better players of leg spin than these Indians, who feed on it at home. It is only a pity that he doesn't trust himself to give the ball a little more air a little more often'.

Perhaps the highest praise was that from former Australian captain, and leg spinner, Richie Benaud who wrote that it had been a 'fine debut by Hobbs' and that in his opinion he had been the pick of the bowling attack. 'For what it is worth, I am quite certain he is a far better bowler than I was when I first represented Australia and I tip him to have a good future in English cricket.' Benaud was 21 when he made his Test debut in 1952 and went on to take 248 wickets in 63 matches, if Robin could even half-emulate his achievements he would be doing well. Brian Chapman, writing in *The Daily Mirror,* was equally fulsome in his praise for Robin whom he described as an 'an outstanding young leg-break bowler', Chapman also revealed some of the background of Robin's selection.

'The intriguing thing about 25-year-old Hobbs is that he got his first Test chance almost by a fluke. Had Bob Barber been available, Hobbs would still be waiting on the side-lines. He did his early stints with Chingford, which happens to be the home club of Douglas Insole, chairman of the England selectors. Hold everything. That, too, nearly ruled Robin out Douglas told me yesterday: "I was so worried about possible charges of nepotism that I waited for someone else on the committee to put Robin's name forward.'"

Robin felt brilliant; he'd made a decent start to his international career and could also look forward to the second Test at Lord's, having been guaranteed his place. Perhaps the proudest spectator at Headingley was Reg Hobbs, who had travelled up from Walthamstow to watch his son's England debut. "I've still got a silver salver he presented me after the season with an inscription on it – *It's been a long way* – which was right, it was only six years since I was playing for the Essex second team."

When Robin returned to Essex and met up with his county team-mates there was plenty of ribbing amongst the pats on the back which helped him keep his feet on the ground. In between the first and second Tests Robin played in the Championship against Glamorgan at Cardiff and his performance would surely have pleased the England selectors. In a 27.3-over spell where he spun and flighted the ball adroitly, he was rewarded with figures of six for 50 and a total of nine in the match; confidence was high.

After their second-innings heroics at Headingley, India came crashing back down to earth in the second Test at Lord's. They may well have thought their luck was in when they won the toss but it was a day when winning the toss was a mixed blessing. India chose to bat but were rueing the decision when they were all out for 152 inside 55 overs. Only Wadekar was able to repeat the form he had shown at Headingley with a graceful innings of 57. Robin wasn't required to bowl as England's opening pair, John Snow and David Brown, took three wickets each, with two for D'Oliveira and one for Illingworth. Wicket-keeper John Murray took six catches which equalled the record held by the Australian Wally Grout and South African Denis Lindsay.

Although he didn't bowl, Robin was able to demonstrate his effectiveness in the field. With the score on 144-8 the Indian number nine Prasanna knocked the ball out towards mid-wicket and called Bedi for two runs. Attempting a second run may have been on against most of the other fielders in the England side but as the ball went down the slope at Lord's towards the Tavern, Robin athletically covered the ground from deep mid-wicket, collected the ball and arrowed it perfectly into the gloves of Murray who was able to complete the run out with Prasanna two yards short of the crease. In many ways Robin was ahead of his time compared to the pedestrian fielding of many of his contemporaries. Brian Scovell rated Robin as an 'exceptional fielding talent' in his favoured position of cover/cover-point and it was this aspect of his game which almost alone would earn him a place on future tours and in the Essex one-day matches under Brian Taylor's captaincy.

England scored 386 in their first innings thanks largely to 97 from Ken Barrington and an elegant 151 from Tom Graveney.

Graveney was a classical batsman, very stylish in everything he did. You'd never see him try and hit the ball for six, he was very graceful, great cover drives. Every day of his life, whether it was a Test match or a county match at Worcester, he'd go out to the nets for 10 minutes and that was all he needed.

After passing 300 with only three wickets down a clatter of England wickets fell and Robin found himself striding to the crease with the score at 365-7. He decided he wasn't going to hang around and deposited Bedi into the Tavern. Unfortunately for Robin, and the Lord's crowd, the fun didn't last long and he was out shortly afterwards bowled by Bedi for seven. England ended on 386 all out and India started their innings 234 runs behind. After Engineer was dismissed early in the innings by Snow, Kunderan and Wadekar steadied the ship taking the score along to 60 but when Wadekar became the second wicket to fall it was the signal for the floodgates to open. Ray Illingworth was the destroyer in chief taking 6-29 off 22.3 overs but, according to John Woodcock in *The Times*, the wickets were 'of no great intrinsic value. If a chance was missed in the field no one doubted that another, equally good, would not be long in coming.' Disappointingly for Robin, whilst Illingworth was cashing in, he only bowled six overs and ended wicketless with figures of nought for 16 as India were bowled out for 110. The Indians were thoroughly outclassed in what actually amounted to only two-and-a-half's day cricket due to play lost to wet weather.

England v India at Lord's, June 1967. Shortly after depositing Bedi for six into the Tavern, Robin has his off stump knocked back by the left-arm spinner.

In spite of his limited involvement Robin wasn't too disheartened with how things had gone.

I knew because it was damp and miserable and the wicket was green that I was hardly going to bowl, I was just in the side really as a fielder. I was surprised to bowl six overs quite honestly. I wasn't too fussed not to be bowling as long as the side was winning, and I was the fifth-choice bowler, which was fair enough, I didn't have any problems with that.

Following the early conclusion of the game there was some waiting around pending the arrival of the Queen and the Duke of Edinburgh to whom both teams were presented.

Presented to the Queen. Several months later Robin would meet her sister in less formal circumstances in the West Indies.

The last match in the series at Edgbaston would, at best, offer India the chance to salvage some pride and Robin was hoping to play a greater role than he had at Lord's although he very nearly missed the match. It was touch and go as to whether he'd be able to play after suffering with a stomach complaint but in the end he declared himself fit, reckoning that with India's weak batting the game would be unlikely to last five days.

Boycott returned to the side having served his one-match punishment and Colin Milburn was also brought in with Edrich and D'Oliveira dropping out. On winning the toss England opted to bat. Boycott and Milburn put on 63 for the first wicket before both openers fell in quick succession and by the time Ken Barrington became the fifth wicket to fall England were 182-5. A slump soon became a collapse with England sliding to 191-8 until Snow, batting at 10, dug in and kept Murray company; together they added 50 for the ninth wicket before Snow fell to Bedi. Robin, batting at number 11, strode to the crease with the score on 241-9 and together he and Murray pushed the score past 250.

'Robin wasn't a great batter,' recalls Murray,

'But what he could do quite well was block and stick around, the moment he tried to play any shots he was always going to get out. All that I required of him was to stick it out, simple basics. I told him I'll try and take as much of the bowling as I can and you stick around which he did very successfully.'

By the time Murray was last man out for 77 they had put on 57 – a new 10th-wicket record for England against India; one which stood until 1982. The last two wickets had salvaged the innings, adding 107 runs to see England's first innings close on 298. Robin finished undefeated on 15 which was to remain his best score in a Test cricket. "John Murray and I were good friends," recalls Robin, "he was a good player. I just stuck around with him and thoroughly enjoyed it. I remember feeling quite proud when we came off, the last two having put on fifty."

England's opening bowlers Snow and Brown made early inroads into the Indian batting which was again found wanting as they were reduced to 41-5. Close then turned to the spin of Illingworth and Hobbs. The last five batsmen put up more resistance than the top order, but only just, the innings only lasting 36.3 overs as India were bundled out for 92. The spinners shared the last five wickets with Robin achieving his best Test match figures of three for 25 – Subramanya, bowled for 10, Bedi, caught and bowled for one and Chandrasekhar, stumped by Murray for nought.

England had a lead of 206 but Close chose not to enforce the follow-on. To many observers the decision to bat again appeared to be financial rather than tactical with the game's administrators eager for the revenue of a third-day crowd. Close top-scored with 47 but Robin could only manage two before being the last man to fall with the score on 203. At the end of day two India were left with three days to chase a target of 410 which, if achieved, would give them their first Test-match victory in England.

The England team booked out of their accommodation at the Raven Hotel in Droitwich after breakfast on the morning on the third day, such was their confidence in forcing a quick result. In fairness many cricket commentators and reporters did exactly the same, convinced that the Test would finish at some point that day.

A crowd of around 10,000 turned up on the Saturday and witnessed the Indians putting up sterner resistance in their second innings. The opening pair of Engineer and Kunderan had put on a stand of 48 before Robin made the breakthrough with his first ball as Engineer drove carelessly and gave a simple catch to Barrington at extra-cover. By tea India were only three wickets down and for a time it seemed that England and the assembled cricket media would be scrabbling around trying to book back into their accommodation, not only for the Saturday night but Sunday too as it was a rest day.

Wadekar and Pataudi held up England in a fourth wicket stand of 83 but once Wadekar got himself out, Pataudi, Hanumant Singh and Subramanya all soon followed. From 207-7 the Indian tail went down all guns blazing as they added 70 runs in the final hour. Robin took the eighth wicket to fall, bowling Prasanna for 15, and then caught Venkataraghavan off the bowling of Close. India were finally dismissed for 277. Robin was pleased with his performance in the Test.

I bowled quite well in that second innings and could have had a four-for. Closey was a golden-arm bowler, when he came on he got wickets, how he got them nobody knew but that's how he did it. I took a couple of good catches off his bowling at mid-wicket. They weren't a bad side actually but the conditions weren't good for them, the wickets were green.

England won by a margin of 132 runs and Close had kept his word that Robin would play all three matches. Robin finished the series with nine wickets at 28.78 and an economy rate of 2.31 and felt satisfied with his efforts which compared favourably with the other bowlers.

I'd contributed to the success of the team and thought at the time that it was a fair return for my first three Test matches. The first Test was a good one to bowl leg breaks but the Lord's and Edgbaston Tests weren't great conditions so I was quite satisfied overall and I would have been disappointed if I hadn't been picked for the next one against Pakistan.

Having made a decent start to his international career, Robin was named in the 12 for the first Test against Pakistan at Lord's starting on 27 July. Geoffrey Boycott dropped out of the side before the start of the game due to the death of his father, his place being taken by the Middlesex opener Eric Russell. On winning the toss England elected to bat. Colin Milburn soon fell for five but Barrington and Russell added 77 for the second wicket before Russell was bowled by Intikhab Alam for 43. Having warmed up with three big fifties against India, Barrington went on to record his first Test-match century of the summer, and his first in a Test match at Lord's.

He was in his element and together with Graveney recorded a double-century partnership to take the score up to 282-2 at the close of day one. Having been in such a strong position overnight England soon found themselves in trouble with the pair adding just one run between them early on day two. Worse was to come with Close and Murray both falling with the score on 287 and by the time Illingworth was bowled by Asif Iqbal for four England had lost five wickets for nine runs.

Basil D'Oliveira restored some dignity to the innings and, aided by Ken Higgs, pushed on the score to 352, before Higgs departed lbw to Mushtaq Mohammad for 14. John Snow swiftly followed but Robin, batting at 11, hung around with D'Oliveira long enough to see him reach his half-century before he was the final wicket to fall having scored 59 in England's total of 369.

Ken Higgs took the first three Pakistan wickets to fall in their reply and when Robin dismissed Majid Khan caught and bowled for five the score stood at 76-4 with England's first-innings total of 369 a long way off.

> I was bowling that evening from the Nursery End at Majid Khan who was a great player. I seemed to get him out whenever I played against him, I don't know if he felt sorry for me! I caught and bowled him and then in came Nasim-ul-Ghani and in the same over he hit one back at me and although I was a good catcher off my bowling it ricocheted off my hands towards Basil D'Oliveira at mid-on but it just didn't carry to him otherwise I'd have got two in one over. Of course the next morning Close opened with the seamers and Nasim-ul-Ghani got out to Snowy and then there was the stand between Asif and Hanif.

Pakistan started day three on 78-4 and were soon 99-6 and facing the threat of following on. Intikhab Alam fell with the score on 139 with 30 still required to make England bat again. Asif Iqbal, batting at number nine, joined his captain Hanif Mohammad and between them they turned the tide for Pakistan. Writing in his report for *The Times*, John Woodcock felt that spin had been underused by England.

> 'The two leg-spinners, Hobbs and Barrington, were regarded virtually as supernumeraries by a captain who, only last week saw his Yorkshire side go down

to Barrington. By tea Hobbs had bowled just nine overs, and the innings was 117 runs old when Barrington was called for. This is captaincy of the modern type, based on restrictive orthodoxy, with seldom a trace of imagination.'

EW Swanton, in his third-day report for *The Daily Telegraph*, was similarly perplexed by Close's reluctance to make more use of Robin's leg breaks. 'One's only criticism is that he [Close] seemed to under-use Hobbs, whose duel in mid-afternoon with Hanif was just about the best thing of the day.' Due to the generosity of England's fielders Pakistan closed day three on 233-7, Hanif had reached his century and Asif was on 56.

For England, the morning session of the fourth day was error-strewn and for Robin it was arguably a career changing passage of play. In his most impressive spell of leg-break bowling in Test cricket – 17 overs for just 17 runs – Robin had four chances wasted. By this stage in the game a patch of rough had formed at the Pavilion End due to the bowlers' footmarks and Close, quick to realise how he could best exploit it, brought on Robin to bowl from the Nursery End with a ring of close fielders.

Observing this absorbing passage of play, the Pakistan umpire and writer, Qamaruddin Butt, remarked of Robin's bowling that morning 'I had umpired two matches of the MCC (under-25), in which Hobbs had played. I did not see Hobbs bowl with such viciousness as on that day. There was a hint of desperation in Asif's play. He developed an alarming affection for the cross bat and began to take the sauciest liberties.'

Having only added three to his overnight score, Asif hit a full toss from Robin, in his second over of the day, straight to short mid-wicket where it was dropped by Eric Russell. In his third over, Robin bowled a leg break which Hanif pushed forward to, the ball came off the outside edge and agonizingly past Close's right shoulder before he could react at silly-point. Close was renowned for his brave fielding near to the bat but a number of cricket writers that summer felt that he was standing too near. Just a few feet further back and it would have been a straightforward catch, where he was he had practically no chance.

In an attempt to hit Robin out of the ground and, hopefully for Pakistan, out of the attack, Asif used his feet to dance down the wicket and twice should have been stumped but Murray fumbled the ball on both occasions. Murray, a naturally stylish 'keeper, was, in his defence, hampered by a patch of rough on the pitch. 'I remember one I missed,' recalls Murray, 'Rob pitched it in the rough outside leg, it bounced and it hit me up on the top of my chest.' Robin's misfortune that morning was best summed up by John Woodcock writing in his report of the day's play in *The Times* – 'Hobbs, operating round the wicket for much of the time, bowled the first 17 overs of the day from the Nursery End for

17 runs and a month's share of frustration.'

Hanif Mohammad carried his bat for 187 as Pakistan were eventually dismissed for 354, only 15 runs behind England's first-innings total. Pakistan's last four wickets had added 255 runs. Robin took one for 46 off 35 overs but with a bit of fortune could have taken four wickets which, as he says, "could have changed my life". At the close of play on day four England were 131-4 in their second innings, an overall lead of 146. Pakistan had fought back superbly and had put England on the back foot for the first time that summer.

England v Pakistan at Lord's, July 1967. Hanif Mohammad leaves the field 187 not out at the close of the Pakistan first innings. Robin took one wicket but it could have been four.

Pakistan weren't able to make a breakthrough in the first session of the final day when quick wickets would have given them a great chance of forcing a win. The fifth-wicket partnership of 104 between D'Oliveira and Close was enough to see England to safety and they declared on 241-9. Pakistan were set a target of 257 but never really looked like chasing it down, finishing on 88-3 from 62 overs. Robin toiled away for 16 wicketless overs, bowling nine maidens and finishing with none for 28. It could have been so different as he was left to reflect.

In Pakistan's first innings Hanif got 187 and Asif got 76 and I bowled 35 overs and got one for 46. Well, you can't do much better than that as a leg spinner. It's bloody ridiculous bowling 35 overs. I could have got four for 40. I did feel unlucky not to have played in the next Test. To bowl 35 overs for 46 and get dropped. And then 16 overs for 28 in the second innings, I think I felt hard done by.

Eric Russell's dropped catch was a dolly but in all fairness John Murray's missed stumpings around the wicket weren't easy. There was some rough outside the leg stump and if you're pitching it there and it's going between bat and pad it's not easy. I felt pretty down and with Derek Underwood looming on the horizon I wasn't surprised to be left out for the next game.

If things had gone my way I could have ended up with bloody good figures and could have stayed in the side for another Test but I think by then the selectors probably decided that unless I did something exceptional, like getting four or five wickets in that innings, this was probably the last chance for a while. Four Tests on the trot, we need to change it. I think I was lucky to play four on the trot. But that's what they did in those days. I missed out on the next Test and Underwood got a five-for.

Despite taking only one wicket, match sponsors Horlicks expressed their appreciation of Robin's efforts and bad luck by awarding him a share of the £100 England bowling prize. Ken Higgs took the other half.

Robin didn't play in either of the last two Tests of the summer. At Trent Bridge England won by 10 wickets with Derek Underwood taking five for 52 on a wet wicket. In the final Test of the summer, despite Asif Iqbal's second-innings score of 146, England won comfortably by eight wickets to take the three-match series 2-0.

Life as an international cricketer for Robin in the 1960s was vastly different to the modern era of central contacts. At that time, and for the best part of 30 years afterwards, England cricketers would turn up to play a Test match straight after a county game and at its conclusion would head straight off to play another county match. There was no back-up team of coaches or data analysis to refer to.

You'd turn up, the skipper would talk a certain amount of tactics on the morning of the Test match depending on whether you won the toss or lost the toss and said "right we're going to aim to get 400" or "we're going to aim to get them out, OK let's take the field lads. Good to see you", and that was it.

Nor was there a team-England ethos.

In those days players kept themselves to themselves. I don't think there was that team spirit, if we won we won, if we didn't win so be it so long as I got runs I'm happy. There's nothing wrong with that, but you arrived the day before, you had dinner, you played the Test, and then you went back to your counties. It's nothing like it is now with a week preparing and getting to know people. Of course that changed when you went on tour, you found out exactly who were the nice guys and the ones you wanted to be with.

Although England had won five and drawn one it wasn't a great or memorable summer for Test cricket, much of it was as disappointing as the damp weather. Both India and Pakistan were still in their relative infancy as far as Test cricket was concerned and the contests were mostly one-sided. From Robin's recollections it appears there wasn't a great deal of excitement or enthusiasm amongst the England players that summer.

People didn't say a great deal, you just sat there and watched the cricket and it went on and at the end of play you went back to the hotel, there was never really much thought of how many we were going to get, it was just a matter of 'Oh well, we'll bat for two days and see what we can do after that.'

Basil D'Oliveira, still relatively new to Test cricket, certainly felt that the games lacked the tension one would normally associate with international cricket recalling that 'I hardly bothered to watch a ball from the dressing-room, compared to the previous summer against the West Indians, when I was glued to every bit of it.'

Perhaps the lack of excitement on the field led some of the players to search for entertainment off it and larger-than-life character Colin Milburn was at the centre of it. Geoffrey Boycott recalls Milburn taking him out for the night during the Test match at Lord's in 1966. They ended up at Raymond's Revue Bar in Soho complete with strippers, exotic dancers and near-nudes swimming in a large glass tank. The late night possibly affected Boycott who was out cheaply in England's second innings but Milburn went on to score 126 not out. Milburn possibly enjoyed the experience so much that he looked to repeat it during the first Test against Pakistan at Lord's in 1967. Boycott wasn't playing – although one wonders if he'd have been up for it again – so Milburn invited Robin and D'Oliveira along.

"Colin Milburn was very friendly with the comedian Dave Allen," remembers Robin.

He came to Lord's and took us out on one of the nights. We stayed out all night during the Test match and turned up the next day at eight o'clock for breakfast. We spent the whole night in Soho at Raymond's Revue Bar although I don't remember a great deal about that night, it's all pretty bleary.

Enjoying themselves off the field was pretty commonplace and so the players wouldn't have thought they were doing anything out of the ordinary even in the middle of a Test match.

I think that as you did that quite often playing county cricket it didn't come as a surprise. There were no restrictions, everyone assumed that you'd go to bed around 11 o'clock, go to sleep and get up next morning. I don't think the management knew about it, I don't think they'd have been too happy.

Having lost his England place, Robin returned to county cricket and in August was in the Essex side playing Yorkshire at Scarborough. Having had reasonable success early on in his career against them, Robin always looked forward to these fixtures and was usually confident of taking wickets which was particularly satisfying against a county which had a reputation for not believing in leg spin. According to David Acfield this was partly the legacy of uncovered wickets "leg spin doesn't work as well on uncovered wickets as finger spin, it's as simple as that, they haven't got the accuracy or the pace to do it." Yorkshire didn't believe in it and they didn't play it particularly well either which may well have been due to a lack of exposure to it in the nets and in the middle; a wider issue nowadays according to Robin.

It's a bit like England playing today, they can't because they don't see spin, or very little spin, in England. When they come up against guys like Nathan Lyon their performances are poor because they don't know how to play it.

Robin's confidence at Scarborough was well-founded, he took seven wickets in the match including England colleagues Boycott, Close and Illingworth, as Essex beat Yorkshire by nine runs which, after being dismissed for just 87 in their first innings, was some achievement given Yorkshire were the powerhouse side of the '60s.

That was one of the great victories we had in the years I played for Essex, the game was a complete turn-around. We were all out for 87, they got 214 in their first innings, we got 245 in our second and then bowled them out for 109. When you look at that Yorkshire side – Boycott, Sharpe, Padgett, Hampshire, Taylor, Close, Illingworth, Binks, Wilson, Nicholson and Trueman – to concede 131 on first innings and to beat them on their home soil was monumental. David Acfield bowled very well in their second innings, he got five for 32 off 24 overs. It was a really special victory, Tonker was so proud.

It was a massive morale boost for Essex who were leading a precarious existence; financial woes still beset the county and the playing staff had been cut to the bone with only 12 professionals on the staff. It was a tough time in the club as Robin remembers.

We couldn't afford more than 12 players, we were in such a state financially at the time that Doug Insole's father used to go round the ground at home matches with a blanket asking for donations of Green Shield stamps to keep the county going. Things were so perilous that David Bradford, who later became David Acfield's father-in-law, and Johnny Welch, who was the second-team captain, both put their hands into their pockets and paid the players wages for a couple of months that season, that's how bad things were.

A changing of the guard was in effect; Barry Knight had left under a cloud earlier in the year and Trevor Bailey, having handed over the captaincy before the start of the season, made his final first-class appearance against Middlesex at Lord's in August. It may not have been apparent at the time but the seeds were being sown which would see Essex achieve success a decade later. Keith Boyce had emerged as a serious allrounder to fill the gaps left by Knight and Bailey, younger players like Ray East and Acfield had started to establish themselves, John Lever made his debut for the club and the following year Stuart Turner was re-engaged.

As a young player John Lever was initially wary of Robin and his reputation as a sharp and quick-witted joker in the changing room. Lever was never entirely sure if Robin was laughing with him or at him: 'As a youngster coming in to the side I didn't dare open my mouth because I knew I was going to get set up somewhere along the line. He was a terrible piss-taker but that was all part of the changing room scene.' When he made it onto the playing staff Stuart Turner was similarly in awe of Robin and his sense of humour.

'He used to wind Tonker up sometimes just for the hell of it, little quips here and there and Tonker being the sergeant-major type that he was would tell him to just button it. "That's enough Hobbsy, let's get on with the game!" Even Tonker's blue-eyed boy would sometimes push it too far. Funnily enough Hobbsy has got piercing blue eyes, he always used to remind me of Peter O'Toole in *Lawrence of Arabia*.'

The likeness to the actor – himself a great cricket lover – has been noted by many including David Frith, Mike Brearley and Intikhab Alam, and despite the numerous charity matches they both played their paths never crossed; a shame as they would surely have enjoyed each other's company. According to Robin, the O'Toole link initially occurred in the mid-sixties as Essex were heading to a match against Gloucestershire.

We were driving on the Oxford Bypass going down to Bristol and we stopped at a pub to have a beer. We were in one bar and there was a group of people in another bar and I don't think I've got any resemblance to Peter O'Toole at all, but these people started pointing and as we left they all came out of the other bar and met us: "Peter O'Toole! What's he doing here?" I said "I'm not Peter O'Toole", "Yes you are, it's Peter O'Toole with his friends, look!" That's how it started.

Once again Robin's season would conclude at the Scarborough Festival playing representative matches for Tom Pearce's XI versus Pakistan, an England XI versus a Rest of the World XI and finally, on 9 September, MCC versus Yorkshire. Robin had gone into the match against the county champions with 90 first-class wickets for the season and despite defeat for MCC, a superb all-round personal performance saw him break the 100 barrier for the first time in his career in the final first-class match of the 1967 season.

Conditions were perfect and the Scarborough crowd basked in the September sunshine, soaking up the final throes of the season. The Yorkshire side had received a tremendous ovation from the 5000-strong crowd but the champions were in trouble from the start of their innings and were dismissed for just 145. Robin had troubled Yorkshire all through his spell. In his second over he deceived Barry Leadbeater to clip the leg stump and in his third John Hampshire was caught by Roger Prideaux on the boundary. Ray Illingworth set about improving the position with a breezy innings of 40 but at the other end a superb diving catch by Tony Greig at silly mid-off accounted for Richard Hutton for two off Robin's bowling. A second catch by Greig, this time a simple one at mid-off, gave Robin his fourth wicket of the innings as Illingworth mistimed his shot, and his five-wicket haul was achieved as Jimmy Binks was caught at short-leg by Keith Fletcher to enable Robin to finish with five for 41.

MCC also struggled in their first innings and were dismissed for 132 giving Yorkshire a slender lead of 13 runs. The champions were more disciplined in their second innings but their fallibility against leg spin was acutely demonstrated by Robin who took six for 116 in 30.2 overs of controlled and accurate bowling. Geoffrey Boycott was the backbone of the Yorkshire innings with 86, using his feet well to combat Robin's leg breaks. Boycott didn't have as much success trying to sweep good balls pitched on middle and leg which, in the end, proved to be his downfall. He survived two lbw appeals playing the shot but was third time unlucky as he finally fell to Robin's bowling. In spite of his bowling efforts Yorkshire went on to win by 39 runs but Robin's match figures of 11 for 157 had seen him to 101 wickets for the season at an average of 23.77. He was in good company with a number of his contemporaries also breaching the hundred barrier. Pat Pocock, a mere babe at just 21, had 112 wickets to his name at an average of 18.22, better than experienced rivals Ray Illingworth with 101 at 15.97 and Fred Titmus 106 at 20.35, but leading the field were a pair of left-armers. Veteran Tony Lock of Leicestershire had 128 at a shade over 18 but the leading spinner was Derek Underwood who'd amassed 136 at 12.39 and had lived up to his nickname of 'Deadly' on English wickets

It had been an excellent season for Robin; on top of 101 first-class wickets he had made his Test match debut and been selected for his second major overseas tour with England. Unlike South Africa in 1964/65 Robin could now seriously expect to play a part in the upcoming series in the West Indies – a place where he'd enjoyed considerable success and forged his reputation as a leg spinner of genuine promise on the Cavaliers tour in 1964.

Chapter Nine

*From then on I knew I wasn't going to play, all I was good for was carrying the
drinks and organising the parties.*

THE SQUAD FOR the 1967/68 tour of the West Indies was announced at the
end of August and, having been dropped for the final two Tests of the summer
against Pakistan, Robin had waited anxiously to find out if he'd been selected.

Deciding which players would be included in the tour squad stretched
back many months with the seeds being sown in England's 1966 home series
against West Indies. England had lost that series 3-1, their consolation win
coming in the fifth Test at The Oval when a number of changes were made to the
side, including Brian Close being handed the captaincy. It was hoped that Close
would bring a more combative attitude to the side and the selectors faith was
well justified as England won by an innings and 34 runs.

Reflecting on the 1966 series in *The Cricketer*, the chairman of selectors,
Doug Insole, also gave a few pointers for the future. 'We have the Tests against
India and Pakistan next summer to see if any new talent has emerged….I think
that young spinners like Pat Pocock, Derek Underwood and Robin Hobbs are
tremendous prospects….I don't think we should play anyone next season who is
not prepared to go to the West Indies the following winter.'

One key member of the England side during the 1967 season would
definitely not be joining his team-mates in the West Indies. The English cricket
authorities had seemingly held doubts about Close's combative approach, and
were concerned about allowing him to take charge of the potentially explosive
tour to the West Indies. If MCC were looking for an excuse to get rid of him, Close
duly obliged as he was accused of using time-wasting tactics to enable Yorkshire
to earn a draw in their County Championship match against Warwickshire.
The MCC Committee vetoed the selection of Close and instead turned to Colin
Cowdrey to lead the side.

Despite losing the England captaincy, Brian Close did go to the West Indies as
a writer and in this capacity he offered some insight into the thoughts of the
selectors during the 1967 home series against India and Pakistan.

'It was feared that the summer of 1967 would be such a walk-over that England players would not be given the tough build-up they needed for the West Indies.... The months of June, July and August proved the opposite, which meant that England were forced to pick the best possible side they could muster at the time. I know because, as England captain, I was a member of that selection panel.

Yet each selection was made with a further thought in mind – the tour to the West Indies which followed and the gradual build-up of England's strength for the visit of Australia in 1968 and the winter's tour that followed to South Africa.

This is why experiments were kept down to the minimum despite the chances offered by playing against two of the weakest countries engaged in international cricket. Only two were made while, in the main, we stuck to the tried and trusted players who were certainties to go to the Caribbean.

Robin Hobbs was the obvious candidate. He had been blooded to touring on Mike Smith's successful South African venture in 1964/5, although he did not play in a Test match. He had confirmed his potential during the winter on the MCC Under-25 tour during their six weeks in Pakistan. It was not only his bowling but his superb ground fielding in the covers or mid-wicket and his fighting qualities which made him attractive as a West Indies candidate.'

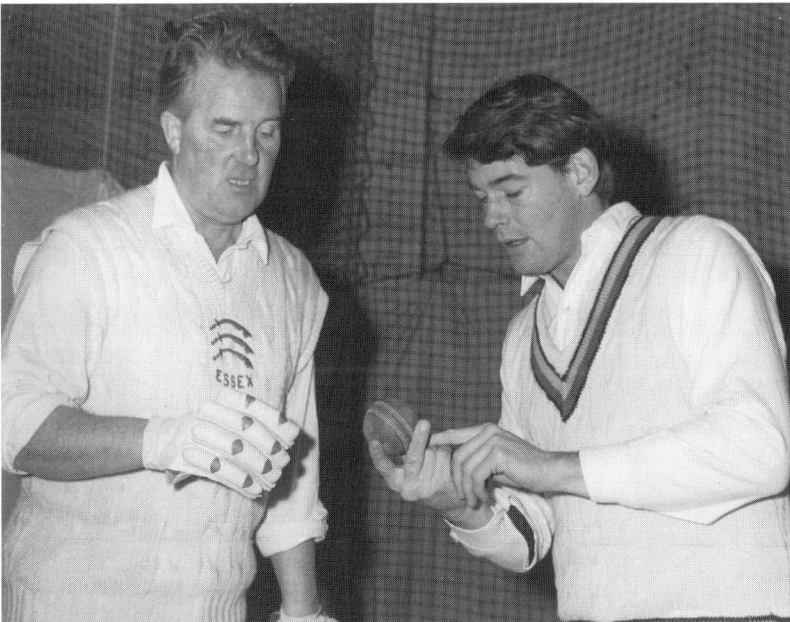

Pre-West Indies tour practice, December 1967. Discussing grip with Essex coach Frank Rist at the Ilford Indoor Cricket School.

Close obviously rated Robin and although he was the England captain when Robin was dropped for the second and third Tests against Pakistan it seems he'd already done enough to be selected for the tour. During the Pakistan series experiments with other selections were made. Close thought that Derek Underwood was pushing his claim strongly, although there were doubts about his penetrative ability on hard surfaces and the under-25 tour to Pakistan seemed to confirm this suspicion. According to Close 'It was decided to give Underwood a chance to prove otherwise in the second Test against Pakistan on the Trent Bridge wicket – the best batting wicket in the country and perhaps the nearest we will find in this country to the West Indies conditions.'

Underwood was a success at Trent Bridge but, in the words of Close, 'the selectors were told nothing they did not already know.' Rain had spoiled England's plans and on a pitch well suited to Underwood he took advantage of the situation taking five for 52 to help England to a 10-wicket victory. Having been dropped by England that summer, Robin was still confident of making the squad for the tour.

> *Having played four Tests and then being left out after Lord's, I probably deep down still thought I had a good chance of going to the West Indies, mainly because Underwood had not had a great tour of Pakistan with the under-25s. The selectors believed that he wasn't the right type of bowler to succeed in the West Indies but I had my doubts about that because I think that Derek Underwood was probably successful on most pitches. If he played today on flat wickets he'd still bowl you 35 overs and take something like three for 70, if it did turn a bit he'd get six for 50. I still thought I had a chance of going to the West Indies and I didn't think that having been dropped I wouldn't get picked.*

Derek Underwood, despite his outstanding record during the season, was not included when the tour party was announced on 30 August 1967 and by coincidence Robin would be coming face to face with him that day as Essex were playing Kent at the Crabble Athletic Ground in Dover.

> *When I got picked to go to the West Indies we were playing Kent. I knew they were going to announce it on the 10 o'clock news so I went down to the beach and sat on the shingle with my radio and they did it in alphabetical order. "Higgs, Hobbs….." I thought, Christ I'm going to the West Indies.*

After hearing that he had made the tour party Robin headed off to the ground. Underwood had heard the news too; he'd been filling up his car at a petrol station when it was announced on the radio. He was appreciative that Robin and Keith

Fletcher took the time to commiserate with him, Robin in return was grateful of the Kent spinner's best wishes. "Derek was the first to congratulate me, he's never been any different. That takes a lot of doing that does." For once, being an English wrist spinner was deemed to be an advantage.

In that game Essex won the toss, decided to bat and were bowled out in their first innings for 93. Robin was out for a pair, run out for nought in the first innings and in the second innings caught by the man who would be his skipper in the West Indies, Colin Cowdrey. Was Robin perhaps distracted and dreaming of the Caribbean? Not quite, it would appear.

We had a chap on our committee called David Bradford who was the father of Helen Acfield, the wife of David Acfield. He was a great supporter of Essex cricket club and paid our wages for a year when things were very tight. He was also a director of Townsend Ferries and the night before that game he'd taken us to Calais. We got back at about 7am in the morning so the guys weren't in the greatest of nick to play county cricket after spending all night over in Calais. That's probably why we were all out for 93.

The England team flew out from Heathrow to Barbados for the start of the three-month tour on 27 December 1967. "We had a get-together with Colin Cowdrey prior to the tour," recalls Robin, "we went to Crystal Palace for two days of intensive training, it was a shambles." In spite of a lack of meaningful practice before departure the touring party were in high spirits according to Robin.

We had a good side, it was a mixture of old and young players. I think we went out there with a fair amount of confidence because we had a very good fast-bowling attack together with Titmus as the spinner, Pat Pocock and myself as young players. We had John Snow, Ken Higgs, David Brown and Jeff Jones, which was a formidable pace attack. The spirit was good and we went out there thinking we had every chance of winning.

In his assessment, written before the start of the tour, Brian Close wrote that Robin was

'Probably the find of the 1967 season now that he has discovered the googly, which was so obvious in his early days that any batsman could pick it out. He would need to change his bowling habits in the West Indies. To get the most effective use on the slower English wickets he has been forced to quicken his delivery. If he could slow it down in the Caribbean he would get more benefit from the extra bounce. His one fault is getting ruffled when he does come under the hammer from batsmen, something slow bowlers should control, although it is a good trait in fast bowlers. His fielding is a tremendous asset and I expect him to become the most popular player with the crowds. In Pakistan on the MCC Under-25 tour spectators often chanted his name in the same way soccer crowds chant the name of their favourite players over here.'

Even though England had been thoroughly outplayed by West Indies in the 1966 series they were confident as they headed out. The West Indies were an ageing team and considered to be in decline, an opinion shared by Robin and his team-mates at the time.

The West Indies fast bowlers, Charlie Griffith and Wes Hall, were coming to the end of their careers and when you looked at the back-up bowlers they had there weren't any who were as quick as them. I don't think the England batsman on that tour feared the pace attack.

Woah! We're going to Barbados. Heathrow Airport, 27 December 1967.

Arriving in the Caribbean just after Boxing Day, Robin and his England colleagues threw themselves wholeheartedly into the festive spirit.

When we landed in Barbados there was a 24-hour party going on at the hotel and we entered into it, we were up 24 hours when we arrived, drinking and dancing with all these young ladies and everything else. That's how we started the tour. I can see Jonesy now, he was so drunk – he was our opening bowler, we'd just arrived in this hotel – he was so pissed that he kept dropping his glass, it smashed, he'd go and get another one, fill it up. These blokes, in prime condition, were representing their country in two weeks' time! It was accepted in those days, it's what you did. You wouldn't do it now.

The first warm-up game of the tour was against Barbados Colts which included 16-year-old Gordon Greenidge in their side. England made changes for the next game versus the President's XI at Bridgetown and Robin found himself dropped, with Titmus and Pocock as the preferred spin attack. Once again Brian Close demonstrated how highly he personally rated Robin: 'I should like to have seen Hobbs given another chance. I believe that he was capable of becoming the match-winning bowler of the tour, especially as the West Indian batsman had received little opportunity to test their reactions against a leg spinner of any quality, apart from David Holford, within the last two years.'

Robin was also excluded from the Trinidad match played at Port of Spain from 9-11 January. The first Test would start on 19 January and Robin's chance of selection had seemingly disappeared. There was however one further warm-up game to be played against the Trinidad Colts on January 15-16. A number of the England batsmen took advantage of some friendly bowling as they racked up 400-6 declared. Colin Milburn made his bid for inclusion in the opening Test by scoring a century before lunch on the first day. The second day of the Colts game would provide the bowlers with their opportunity to stake a claim for a Test spot.

Robin responded by taking six for 59 as the Colts collapsed to 121 all out in their first innings. They made a better fist of their second attempt, following on, and eventually closed on 119-4 with the match ending as a draw. Robin's second-innings bowling figures of two for 53 gave him an overall match analysis of eight for 112 and was good enough to earn him a place in the side for the first Test when it was announced two days later.

Colin Cowdrey, in picking a team not to lose the first Test match at Port of Spain packed his side with batsmen. To many this was another example of the defensive mind-set which Cowdrey displayed in his captaincy. Close also viewed it as a safety-first policy believing that the inclusion of Robin was the only attacking move. However, he felt that there was some justification for the policy, England had made an unimpressive start to the tour, they were without a win and could not afford to lose the first Test of a five-match series.

M.C.C. CRICKETERS TOURING WEST INDIES & GUYANA, 1968

Standing: J. JENNINGS, (Physiotherapist)   A. KNOTT,   I. J. JONES,   P. I. POCOCK,   D. J. BROWN,
J. A. SNOW,   B. L. D'OLIVEIRA,   C. MILBURN,   R. N. S. HOBBS,   L. E. G. AMES, (Manager).

Sitting: G. BOYCOTT,   K. HIGGS,   T. W. GRAVENEY,   M. C. COWDREY, (Capt.),   F. J. TITMUS,
K. F. BARRINGTON,   J. M. PARKS,   J. H. EDRICH.

The official MCC West Indies tour party picture.

Having won the toss and chosen to bat, England got off to a great start to the series by scoring 568, with 143 from Barrington and a fine 118 from Graveney. Early on the third day much-feared Charlie Griffith cleaned up the last three England wickets to record first-innings figures of five for 69. Robin was among his victims that morning.

I got out hooking, I never hooked in my life. I tried to hook Charlie Griffith who was a very quick bowler but he wasn't very quick on the third morning. It went straight up in the air and I was caught by Basil Butcher at mid-wicket.

In reply West Indies were all out for 363 and England had a lead of 205. Clive Lloyd top scored with 118, his maiden Test century in his first home Test series.

In the West Indies first innings Robin bowled 15 overs taking one for 34. His wicket came as he bowled Deryck Murray a full toss, short and wide outside the off-stump, Murray's eyes lit up and he looked to launch it out of the ground but lifting his head as he did so he only succeeded in mishitting the ball and D'Oliveira ran in from deepish mid-on to take the catch.

England enforced the follow-on and very nearly snatched victory on the final day. By mid-afternoon West Indies were 164-2, only 41 runs away from making England bat again, and with eight wickets in hand a draw seemed inevitable. Robin then started a remarkable collapse by dismissing Rohan Kanhai who stepped out to drive but in mistiming his stroke hit a return catch which Robin, moving swiftly to his left, neatly caught. "I came on and got the breakthrough, I caught and bowled Kanhai. We had them in a hell of a mess, we had them by the balls." Clive Lloyd fell at 167-4 and when Holford was bowled by Titmus West Indies were reeling at 178-5, still 27 runs behind.

David Brown came back on to replace Jeff Jones and in the last over before tea he took three wickets as West Indies collapsed to 180-8, six wickets had gone down in an hour. One session left in the Test for England to get the final two wickets for victory. West Indies still need to score 25 runs to make England bat again but while Garry Sobers was in the middle they still had hope. His new batting partner, Wes Hall, led a charmed life as he played and missed several times early on in his innings. According to Cowdrey, 'Hall offered a sharp chance to Geoff Boycott at short-leg. It would have been a difficult but straightforward catch to any specialist in that position but Boycott, who was only one of many fielders crowded round the bat, was not accustomed to fielding there'. Hall was able to keep England at bay and along with Sobers held on in unbroken 9th-wicket partnership of 63 to save the Test. It was a frustrating end to the game according to Robin.

They saved the game, Wes Hall and Garry Sobers, but Boycott dropped Hall twice at short-leg, he never fielded at short-leg in his life. The ball lobbed up and he dropped them both. But for that we would have won the game. If Brian Close had been captain we'd have won by a street, he was more attacking, Cowdrey was defensive, so defensive. If Close had been captain we'd have won the series 3-0.

Having been left out, John Snow came back into the side for the second Test in Jamaica. He hadn't been fit enough to be considered for the first Test although there also appears to have been concerns about his attitude in the early part of the tour. "I think it was a combination" says Robin,

Snowy was an interesting character, a nice guy but not everybody's cup of tea and I

don't think that maybe he really tried in the matches leading up to the first Test. He was never really a great bowler for Sussex but he used to turn it on when he played for England. I think the selection committee might well have thought that in the first Test match he wasn't really worth his place because he hadn't tried.

Once he was recalled though, Snow demonstrated his immeasurable worth to England, taking 27 wickets in the series. Snow's gain was Robin's loss as he was dropped for the second Test. This was undoubtedly a major disappointment, Robin had been selected for the tour over spin rival Derek Underwood as it was expected that the pace and bounce of the Caribbean pitches would be well suited to his bowling. Four years earlier he'd achieved great success in the three matches he'd played at Sabina Park for the Cavaliers against Jamaica benefitting from what was one of the hardest, bounciest surfaces in world cricket.

I'd bowled quite well in the first Test and I fully expected to play in the second at Sabina Park but Cowdrey left me out, he gave me the old pat on the shoulder, "Well played Robin but we're going to play a seam bowler" – he didn't have a lot of time for spin either, nobody did! I was frustrated at being left out for that second Test. At Trinidad the wicket was slow and low, it turned a bit but it didn't bounce. Sabina Park was like concrete, it was rock hard, it bounced like a tennis ball and I thought of all of the Tests I would have played the second Test would have been the one.

I think that if we'd have won the first Test I'd have played in the second, he would have kept the same side. I felt particularly pissed off with Cowdrey, I thought Christ Almighty I'd done alright in the first Test why change the side? Certainly Snow had to come back but I was the easy option to drop, wasn't I. "Oh, we'll leave Hobbsy out, leave the leg spinner out and bring in a quick bowler, he'll be happy as 12th man, he doesn't really want to play anyway." From then on I knew I wasn't going to play, all I was good for was carrying the drinks and organising the parties.

So I didn't play again except in the tour games against the Leeward Islands, the Windward Islands and any other islands they could find. They came out like kamikaze pilots they did, they tried to hit you into the sea. The standard in those days wasn't great. They didn't defend many balls; if it was tossed up they'd have a go at it. I was a reasonable bowler, I knew they were first-class games and I knew I was going to play in them so I was going to make the most of it. I think I got five wickets against the Leeward Islands which is not saying a great deal. I came back top of the tour averages which was nice, nobody looks to see where you actually got those wickets "Oh, he's top of the averages, why didn't he play more Test matches?"

After Jamaica, England headed for Barbados where the third Test was scheduled to start on 29 February. Between matches the players had a number of social functions to attend, one of which Pat Pocock remembers well.

'When we were in the West Indies we got an invite to a cocktail party given by Princess Margaret and her husband Antony Armstrong-Jones at Oliver Messel's house. Messel was Armstrong-Jones' uncle and he had a beautiful house on the beach in Barbados. Hobbsy had had a bit to drink and he wanted to know from Princess Margaret why England kept giving away the Commonwealth. "Why are we giving away the Commonwealth when all these people died fighting for it and now you're giving it away?" Her face was like "How do I get out of this?" That was Hobbsy for you, he was always comical the whole time even when he didn't mean to be.'

Robin recalls the evening well, it was quite surreal for a commoner from Essex to be mixing with royalty.

There was a BBQ and Princess Margaret had to cook the first sausages and burgers. I said to this poor woman "Why are they making you do that?" She smoked Marlboro same as me and so we got on to chatting about things. I had a Mini Moke and I took her to this discotheque afterwards, had a bloody good evening with her, a bit of fun and a laugh, and dropped her back at her place. Two days later I went down to the airport as my job was to and pick-up the up-to-date newspapers off the plane from England, she was flying off to Mustique with her husband and she walked past just a few feet away. I said "Hello, how are you?" and she walked straight past, didn't even look at me.

Fred Perry hosts the off-duty tourists, Runaway Bay, Jamaica.

When he wasn't entertaining royalty in his spare time, Robin also did a spot of water-skiing – an activity he'd really got the bug for on the 1964/65 South Africa tour. The opportunity presented itself when the players were at Sandy Lane beach in Barbados. 'Visually you'll never see anything funnier', recalls Pat Pocock, still laughing nearly 50 years on.

'At Sandy Lane, we get invited to go along because someone is going to turn up with a boat so we can water ski. So we're laying around on one of the loveliest beaches in the whole of the Caribbean and this guy – a real flash harry bloke – is on the skis, he's laying it flat, he's cutting in, zooming around, he's going at a hell of a speed. The bloke comes round parallel to the edge of the beach, let's go of the tow rope, stops and sinks down to a foot of water and very coolly bends down, picks his skis up and comes in.

Well, when it's Hobbsy's turn he does exactly the same thing except he comes in he is at right-angles, twice as fast as he should, and he leaves it about 30 yards too late to let go of the tow rope. So he comes in, and there's about six or seven of us laying on the beach watching, and Hobbsy's coming in quick and of course his skis go 'zonk' and he hits the sand at about 25 miles an hour, flies through the air and goes over and over and over and gets back up covered in sand and we cannot breathe we are laughing so much. If it happened today somebody would have had a phone and they'd have filmed it and it would have gone viral all over the world because to this date it's still the most comical thing I have ever seen in my life.'

Sandy Lane beach would also be the setting for a more serious and bizarre incident which would rob England of their vice-captain and most experienced spin bowler for the rest of the tour. A number of the England players were enjoying a day's relaxation on the idyllic beach and swimming in the sea, including Robin.

I was very lucky, very lucky indeed. We were at Sandy Lane which was very pukka. There were four of us, Titmus, Cowdrey, myself and Ollie Milburn when this little motorboat, a hire boat from one of the little islands came about. The England players swam up to the motorboat and as they were out of their depth they held on to the side and chatted. Titmus was opposite me and we both had our feet up underneath the boat. Ollie Milburn was diving underneath this bloody thing, the thought of it now. Suddenly there was a bang and Fred said "Christ my foot!" Suddenly you think it's a shark, some shark has got you.

Unbeknown to the four of them the motorboat had an unusual design, instead of being at the usual position of the back of the boat, the propeller was immediately underneath the centre of the hull. When Titmus had let his legs float up beneath the boat, the propeller instantly severed two toes from his left foot and left two others hanging by their skin. Robin was fortunate to have escaped unharmed having also had his feet bobbing up underneath the boat.

We got him to the shore and wrapped his foot in towels, somebody phoned an ambulance but it didn't turn up so we bundled him into a car, Cowdrey drove, I was in the passenger seat and Fred was in the back seat with towels wrapped around his foot. We drove him up the west coast of Barbados to this hospital where there were two surgeons who were used to injuries in the ice hockey world, they took him straight in, amazing these two guys, they did a good job on him, and he was out in 10 days.

Cowdrey said that as they hauled Titmus out of the water and saw the terrible sight of his leg 'I was as close to personal panic as I have ever been in my life.' According to Robin "Cowdrey was crying his eyes out." As much as he was concerned for the welfare of his vice-captain, Cowdrey was panicking about the identity of the driver of the motorboat being revealed in the press. Although there were a number of journalists present at Sandy Lane that day it didn't come out for a number of years that the mystery driver of the speedboat was in fact the England captain's wife, Penny Cowdrey. Titmus himself stressed that she was innocent of any blame but that the potential headline 'England skipper's wife chops off his deputy's toes' was one which Cowdrey was understandably keen to avoid.

Titmus felt that it was an illustration of the good relationship that the players had with the press in those days that Penny Cowdrey's name was never mentioned. Robin agrees that the relationship was pretty different in those days.

They were the old school of reporters, you could say things to them discreetly and they wouldn't put it in print. I got on well the press, they were decent blokes most of them, there were one or two scallywags but overall they were good blokes. Everybody knew it was Penny Cowdrey, she was actually driving the boat but it was doing no more than one or two knots an hour, it was just ticking over. She was in the boat, she was in the driver's seat, and then Titmus lost his toes. They covered it up for quite a long time, I don't know why, it was probably Cowdrey who didn't want people to know that it was his wife who driving the boat, so what, it could have been anyone. It didn't come out until much later that it was her.

I can remember the reporter Crawford White arriving, having heard the news, before we actually took Titmus off to hospital. White was one of the guys who dug up the dirt, nothing against him, he was a nice enough guy. EM Wellings was another one, they were catering for a different readership whereas the Swantons and the Woodcocks, they were reporting the cricket, they weren't reporting what else went on. I'm sure they did know what happened, they must have done. Word gets around, somebody must have said it "Hey, it was Penny Cowdrey but don't tell anybody."

Any slim hope Robin may have had about playing in the remaining Tests was shattered as the England management summoned left-arm spinner Tony Lock, who had been playing for Western Australia, to fly in as Titmus's replacement. "I think I felt pretty disappointed at the time. Why bring in somebody from the other side of the world when you've got Pocock and myself here."

The third Test, played at Bridgetown, ended as a draw and although he wasn't in the team Robin was 12th man and acting as a specialist substitute fielder and England used him to good effect, sending him on to the field and geeing up the team when it was needed. In West Indies second innings, Robin displayed his fielding prowess by running out Basil Butcher for 60. It would have been a safe two against the majority of England's fielders, but Robin, on as a substitute for John Edrich, beat Butcher by a yard with his return throw to wicket-keeper Jim Parks. It brought to an end a 100-run partnership for the fourth wicket between Butcher and Clive Lloyd; a moment Cowdrey would fondly recall in a letter to Robin many years later: 'I shall always enjoy your superb run-out at the vital moment.'

With the series all-square at 0-0 after three Tests the teams would meet up next at Port of Spain for the fourth Test. Tony Lock, who by now had arrived from Australia, was included, along with Robin, in the team to play in the tour match against the Windward Islands in St Lucia. The match was eventually abandoned but not before Robin had scored 40 in a total of 215 and taken five for 50 as the Windward Islands were dismissed for 165.

He arrived and in the next tour game, which was against Windward Islands, I got five for 50 and Lock got three for 62 and I was over the moon thinking well I've got a chance of playing now but obviously they recognised these kamikaze West Indian batsman were not quite as good as the Test players. I think it did probably hurt a little bit but as it transpired it was the right decision because he saved the last Test when he scored 89 in Guyana.

Writing in *Playfair Cricket Monthly* at the time, Rex Alston was of the opinion that Robin could count himself unfortunate.

'After Titmus, the really unlucky man in the party is Hobbs, who is the only one unlikely to play again in a Test on this tour now that Lock is available. He was picked as a leg spinner, but finds himself unable to command a place because Barrington, picked for his batting, has proved himself more penetrative. Moreover, by his speed and agility in the covers, and in the outfield, he lifted the standard of our cricket. Life is hard for some on every tour.'

In the decisive fourth Test Robin at least had a walk-on part. Garry Sobers, frustrated at England's tactics, decided to declare, setting England a target of 215 with 165 minutes left in the game. According to Brian Close, this played into England's hands with players well used to run chases in county cricket, the West Indies were further hampered by only having three fit bowlers as Griffith had pulled up with a thigh muscle injury during England's first innings.

Robin got an early indication of Sobers' intentions.

I was sitting on the side in my whites as 12th man as England were being flogged all-round the park and Sobers said "All right lads get changed" and I thought what's going on? Me being me I ran on to the field to Cowdrey and said "Hey skip, they're going to declare."

It was as intervention which Cowdrey was to fondly recall in his autobiography and interviews in the years which followed.

Once the declaration came Cowdrey walked into the pavilion to discuss the game plan with his team. It was a moment that's still clear in Robin's mind.

Cowdrey sat in his chair and said "Well that's it, well done lads, play it out for a draw" and Edrich and Barrington were aghast "A draw! They've only got three bowlers. It's 200 in 40 overs, we can walk this". "Oh no, no, no" replied Cowdrey "we don't want to lose it". "Lose it!" Barrington said. They went out there and they smacked them off. Cowdrey didn't want to go for them, he wanted to block them out. You're never going to get a better opportunity of winning in the Caribbean.

Had Ken Barrington not been so insistent, Cowdrey might not have pursued victory but once convinced that a win was possible both he, with 71, and Boycott, with 81 not out, batted well to reach the winning score of 215 with just three minutes to spare. Sobers gamble had backfired and certain sections of the West Indies supporters made their feelings known as Robin witnessed – "The next day after we won, poor old Garry, there were effigies burning in the street."

The England team, however, were jubilant and on arrival back at the Queen's Park Hotel, Ollie Milburn led the others in a celebratory sing-song.

According to Cowdrey, Milburn made a major contribution off the field by keeping the tour party entertained, particularly with his renditions of Tom Jones songs, and especially *The Green, Green Grass of Home* which became the unofficial tour song. Despite not featuring in the Test matches, Milburn – Robin's room-mate throughout the tour – had a fabulous time.

> *He enjoyed life did Colin, he really did. He got out in the early games, unfortunately if there was a bad lbw decision he'd get it, but he took it all in his stride. He never looked like playing a Test match but he thoroughly enjoyed himself, he was a great part of the team. I can see him now, sitting in the pool in Barbados in one of those great big rubber inner tubes, scorching down at nine o'clock in the morning it was and the bus was just going to the Test ground. I always went with the team because I was 12th man but they didn't need Ollie. He enjoyed a drink and he used to sit in this inner tube and as the bus was leaving he'd raise a glass and call out "Have a good day Tom!" Tom Graveney hated him; he'd be sitting in the coach ready to go and would say "What a bloody disgrace, look at him sitting there, he's getting the same money as me and here I am going off to fight against the West Indies". He used to wind up Tom Graveney, he really did, but he was great value was Colin, there was not a nasty thing in him, he was a social animal.*

The battle for the series was not yet won and there was a dramatic scare in the final Test at Georgetown, Guyana. Cowdrey and Alan Knott rescued their side from disaster after they had slumped to 41-5 in their second innings chasing 308 to win. England were ultimately indebted to unlikely batting hero Jeff Jones for his sturdy defiance in the final over of the match.

> *The most exciting part of the whole tour was when Jeff Jones defended the last over in Guyana off Lance Gibbs. We never thought that he'd last an over. Some people were locked in the toilet, people didn't watch, and to win it, to win the series. We should have won the first Test, there's no question about that and I think we would have won the second Test but for the fact that D'Oliviera dropped Sobers on nought and he went on to get a hundred and the game was taken into the sixth day because of the riots, we should have been 2-0 up. The third Test was drawn, the fourth Test would have been irrelevant with the declaration, we'd have still been two up. We were a better side throughout the series.*

Robin topped the tour bowling averages but happily admits that he didn't bowl against stronger teams like Barbados. Brian Close was of the belief that Robin and Ken Higgs' time would come again – 'The wickets were not suited to them, but that does not leave them out of the Test reckoning at home.'

Robin's reputation as an excellent tourist had been enhanced. Cowdrey wrote congratulating Robin on his contribution to the tour and for his help and loyal support, adding that he'd 'never toured with a better tourist'. Cowdrey also took the opportunity to express his regret at the lack of playing opportunities for Robin; 'I am only sorry that you did not play a bigger part in the Tests.'

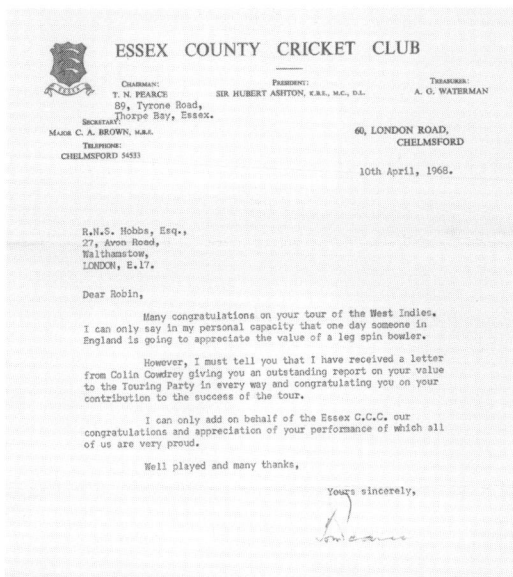

ESSEX COUNTY CRICKET CLUB

CHAIRMAN:
T. N. PEARCE
89, Tyrone Road,
Thorpe Bay, Essex.
SECRETARY:
MAJOR C. A. BROWN, M.B.E.
TELEPHONE:
CHELMSFORD 54533

PRESIDENT:
SIR HUBERT ASHTON, K.B.E., M.C., D.L.

TREASURER:
A. G. WATERMAN

60, LONDON ROAD,
CHELMSFORD

10th April, 1968.

R.N.S. Hobbs, Esq.,
27, Avon Road,
Walthamstow,
LONDON, E.17.

Dear Robin,

Many congratulations on your tour of the West Indies.
I can only say in my personal capacity that one day someone in
England is going to appreciate the value of a leg spin bowler.

However, I must tell you that I have received a letter
from Colin Cowdrey giving you an outstanding report on your value
to the Touring Party in every way and congratulating you on your
contribution to the success of the tour.

I can only add on behalf of the Essex C.C.C. our
congratulations and appreciation of your performance of which all
of us are very proud.

Well played and many thanks,

Yours sincerely,

At least Tom Pearce appreciated Robin's efforts. 'One day....', it
has yet to come.

Chairman of selectors, Doug Insole, was evidently pleased with Robin's conduct having received 'glowing reports of your performances on tour'. Like Cowdrey, Insole also appreciated Robin's contribution as a happy tourist. 'I think you have every reason to be satisfied with your results on the field – I certainly am – but to be able to make a real contribution to team spirit and to the keeping up of morale is a bonus which is appreciated by anybody who knows anything about touring sides, and the Skipper is obviously very much aware of it.' Essex chairman Tom Pearce also shared Insole's local pride but added a hint of frustration in his letter congratulating Robin. 'I can only say in my personal capacity that one day someone in England is going to appreciate the value of a leg-spin bowler.'

And so, in spite of having a good tour and receiving congratulations from all corners, Robin didn't think he had a future at Test level – "I knew I wouldn't get picked for the Ashes in 1968 and I didn't think I'd ever get picked again."

Post-tour reception, April 1968. Lord Mayor Sir Charles Trinder entertains. David Brown, John Snow, Pat Pocock, Jim Parks, John Edrich and Robin politely sip drinks and look uncomfortable.

Chapter Ten

I didn't bat, I didn't bowl and I didn't even bloody well field.

DESPITE PERSONAL CONGRATULATIONS for his contribution to the success of the West Indies tour from both the England captain and chairman of selectors, Robin wasn't selected for any of the home Tests in the 1968 Ashes series. It was a bit of a damp squib and Australia retained the urn with the series drawn 1-1. England used 20 players with the bulk of the spin provided by Derek Underwood and Ray Illingworth. The only other specialist spinner to be used was Pat Pocock and he was dropped after the first Test despite taking six for 79 in Australia's second innings.

Essex would go on to finish 14th in the Championship and Robin attained the third-best match analysis by a bowler that season with 13 for 133 against Worcestershire at Chelmsford; he was pipped however by his team-mate Ray East who took the top honours with 15 for 115 against Warwickshire at Leyton. In spite of East's Herculean efforts, Essex managed to lose the match by 50 runs. East became a key member of the Essex side and Robin recalls that his progression from village to county cricket in such a short space of time was quite incredible.

Ray really came from nowhere, he was an East Bergholt boy playing village cricket for a very ordinary side and he was a natural cricketer. In his fifth game for Essex at Ilford against Gloucestershire in 1966 he took five caught and bowleds which was something special. He had a terrific action, a natural cricketer and in any other age he'd have played for England. He was a very humorous guy and probably that was held against him in a lot of ways because he did a lot of silly things on the field which you wouldn't be allowed to get away with now. You've only got to look at his record for Essex; he got over a thousand proper wickets, not messing around at Scarborough festivals and things like that.

The 1968 season brought with it a momentous change in domestic cricket as counties were now allowed to sign overseas players under the new immediate registration rule. Essex, at the time still very much governed by financial restrictions, opted to sign Lee Irvine, a relatively obscure batsman from South Africa, rather than go for an expensive established Test player. It turned out to be a very astute piece of business according to Robin.

The April nets, 1968.

Lee was a fabulous competitor. The South African wicket-keeper at the time was Denis Lindsay who was a good 'keeper, no better than Lee but a good batsman. Lee grew up with Procter and Richards, they all came over at the same time. If they hadn't got banned from Test cricket he could have played for 10 years as a wicket-keeper batsman. He was a bloody good player, a pugnacious left-hander, he had a good eye and hit loads of sixes. He had two great seasons with Essex and one of his biggest regrets is that he didn't come back for a third year.

Throughout his career Robin wasn't used as much as he perhaps should have been in the one-day game but there were some standout moments. On 4 May 1968 Essex were playing against Middlesex at Lord's in the first round of the Gillette Cup. After 59 overs Middlesex had been restricted to 150-7 and Robin hadn't been used at all in the innings before Brian Taylor asked him to bowl the last of the 60 overs. Robin's first three balls went for 11 runs but he then dismissed Ronald Hooker, John Price and Robert Herman to complete a hat-trick and bring Middlesex's innings to a dramatic conclusion.

An equally impressive performance – this time with the bat – followed in June as Robin scored his maiden first-class century in the County Championship fixture against Glamorgan at Valentines Park during the Ilford festival week. Essex, in their first innings, were in trouble at 185 for 7 when Robin walked out to join Stuart Turner in the middle. It was a gloriously sunny afternoon which had attracted a bumper crowd. Glamorgan must have been looking forward to wrapping up the Essex innings for little more than 200 but the pair took the attack to the Glamorgan bowlers who came in for some severe treatment.

Stuart Turner remembers it well, it was only his second first-class match since rejoining the county after being let go at the end of the 1965 season as part of the general cost-cutting measures of the day. Farcically he wasn't aware that he was no longer an Essex player. 'I didn't know I'd been released,' he says, still with a hint of bewilderment more than 50 years later. 'I turned up in 1966 for pre-season training and was told: "What, didn't you get a letter?"'

Determined to make to make the most of his second chance, Turner remembers being in single figures when Robin came in to bat.

> 'He came out to join me just before tea and I had seven or eight. We went into the pavilion for tea and as we went back out Fletch said to me "Good luck Stuart" and he turned to Robin and said "See you in a minute Hobbsy" which I thought was a bit unkind. Of course a couple of hours later he had to eat his words because we ran riot a little bit, we scored them very quickly.'

Turner looked the more accomplished batsman but Robin, with a series of short-arm strokes, hit all round the ground with extraordinary strength. Tony Lewis, the Glamorgan captain, tried all his bowlers but none looked likely to succeed until Robin, having just reached his century, was caught by Lewis at mid-on off the bowling of Don Shepherd. Robin had hit 13 boundaries and in just under two hours he and Turner had put on a partnership of 192 during which Robin passed his previous highest score of 48. Recalling Robin's innings in the November 1975 issue of *The Cricketer*, Lewis observed that 'He would be first to admit that something genuinely fast often finds him wanting, but on that day eight years ago Jeff Jones, Glamorgan's England fast bowler, had left the field injured, so Hobbs made hay in the most violent way.'

Lewis was spot on in his assessment of Robin's susceptibility to genuine pace – not uncommon in tail-enders of any age – but that's not to diminish his achievement in reaching three figures. Although Jones had left the field, Glamorgan could still call on the services of Tony Cordle, Don Shepherd and Peter Walker. Even if they couldn't match Jones' pace they were all experienced and proven first-class bowlers. Glamorgan also had left-arm seamer Malcolm Nash in the side; it was only his second season in first-class cricket although he would go on to become one of the best new-ball bowlers in county cricket with a happy knack of dismissing top-order batsmen. 'That was a bit of a nightmare for us,' says Nash as he reflects on the match 50 years later, 'we just could not get Turner and Hobbsy out, it was unbelievable. Hobbsy was a swashbuckling sort of guy, that's the way he played his cricket; there was no real defensive stuff in that innings, he played himself in a little bit but then he smashed it everywhere.' Stuart Turner has slightly fonder memories:

> 'One could say we were rather fortunate in that Glamorgan had lost their best bowler, but Tony Cordle was no slouch, nor was Malcolm Nash with his left-arm-over in-swingers. Don Shepherd was an icon of that time, he wasn't an off spinner, he came off a longish run and bowled off cutters, he was a little bit like Derek Underwood who at times bowled a lot quicker than the average left-armer. Shepherd was a master of line and length and a very difficult bowler to score off but I always tried to be positive when I batted. Hobbsy was quite unorthodox in the way he played, he wasn't a classical batsman, if the ball was there to be hit he'd hit it, he had his own way of defending when he had to defend and at times it wasn't particularly pretty. He was great fun to bat with and we also ran some pretty ridiculous singles, one would almost say suicidal, that's the way we played it.'

David Acfield similarly remembers Robin's running between the wickets as being unbelievable. According to Acfield, Robin never hurried, preferring instead just to beat the throw. Occasionally he did commit suicide but quite often he'd receive four overthrows from a fielder amazed at his ludicrous audacity. 'Half a run quite regularly became a five when he was at the wicket', says Acfield.

Robin and Turner had largely kept pace with each other on the scoreboard during their partnership before Robin got his hundred and was out almost immediately afterwards. That left Essex eight wickets down and Turner only needed around half-a-dozen runs to get to his century but he was worried that he was going to run out of partners. Fortunately he was able to record his maiden first-class hundred, scoring 110 not out before Brian Taylor declared the innings on 385-8. With a century and seven wickets in the match it turned out to be another memorable performance for Robin, something which he regularly seemed to manage against Glamorgan, as Essex went on to record a victory by an innings and 84 runs. 'I don't think we could read him terribly well' laughs Malcolm Nash, 'I certainly had trouble. Being a left hander it spun into me – normally I'd hit with the spin but it was a bit like facing Underwood when he came on – and he did me both innings in that game at Ilford.'

Nash would go on to play over 300 times for Glamorgan but sadly for Jeff Jones it turned out to be his final County Championship appearance. He'd damaged shoulder and elbow ligaments and missed the rest of the summer; worse was to follow as a specialist discovered arthritis in his elbow joint and a wearing of the bone. Despite changing his action Jones was forced to retire from county cricket at the age of 27, a sad loss to the game for this popular player as Robin recalls.

Jonesy was a great bloke to tour with, he had a good sense of humour and was a great trier. I very nearly got his lad Simon to play for Essex because Jeff didn't want him to bowl on the wickets he did in Glamorgan. Simon came down for a week or so but couldn't settle so he went back to Glamorgan.

Robin bowling in 1968.
To a suburban backdrop the effort of making the ball turn on a green English wicket is clear to see.

As was by now an end-of-season tradition, Robin played three matches at the Scarborough Festival in early September, producing some solid performances. For an England XI versus a Rest of the World XI he took five for 73 in the second innings which included the West Indian quartet of Nurse, Lloyd, Butcher and Sobers, for a duck. Robin's other victim in his five-for was Graeme Pollock who also fell for a duck. "I got Pollock out with a double-bouncer," says Robin with a tinge of embarrassment. "He tried to hit it into the wharf at Scarborough, it the one that got Sobers was a genuine ball." There were certainly no tailenders in this illustrious quintet.

In the Rest of the World first innings, Robin had taken just the one wicket – Hanif Mohammad stumped by Jimmy Binks for 19. If only John Murray had been able to do this a year earlier at Lord's, Robin's Test career could have been so different. Playing once more for an England XI, this time against an England under-25 XI, Robin took four for 98 which included the wicket of Keith Fletcher, although his county colleague had, by then, scored 112.

In the final match of the Festival Robin took another five-wicket haul, this time with five for 71 for MCC versus Yorkshire, including the wicket of Brian Close, bowled for one. Having played against his county colleague Fletcher earlier in the Festival they now found themselves in the same side and together at the crease with the MCC score on 244-8 in reply to Yorkshire's first innings total of 199. Writing for *The Guardian*, Brian Chapman's account of Fletcher and Robin's partnership captures wonderfully the excitement of the occasion.

'The MCC first innings ended as it began, with an explosion of runs in Yorkshire's face. Fletcher and Hobbs scorched to 78 for the ninth wicket in 28 minutes, positively out-Milburning Milburn. When the Essex men came together Fletcher was well set at 67 and primed his shots beautifully: he had merely to accelerate. Hobbs, who was in no danger of being confused with his immortal namesake, was suddenly seized with a demonic spirit which inspired him to fling his bat with some purpose. Perhaps he was stung by Binks' gesture in pointing to the pavilion when a run-out appeal was rejected.

Like most leg spinners, Hobbs is of an original turn of mind and he accepted this as a signal to mow a destructive swathe through Yorkshire's bowling. Twice he clouted Close – drove, mot juste – to the screen, then square cut him with quiet pride. A ball from Wilson he lifted clean over the Trafalgar Square stands, though admittedly they are low as stands go, and the entire field broke into amazed applause.'

Robin was finally bowled for 31 by Tony Nicholson but he'd stuck around long enough to support Fletcher who ended on 113 not out, an innings which along with his 112 for England under 25s had given him a great deal of satisfaction during the Festival. Neither Robin nor Fletcher could repeat their form in the second innings and the final first-class match of the 1968 season finished as a draw.

England were due to tour South Africa in 1968/69 but it was cancelled due to the controversy surrounding Basil D'Oliveira's initial exclusion and eventual inclusion in the tour party. Despite a previous good tour of South Africa in 1964/65 and a decent season in 1968 in which he took 83 first-class wickets at 23.95, Robin never felt that he had a serious chance of being selected but was heading for South Africa regardless as he and Isabel were due to get married there. "I was totally out of the frame for England", he remembers. Robin and Isabel were married in church in Pretoria on 26 December 1968 with the reception held on the farm where Robin had been lodging. There weren't many of Robin's friends there because of the distance involved but it was a lovely day and everything went to plan. Robin's best man was Derek Hill, a first-class cricketer for Northern Transvaal and the son-in-law of the couple whose farm he was staying on.

Robin and Isabel on their wedding day, Pretoria, 26 December 1968.

Robin had intended to stay in South Africa with Isabel for the remainder of the winter but following the cancellation of the South Africa series a tour of Ceylon and Pakistan was hastily arranged in its place and Robin was suddenly back in the frame for England. It was intended that the tour party would be the same 16 players that had been selected for South Africa but following the withdrawals of Boycott and Barrington – both for health reasons – the selectors decided to reduce it to 15 players and Robin would replace the two batsmen as another spinner would be needed for the sub-continent. "I received a telegram telling me to return to England as soon as possible", recalls Robin, "I was supposed to be coming back by boat with Isabel but I had to fly back because there were several functions in London to attend before the tour party headed off."

Writing in *Playfair Cricket Monthly*, Rex Alston felt that the balance of the squad wasn't quite right, having originally been picked with South African conditions in mind. With Boycott and Barrington's withdrawals Alston's opinion was that 'MCC have made the best of a bad job by selecting leg-spinner Hobbs, whose fielding may have tipped the scales in his favour against other candidates like Birkenshaw or Don Wilson.'

An imbalance of the tour party was the least of England's problems; internal unrest in Pakistan meant that the country was as good as engaged in civil war. This was no time and place for a cricket tour but incredibly it was sanctioned and encouraged by a British Foreign Office keen to demonstrate support for the Pakistan President, Ayub Khan, who was considered a vital ally in the Cold War.

All of this was still to come as the tour party headed off to the peace and tranquillity of Ceylon for the first leg of the tour, arriving in Colombo on 22 January 1969. The four warm-up games were played in a festival spirit and in between the players relaxed playing golf and basking on the idyllic sands of the island's beautiful beaches.

We played in Kandy and Colombo, there were thousands of people watching. I used to toss it up and got smacked all over the park, I got one for 70 in eight overs and one for 60. Everyone was happy, people were running after the ball for the sixes and our captain, Colin Cowdrey, must have been thinking 'He's a bit expensive this bloke!'

After the serenity of Ceylon the tour party flew on to Pakistan where they'd be playing three warm-up games before the start of the Test series. Robin played in the first of these games against the Control Board XI at Bahawalpur, taking two for 71, in an attack which also included fellow spinners Pocock and Underwood.

Despite a good bowling performance, Robin wasn't selected for either of the final two warm ups. At one stage he had been left virtually alone in a hotel in Lahore while the rest of the team had headed off to Sahiwal, some 180 km away, to play a three-day match against the West Pakistan Governor's XI. Without much by way of entertainment Robin turned to pitch and putt to keep himself amused.

The first Test at Lahore was drawn and Robin could only watch from the sidelines twiddling his thumbs, England preferring to go with the spin of Pocock and Underwood. There were a number of interruptions from protestors during the game, particularly on the first and last days, and an air of tension pervaded the ground as the England players were left wondering whether they might be forced to flee at any moment due to the inefficiency of the security forces' efforts to keep control.

First Test at the Gaddafi Stadium, Lahore. February 1969. Standing: Bernard Thomas (Physiotherapist), John Snow, Pat Pocock, Roger Prideaux, Bob Cottam, Derek Underwood, Keith Fletcher, Alan Knott, Robin Hobbs. Sitting: David Brown, Basil D'Oliveira, Tom Graveney, Colin Cowdrey, Les Ames (Manager), John Edrich, John Murray.

The second Test was at Dacca in East Pakistan and before departing a cable was received from the British High Commission there warning that the tour party should not come to that part of the country as their safety could not be guaranteed. When news broke that the team wouldn't be heading to Dacca an angry mob promptly burned down the High Commission. Surprisingly, the following day a further cable arrived from the High Commission assuring that everything was now fine and that the tour should proceed as planned. It was *Carry On up the Khyber* stuff! "Poor old Les Ames was tearing his hair out," Robin recalls, "he spent more time at the High Commission than he did at the cricket."

Incredibly the Test passed off without serious interruption with the organisation of stewarding and security taken over by the student protestors themselves. On the field the match was drawn, Robin once again wasn't selected and Pocock was dropped as England opted to go with three seamers and just one specialist spinner in Underwood. Pakistan on the other hand opted for four spinners and just one seamer.

The one bright light amongst all the turmoil was the arrival of Colin Milburn shortly before the start of the Dacca Test. Milburn – who'd just come to the end of a stint playing for Western Australia – was preparing to sail home to the UK when he was summoned to Pakistan where he was needed as cover due to injury concerns over Cowdrey. The journey from Perth to Dacca took 72 hours and Milburn emerged exhaustedly from the plane to be greeted by the whole England team, his arrival was a huge fillip. The mood was raised even higher by a few laughs at Milburn's expense. Years later Robin stills chuckles away at the thought of that day.

> *When the plane landed we picked him up from the airport. We were staying in a decent hotel but there was a hotel we'd stayed at on the under-25 tour two years earlier which we called the Shag Bag, it was a dreadful hole. We picked him up from the airport, put him on the bus and we dropped him off at the Shag Bag, we told him there weren't any rooms free at the Hilton and left him with his bags outside this bloody hotel.*

After an hour the players returned to collect Milburn but the horror wasn't over for him. By chance his arrival in Pakistan that day coincided with a religious festival which Robin remembers well with a mischievous smile.

> *It was the day of the year when the locals throughout Pakistan slaughtered an ox wherever it stood to feed the local village and so the whole place was covered in blood and carcases. Ollie's reaction was priceless – "F***ing hell, what have I come to, there's blood everywhere!"*

The second Test was drawn and the tour party flew to trouble-torn Karachi for the series finale. By now Robin had given up hope of playing any further part in the tour and had got rid of all his kit, giving it away to grateful locals. Taking a look at the pitch in the days leading up to the Test Robin describes it as being "as flat as a table". Not having played for a month he felt certain he had no chance of being selected and was relieved that he wouldn't have to bowl to a Pakistan batting line-up well used to facing spin and in their own backyard. "Pakistan had a batting order that looked like a world eleven", recalls Robin, "they had Hanif Mohammad, Majid Khan, Shafqat Rana, Asif Iqbal, Saeed Ahmed, Mushtaq Mohammad, they batted down to 11."

To his total bewilderment, Robin found himself selected anyway. The England selectors had originally opted to go with the same bowling attack as in

Dacca but as the wicket dried they felt it would be a slow turner. Bob Cottam was dropped and in came Robin, ridiculously short of match practice, something which he still looks back on with a sense of astonishment.

Cowdrey said to me two days before the game, "You're going to play the next game Robin, we think you're the chap to bowl them out."
I said "You're f***ing joking! I haven't played or bowled a ball for five weeks."
"We'll sort that out this afternoon" he replied.
"Oh really, what are we going to do?" I said with more than a hint of sarcasm.
"We're going to the nets, you and I, and you're going to bowl 50 balls."

And so, with less than two days to go before the deciding Test in the series, Cowdrey and Robin headed for the nets for a special practice. "Oh my God, oh God help us," recalls Robin, "balls were going all over the place and there I was – Hobbs picked for the final Test in Karachi, trying to hide or run away."

Colin Milburn was also brought into the side, replacing Roger Prideaux, and went on to score a magnificent 139 after England had won the toss and, much to Robin's relief, opted to bat first. A number of pitch invasions and interruptions had occurred during the first two days and on the third the situation turned ugly following the death of a prominent anti-government leader. For Robin, short of match practice and contemplating the prospect of a mauling at the hands of the Pakistan batsmen, fate intervened and provided his salvation.

The anti-government protestors had been threatening all tour to disrupt the place and we're playing in the national stadium in Karachi and I'm thinking 'We're 502 for 7, I'm going to have to bowl 25 overs here and I'm going to get smashed for 150 and this is the end of my f***ing life, I can see it happening.' I couldn't bowl a hoop down a hill and they had a batting order I couldn't get any of them out, I would have got nought for 150. And then suddenly God looked down on me. The gates at the far end of the national ground opened and f*** me, about 500 people came bursting in. They set fire to all the hoardings, all the VIP lounges went up in smoke and there were two blokes out there with a f***ing shovel digging the pitch up and if I could have had another shovel I'd have been out there with them. I tell you what, was I happy!

One player who possibly didn't share Robin's elation was Alan Knott who was on 96 not out and approaching his maiden Test century when the mob broke into the ground and brought a halt to the game. The England team took refuge in their dressing room and the Pakistan cricket authorities took the decision to abandon the tour. The players were as good as smuggled out of the ground back to their hotel; they hastily packed their belongings and headed for the airport where Les Ames had managed to get everyone booked on to the first flight out of Karachi. As the plane took off at midnight, Milburn rocked the cabin with a rendition of *The Green, Green Grass of Home* and Robin and the other England players broke into rapturous and relieved applause, flying home "as happy as Larry."

It had been a strenuous five weeks on a tour which should never have been given the go-ahead. Other than Boycott and Barrington, none of the other players had pulled out before the start which, on reflection, may seem surprising but in that era international cricketers were not as financially secure. The original tour to South African would have lasted close to four months, the rearranged one lasted less than two. However, MCC – perhaps mindful of how fraught it might be – still opted to pay the players the same fee which made the ordeal well worth their while. Robin still chuckles at the whole experience: "I got two wickets which cost MCC £1000 – £500 a wicket."

The whole tour had been a farce and the England team had been lucky to escape unscathed, the experience had been even more surreal for Robin and the bizarre recall for the third Test despite him being completely short of bowling practice.

It was unbelievable, I was really sold down the river being picked for that last Test there and I only got out of it by luck, I didn't bowl and came back unscarred by pure luck. I would have been slaughtered, I would have been smashed all round the park so that made up for the missed chances at Lord's in 1967.

Playing in an abandoned Test did however bestow upon Robin a rare and dubious honour which he still sees the funny side of many years later. "I've been one of the few people to have played in a Test series who didn't bat, didn't bowl and didn't even bloody well field."

Chapter Eleven

It took ten coats of paint to get rid of it.

Things were starting to fall into place for Essex at the end of the 1960s under Brian Taylor's sergeant-major style of leadership. Operating with a small squad the county developed an excellent team spirit which Robin was an integral part of. 'Hobbsy was a great team man.' recalls former Middlesex batsman Peter Parfitt, 'He was an outstanding outfielder, and when I say outstanding I mean outstanding – he was in the class of Derek Randall.'

Former Middlesex wicket-keeper John Murray shares his county colleague's assessment of Robin's talent as a fielder. 'He was high class in the field and had a good throw. When you played against him you didn't take any liberties when the ball was going in his direction, you made sure it was past him.'

> *I loved fielding, couldn't wait for the ball to come to me. I was a bloody good cover fielder and also fielded at mid-wicket; towards the end of my career I fielded in the gully which I found a terrific spot. I loved fielding, chasing the ball, getting run-outs which I got quite a lot of.*

But Robin was not alone.

> *In actual fact the Essex side I played in with Lee Irvine, John Lever, Stuart Turner, Ray East, Brian Edmeades and Keith Boyce, they were a bloody good fielding side. Boycie was a better all-round fielder than I was because he could field at leg gully and things like that. I stood out above them, just.*

Peter Parfitt, a left-handed batman who played 37 Tests for England, remembers facing Robin in domestic first-class cricket. 'He didn't spin the ball much,' recalls Parfitt, 'but he was accurate and he had a variation of pace; you could always tell when he was bowling a quicker ball because he used to run up quicker.' Murray, who had experience of keeping to, and batting against, Robin's bowling, agrees with Parfitt's assessment – 'He wasn't a big spinner of the ball but he had good control, he was almost like a top-spin bowler.' It's an assessment that Robin doesn't dispute.

> *I wasn't a great spinner of the ball but I don't think you have to be to bowl leg breaks*

because you've only got to make it spin a few inches. When the pitch did turn I turned it, quite a long way, but I was more conscious of bowling it economically. Most of the wickets you get are people on the drive, you think them out – caught slip, stumped. Alright you get wickets with a bad ball caught at mid-wicket or whatever but you're aiming on getting a guy caught in the slips or in that area and bowling it accurately and not bowling a bad ball. I was a believer in bowling leg breaks and top spinners, a lot of the balls that were bowled as leg breaks went down as top spinners because of where you let the ball go. If you're slightly over 12 o'clock it tends to go on more than turn. So my action was very basic, leg breaks most of the time, I could actually bowl the top spinner as well but I didn't bowl it that often because I found that a lot of the leg spinners were top spinners so I thought there's no point trying to bowl the top spinner if the ball is actually going on straight anyway.

Parfitt recalls that playing Essex was usually a fun occasion particularly with Robin in the side.

'He was absolutely full of chat all the time was Hobbsy, a piss-taker but a fantastic character and a bundle of fun. He was also a member of that Essex 'circus' that was led by Tonker Taylor and then you had Acfield who was a comedian, Lever who was a comedian and that other comedian Ray East. They were hilarious, playing against them was ridiculous. You had to be on your mettle all the time, Acfield would be in the covers somewhere, Lever would be somewhere else and Easty would be chatter-boxing away so there was never a quiet period when you were batting away against that lot.'

Murray similarly recalls that the Essex team 'were a pretty wild bunch' – there was never a dull moment playing against them. 'I always thought that Brian Taylor should have been given a knighthood. They only had 12 professional cricketers during that period and luckily they all stayed fit. Dear old Brian, he tried to keep that lot under control, it was a miracle. But they were all good cricketers.' This was the view from within as well with David Acfield cheerily terming them as 'scatterbrain youngsters'.

Describing himself as Tonker's blue-eyed boy, Robin felt that he was able to get away with things whilst others in the team were less fortunate. John Lever, however, remembers Robin getting the sharp end of Tonker's tongue in the changing room on one occasion when he discovered that the Essex van had gone missing. "Well, where has it gone?" an exasperated Tonker demanded, "I've lent it to Jackie Birkenshaw," confessed Robin, who hadn't foreseen a problem in lending the van to the Leicestershire player as a favour. Ray East had a much harder time under Tonker, they were like chalk and cheese although they became great friends in later years.

Ray was one of the guys in the team Tonker would get stuck into. If he stayed out until one o'clock in the morning and Brian knew about it he did his penance the next day, he had to bowl 30 overs. At Northampton one day he'd bowled about 25 overs and Fletch said "What about giving someone else a bowl?" "No," replied Tonker, "he's got to do 30 overs because he stayed out until one o'clock!" It was a shirt front of a wicket and he bowled, and bowled, and bowled and just before tea he got one to turn; it pitched leg stump and it turned between Tonker, who never layed a glove on it, and Graham Saville at slip and it went for four byes. Ray, being the clown he was, stood in the middle of the wicket with his arms aloft and yelled "I got one to turn lads, I got one to turn." Tonker's face was red, he was not impressed. He walked down the wicket, grabbed East by the scruff of the neck and said "You turned that one on bloody purpose to make me look a complete bloody idiot."

The Essex Circus. A motley crew sponsored by Ford Transit.

Another example of East's fooling around again landed him in hot water with Tonker, much to Robin's amusement. Tonker's rage was increasing to danger levels during a session in the field at Worcester whilst East was clowning around and bowling poorly on a turning wicket. As the players headed back to the changing-room for lunch there was an air of expectancy of the inevitable. They didn't have to wait long. Tonker took off his pads and barked: "Raymond.

Get your blazer on and see me outside!" East duly obliged and headed outside for a bollocking, although – and much to their glee – the rest of the Essex players could still hear every word of it from inside. When Tonker and East came back in, East apologized to the rest of the players for his behaviour and that appeared to be the end of the matter until later that evening in the pub when every couple of minutes Robin would leap up and shout: "Raymond. Get your blazer on, I want to have a word with you outside!" According to John Lever this was typical of Robin. 'He never forgot anything and he was a good mimic as well, and that kind of thing did a lot to build up the spirit in the Essex side. It defused the situation and I think Raymond learned quite a lot from him so that in later years he himself became one of the better defusers of potentially ugly situations.'

Unorthodox batting. Uppercutting Sarfraz Nawaz on the way to 83
at Chelmsford in 1970.

Another joker-in-the-pack at Essex was Keith Pont. At the end of each day's play the scorer used to bring in the bowling figures and handed them to Pont. If they were good figures he'd read them out, if they'd had a bad day he'd say we'll put them in the medicine cabinet to see if they get better.

In one of Pont's early matches for Essex – against Derbyshire at Burton-on-Trent – Tonker decided that the young batsman would field at third-man at one end and fine-leg at the other. Pont borrowed a bicycle off a boy in the crowd and pedalled his way from one position to the other. Tonker was not best pleased but Robin assured him that there was no harm in it; "It's only Burton-on-Trent, there's nobody here", "Alright Rob," he replied "if you think that's alright that's fine by me." When Doug Walters tried the same with Ian Chappell the response was slightly less lenient. Robin was again able to defuse a situation and often found that Tonker would agree with him on matters which he'd occasionally use to his advantage. "There were situations when you were playing against bloody good players," he says,

> Some days when you don't really fancy bowling on a flat wicket, I used to say to Brian "I'll have a little bowl in a couple of hours", "Alright Rob," he'd say, "If you don't fancy a bowl now." "Well no, not really at the moment, I'll have a look at the way things are going" and he used to let me bowl at the numbers 7, 8, 9, and 10 – I shouldn't have got away with it but I did.

One time Robin wasn't able to exert his influence over Tonker was in the Championship fixture against Northamptonshire at Chelmsford in May 1970. Essex were 159-6 in their first innings as Robin, batting at number eight, went out to the middle. Stuart Turner fell soon afterwards but Robin, along with Ray East, added 83 for the eighth wicket and then John Lever did a good job in staying with Robin in an unbroken partnership of 62 to take the score to 314-8. Robin was on 83 not out and looking forward to the possibility of scoring his second first-class hundred when Tonker declared and called them in. 'That was Tonker all over,' says Lever, 'he was never one for personal glory getting in the way of a game of cricket. That's how we played our cricket all the way through and when Fletch took over it was exactly the same, it was a case of "Well, if you want to get a hundred you've got to get it before I want to declare otherwise it doesn't come into the equation."'

Team man Robin celebrates as Leicestershire's Roger Tolchard
is caught by Tonker off the bowling of David Acfield.

Whilst there was plenty of joking and mischief on the field, off it Essex were making serious strides in securing financial sustainability. By the end of the 1969 season the county had registered a profit for the first time since the end of the Second World War and a £15,000 loan from the Warwickshire supporters club had been secured which would pay for the building of the pavilion at Chelmsford. Essex were certainly getting their act together; in the Sunday League they became used to playing to full houses of 6000 and on occasion had to shut the gates. For Brian Taylor, the introduction of the John Player Sunday League was instrumental in honing the skills of his young charges and developing a winning mentality. 'With the introduction of the Sunday League people gave us no chance but we talked for hours about how we would go about this game as a lot of other counties weren't interested. We won seven of our first eight matches and that success started to gather momentum and rub off into the three-day games.'

Stuart Turner believes that the county were improving and, like Taylor, credits the advent of the Sunday games as instrumental in this progress.

'I think we all looked at this game and thought "We can win this" and, because we were an amazing fielding side, we got out of jail so many times with perhaps small totals which today would have been a joke. I think the John Player League did us a lot of good.'

The establishment of a permanent base at Chelmsford marked the beginning of the end of the county's nomadic existence, the end of the circus. It was a change Robin had mixed feelings about; he'd always enjoyed travelling around Essex and has many fond memories of the games he played at the outgrounds.

I've always thought that it was a great shame when Essex decided to stop playing county matches at Westcliff. The pitches were, by and large, so unpredictable that games stick in my memory as some of the most exciting I've ever played in and the match against the New Zealand tourists in 1969 was no exception. The tourist match each year was always eagerly awaited by the players. My memory of the game itself is quite clear. The pitch started very green, but rapidly the top came off and it became a turner which first Ray East and then Hedley Howarth took full advantage of.

Having won the toss, Essex chose to bat were bowled out for only 121. By the close of play the New Zealanders had drawn level with only three wickets down. An excellent display from the Essex spinners – led by Ray East with six for 49 – saw the tourists dismissed for 201 largely thanks to a quick 40 from the big-hitting of Dick Motz who struck Robin for four sixes and two fours in quick succession. "I was hit for the biggest six of my career in that game," recalls Robin, "it was enormous, it cleared the Leigh Cricket Club Pavilion and disappeared down the main road to Hadleigh!"

After a steady start in their second innings Essex suffered a batting collapse as left-arm spinner Howarth eclipsed East's first-innings efforts to claim seven for 43. Robin was the eighth wicket to fall with the score on 102, an overall lead of 22 with only two wickets left. It was a comical dismissal, befitting of Robin's career, and one which gave him an everlasting memory of the game.

Arthur Jepson had the habit [when standing at the non-striker's end] of raising his finger at the end of every over as he tossed the last stone from one hand to the other. Hedley Howarth bowled the last ball, it hit me on the pad well outside the line and I assumed Arthur's finger went up as a matter of habit at the end of the over. I asked their wicket-keeper [Barry Milburn] if the ball was going to hit and he said it was missing another set of stumps.

Robin casually took his place at the non-striker's end as the field switched for the start of the next over but as he looked up he noticed Arthur Jepson at square-leg giving him out lbw. "Arthur had his finger raised and was saying 'Hey, you're out, get out'. Ray East, who was batting at the other end, joined in the chorus and was shouting at me 'Go on Hobbsy, away you go, stop cheating.'"

East went on to score 58 and with the help of Lever and Acfield managed to add another 90 runs for the last two wickets, setting the New Zealanders what appeared to be a formality of 113 to win with plenty of time left.

John Lever made an early breakthrough with the key wicket of the New Zealanders captain Graham Dowling and the Essex spin trio were all soon into the attack applying pressure on a sharply-turning pitch. Wickets began to fall at regular intervals and Essex began to sense that they had a real chance but the match was very much in the balance whilst big-hitting Motz was still at the crease.

I can remember being very apprehensive when Dick Motz came in after he'd smashed me for four enormous sixes in the first innings. He was the one player on the New Zealand side who could change the course of the match within the space of just two overs. This time his luck was out, he took a great heave at a wide leg spinner which Keith Fletcher caught at slip. From then on we were in the driving seat, although the last wicket put on 30-odd runs we were never in danger of losing the match.

Robin's second-innings bowling figures of four for 31 helped Essex to a 15-run victory, the only defeat the tourists suffered in a first-class game outside the Test series that summer. His only regret about the game was that he didn't get to spend time chatting to the New Zealand captain Graham Dowling, the nephew of his old school master, Basil Dowling.

Robin's 1969 season finished with a traditional appearance at the Scarborough Festival and an almost customary five-wicket haul; five for 65 for MCC versus Yorkshire. There was no England tour in 1969/70 but Robin did manage to secure some time in the sun away from the English winter as part of the Duke of Norfolk's XI tour to the Caribbean in February and March 1970. "The Duke didn't really know that people like me existed," recalls Robin, "but he was a great guy, he had a twinkle in his eye and we got on well."

The tour party also included Colin Cowdrey, Tony Greig and Derek Underwood; the team manager was the distinguished *Daily Telegraph* cricket writer EW Swanton whom, according to Robin, the Duke of Norfolk used to enjoy having his sport with.

> *He used to make his life hell. Swanton idolised him because the Duke came from a world he'd like to mix with. The Duke used to sit there, he'd wink at me and then say:*
> *"Swanton!"*
> *"Yes sir" replied Swanton.*
> *"Are the buses arriving shortly?"*
> *"Any minute sir."*
> *Swanton would bow down to him, the old Duke would always take the piss. Anyway at the end of tour we had a whip round and presented him with a salver.*

Robin enjoyed himself on the field too, taking 15 wickets in the three matches including six for 82 in the drawn match against the Windward Islands. On his previous tour of the Caribbean he'd encountered 'kamikaze batsmen' and this style of batting was still very much in vogue he remembers with a grin – "The higher you lobbed it the harder they tried to hit it out of the island."

Essex finished in 12th place in the County Championship in 1970 and but for bad luck with the weather, which robbed them of a couple of victories, they would surely have finished higher. Robin had a fine season topping the Essex bowling averages with 90 wickets at 21.18. In all first-class matches he took 102 wickets at 21.40 and was one of only four bowlers, along with Don Shepherd, Norman Gifford and Fred Titmus, to break the hundred-wicket barrier that season. He was by now an experienced pro', full of confidence and at the top of his game.

I was established then. That year I think I bowled over 700 overs for those 102 wickets which is an incredible strike rate. Suddenly the wickets were fortuitous – long hops, full tosses people got out to; everything went my way. When you're successful in a county season you can't seem to do anything wrong. I went on to bowl every time with confidence, I knew what to bowl and knew the batsmen I was playing against, they were young players. I was 28 and there were lots of kids coming in to the game at 21 or 22. I knew how to play; you only needed two or three overs to get them out.

Former team-mate Stuart Turner feels that Robin was brave in this respect to keep tossing the ball up at times and that he was never scared to tempt batsmen.

'Hobbsy would think, "OK, he might slog me for a couple of sixes but eventually he'll hole out somewhere." Whereas there was a strict contrast if you had him and David Acfield bowling in tandem. David just absolutely hated being hit for runs, he'd get flatter and flatter, he wouldn't loop it, wouldn't throw it up. If he got hit he'd just get flatter and flatter whereas Hobbsy would just toss it up and would be saying to the batsman "Go on then, have a go at that!" and invariably he'd succeed.'

John Lever agrees with Turner on Robin's cavalier attitude. 'You'd see some of the youngsters come in and they'd smash Hobbsy a couple of times but the ball would still go up in the air, higher and higher and invariably he'd end up with three or four wickets which was enjoyable for us and kept the game moving.'

As a proud leg spinner Robin takes some issue with the idea of 'tossing it up'. He naturally prefers the description of 'flight'.

Yeah, you don't toss it up, what is the point of tossing it up? It's a variation of flight, you're not going to get good players out by tossing it up. It's all about varying your flight, there's no point running up and bowling it like a lollipop – that's tossing it up in a benefit game – "Go on boy, hit it for six!" No, every time you bowl you've got to bowl the bloody thing. A lot of players in that era were very ordinary batsmen, and you had more chance of getting them out by "tossing it up" or getting them to have a slog whether you bowled it slower or whatever, wide of the off stump they'd have a swipe at it and it was better bowling it that way because they weren't going to get a bloody edge on it anyway, they would play and miss four balls out of six. Giving it variation in flight, getting it above the eye line, getting them to play an attacking shot at you – not tossing it up.

As an experienced bowler, playing regularly against the other counties, he was able to develop his knowledge of opponents' weaknesses and those players who were susceptible to leg spin.

> *There were certain players in each county side you thought, he's a sitting duck. If I bowl I'll get this guy out with a bit of luck, I don't mind bowling to him, I can't get enough balls at this guy. Stuart Leary at Kent was a bloody good cricketer he used to get 1200 runs a year but he couldn't play leg spin. I knew he couldn't play it and he knew he couldn't play it and I used to get him out on a regular basis – caught Bailey bowled Hobbs. The Notts captain Mike Smedley was another, he was a caught and bowled merchant, he'd be trying to turn it on the on-side and would regularly get a leading edge.*

Whilst there were certain batsmen tormented by leg spin, or new, younger players who'd never been exposed to it at first-class level there were many who played it well but were conventional and, by and large, predictable in their approach; classical English players playing through the V for much of their innings. Bowling to players of the calibre of Graveney, Edrich and Boycott was a challenge but Robin could at least set his field accordingly.

> *Tom Graveney never swept so unless you bowled a rank ball outside the leg stump you didn't need a deep square-leg, he was an off-side player. You knew when Tom came in if he was in good form he'd probably get a hundred but he wouldn't try and hit you over mid-on or mid-off, you knew that 50% of his runs would be through the covers and I knew that my best chance of getting him out was to bowl accurately and hopefully get him caught in the covers or caught and bowled. I got him out a few times. He was very good player but you'd never see him hit the ball in the air so you never worried about having a deep-extra-cover or dropping mid-on or mid-off back because he might hit you for six, he never did that.*
>
> *Boycott didn't sweep either but he was such a good player through the on-side with a straight bat that he didn't need to. I never feared bowling at him because I knew if I bowled a decent ball he'd play it straight, if it was a bit off it went for four. If you bowled it well or accurately you never had any worries about him but then again he had his mate John Hampshire and that was a different ball game. John Hampshire was quite a difficult bloke to bowl at because he was a much more attacking batsman. Boycott was there to look after Geoffrey and to get himself a hundred whether it took two, three, four hours.*

With the experience he'd gained Robin felt that he knew how to bowl to 80 per cent of the players he came across in the game, he also learnt that there were exceptions to the rule, Brian Close being one such example of a player you couldn't set a field to as "he could smash it anywhere". Kent's Alan Knott was "bloody hard to bowl at" as he was so quick on his feet and his batting was full of improvisation. It was this unconventional approach to batting which posed the greatest challenge to Robin as a bowler, players who were nimble footed and happy to come down the pitch forcing him to alter his length and pace and being canny enough to be able get back and cut the shorter balls. The most difficult players in this respect were generally Pakistani batsmen like Kent's Asif Iqbal and Mushtaq Mohammad at Northamptonshire, players brought up on wickets on the subcontinent, adopting a completely different approach to their classically English counterparts. At the time they were the exceptions, early pioneers of the kind of inventive batting now regularly on display.

> Bowling nowadays would be an absolute nightmare with people playing ramp shots. If I was brought up in it I'd probably learn to go along with it but to bowl to these guys who play all these peculiar shots now I would have been tearing my bloody hair out if people reverse swept me. Mushtaq Mohammad was one of the first players to do the reverse sweep and he did a couple against me and I couldn't understand it, it was totally alien. Mushtaq was one of those players I could never get out he must have hit me for a thousand runs in his career. My most memorable wicket was when I got him out at Chelmsford I went around the wicket, it went in the rough, Mushtaq played back, hit him on the glove and he was caught at bat pad by Graham Saville. I might have bowled better balls but that was a wicket that gave me so much pleasure.

Having performed consistently well throughout the 1970 season Robin held strong hopes of being selected for the winter tour to Australia and on 19 August, the day before the England touring party was announced, he bowled Essex to victory in the County Championship with seven for 59 against Derbyshire at Leyton. He was on a high and waited expectantly the following day for the squad to be announced as he and Isabel drove down to Devon. Rain was lashing down on the windscreen as the moment arrived and the news of the squad was broadcast over the car radio. Starting with the captain, Ray Illingworth, the names of the 16 players were revealed in alphabetical order. The announcer reached H on the list – "John Hampshire…", Robin learned towards the radio, holding his breath, anxiously hoping to hear his name, "Alan Knott…" and with that Robin's dream of touring Australia was gone.

"I was bitterly disappointed when the team was selected," he says, "I was devastated. I'm not very emotional but I broke down and that was the last time I cried. I couldn't believe that I hadn't been selected."

David Frith felt that the thinking at the time would have been that 'the Australians eat leg-spin for breakfast', a view shared by Peter Parfitt.

'In 1970/71 Ray Illingworth was always going to go for the finger spinner rather than the leg spinner. Australia was renowned to have good players of leg spin, Australians are very good at hitting the ball through the covers and square of the wicket which helps them with the leg spinner turning the ball away whereas they don't like it getting cramped up and having to try and hit the ball on the on-side. If you're on a worn wicket, the one thing you don't want to be doing as a right-hander is hitting a ball on the off side as you're hitting against the spin. So Robin would always be unlucky in Australia.'

Frith was slightly more optimistic, though, feeling that Robin, had he been selected, 'might just have induced a little indigestion' in the Australian batsmen. Having been on three MCC tours with him, Alan Knott believes that Robin was well able to adapt his bowling to overseas conditions.

'He bowled two different methods. In England he bowled a lot flatter, less spin but very accurate – the Essex wickets made him bowl in this method. When he went abroad he threw the ball up in the air a lot more and spun it more. He bowled so well on the Pakistan U25 tour in 1967, he got the bounce there but not quite enough speed. In Australia they had the bounce but they also had the speed in the wicket which suited leg spinners a great deal so that was a trip really that he was unlucky not to get on, if he'd have got there he could have really shone.'

Despite conditions which may have suited him, Knott suggests that Robin always faced an uphill task in terms of competing with the orthodox spinners of the day, 'That's what did for Robin really,' he says, 'the standard of England spinners was very, very good; to get past guys like Illingworth, Underwood and Gifford even if you were an orthodox spinner – was very difficult.' In addition to Illingworth and his off spin, England opted for Derek Underwood and Yorkshire left-arm spinner Don Wilson. In contrast to Robin's 102 wickets that summer, Wilson had taken 59 at 26.13 and it would appear that Illingworth preferred to go with what he saw as a safer bet in Wilson – his county colleague – rather than a 'luxury bowler' in Robin. As it turned out Don Wilson didn't feature against Australia, his only Test appearance coming against New Zealand once the tour had moved on following the conclusion of the Ashes series.Like Knott, John Woodcock feels that the extra bounce in Australia would have suited Robin but that he wouldn't have enjoyed the tour under Illingworth. England won the series 2-0 but according to the former *Times* cricket correspondent the cricket was very attritional. 'It was done in a very dour way. Ray Illingworth was a very astute captain but Robin just wasn't his sort of bowler. Illingworth hated giving runs away and he also had Underwood who gave nothing away. I don't think

154

Africa in 1964/65.' Robin largely agrees on this point with Woodcock

He's probably right. There no way Illingworth would have had me out on the tour anyway, I never forgave him because he picked one of his own in Don Wilson but looking back it was fair enough. I shouldn't have gone to South Africa in 64/65 so it's swings and roundabouts. Don Wilson went and probably should have gone on the tour I went on, it evened itself out in the end.

Following an injury to Derbyshire fast bowler Alan Ward early in the tour there was speculation that Robin would be flown out as a replacement. He had a job for the winter working in London for Lloyd's Insurance and each day would scour the newspapers for the latest updates from the sports writers reporting from Australia. Jim Swanton in *The Daily Telegraph* was critical of England's tactics early in the tour and the 'ludicrous obsession with speed.' In his opinion the balance of the side was wrong and rather than fly out a like-for-like replacement, what England needed was another spin bowler; 'the obvious candidate is Robin Hobbs.'

With England struggling to bowl sides out in the tour matches and with the first two Tests drawn there was concern that the Ashes series was heading for a stalemate. To journalists like Swanton and Crawford White, the occasional use of part-time leg-break bowlers Keith Fletcher and John Hampshire in some of the tour matches, was as good as an admission that a stock leg-break bowler should have been included in the squad right from the start.

The most vociferous criticism came from Tony Lock, the former England left-arm spinner, who was captaining Western Australia. Lock's arrival in the Caribbean in 1968 as a replacement for Fred Titmus had arguably denied Robin the chance of further involvement in that series, but in an article for *The Daily Mirror* he was fully backing his fellow spinner. 'I find the whole thing laughable. Robin Hobbs, the only class over-the-wrist spinner in English cricket, has just returned 100-odd wickets to complete his best-ever season – and MCC don't pick him to tour. You make sense of that – I can't.'

Things rumbled on in the newspapers for a number of weeks. After the second Test was drawn in mid-December, Chris Lander's headline in *The Daily Mirror* read 'MCC need a "legger" – Hobbs.' In the article Lander noted that Alec Bedser – chairman of the Test selectors – had himself admitted that the England bowling attack in Australia lacked balance. The article also gave an insight into Robin's thoughts at the time with Lander attributing a number of quotes to him.

'Hobbs, the 28-year-old Essex leg-break bowler eased out of a tour place by Yorkshire left armer Don Wilson, said: "I felt bad at the time. Now I just want to see them bring back the Ashes." Hobbs has been on three MCC tours and last season took 102 wickets at 21 runs apiece. "I honestly believe I bowled better than ever," he said. "I don't expect to bowl as well again. I've never taken wickets so cheaply. The boys around the county circuit must be having a laugh watching Colin Cowdrey and Keith Fletcher rolling their leg breaks in Test matches. Surely a leg spinner is needed out there. Every Sheffield Shield side has one 'legger' and some have two.'"

The calls for him to be sent out began to recede as it became clear that England would be sticking with their original selections plus Bob Willis who had already been flown out to replace Ward. In his opinion it was only ever paper talk but the disappointing conclusion of the drawn-out replacement saga spelled the end of Robin's long-held ambition to tour Australia.

> *I think it would have fulfilled my dreams whether I played in a Test match or not. I'd have been a member of the tour party. I think everybody deep down would like to play against Australia; they play the game harder than any other country, no doubt about that. It would have been difficult bowling against them out in Australia – they play leg spin pretty well but I think it's everybody's ambition. If you want to play a Test match, the one you want to play is the one against Australia.*

England went on to win the series 2-0 on the back of John Snow's pace bowling, the end largely justifying the means. The whole situation – from the naming of the Ashes touring party to the speculation about being sent out as a replacement – had left a bitter taste in Robin's mouth and the resentment he felt towards Illingworth would come to the surface again just a few months later.

Having missed out on the Ashes, Robin did get to head overseas, touring Pakistan during February and March 1971 with a Commonwealth XI under the captaincy of Surrey's Micky Stewart. He was returning once more to a country which England had as good as been forced to flee from just two years earlier. Tensions were still running high and the cricket was played against a backdrop of civil unrest as the nationalists in the East of the country demanded secession from the government in the West. The situation was unstable to say the least and would come to a head with the proclamation of Bangladeshi independence at the end of March. In spite of all this and with the experience of 1969 still fresh in the mind, Robin, who'd developed a fondness for the country, wasn't put off.

I loved touring there. The wickets suited me, they spun a bit, they didn't bounce much but they turned a little bit if you gave it a rip. It was a fabulous country to visit – the stunning city of Lahore, Rawalpindi, the Khyber Pass and Peshwar were beautiful places – I really enjoyed my trips there.

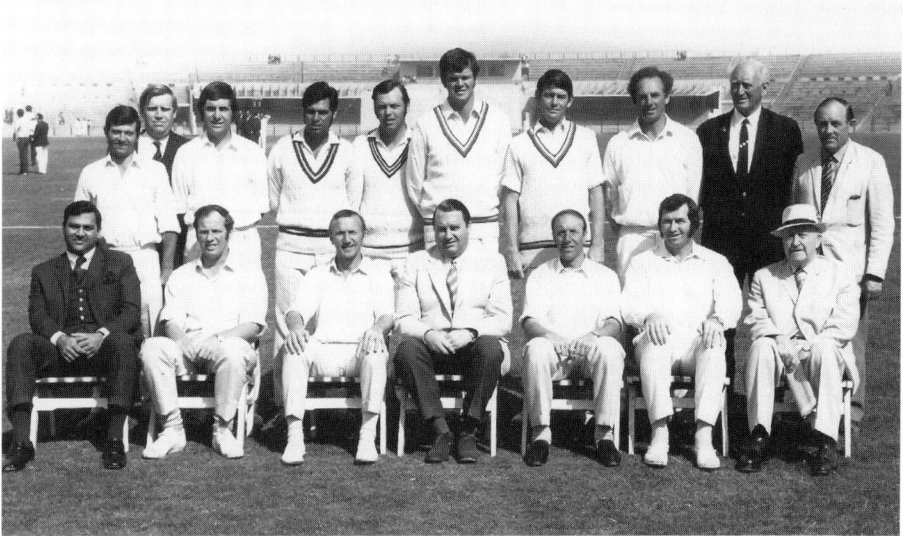

The Commonwealth tour of Pakistan, February/March 1971
The players. Standing: Harry Pilling, Doug Slade, Younis Ahmed, Roy Virgin, Bob Cottam, Robin Hobbs, Don Shepherd, Sitting: Norman Gifford, Micky Stewart, Joe Lister (Manager), John Murray, Neil Hawke.

The first match in Karachi in West Pakistan passed off without incident as the Commonwealth XI lost to a Board of Control for Cricket in Pakistan (BCCP) XI by eight wickets. It wasn't until the team were in East Pakistan that the trouble started, and, as in 1969, the players were in the middle of a game at the Dacca stadium when it erupted. On the fourth day of the match the BCCP XI were struggling, eight wickets down in their second innings and only 128 runs ahead. The Commonwealth side were well placed to win the match and square the series; that was until fires were started on the terraces and rioting students invaded the pitch. Invoking the wartime spirit of 'Keep Calm and Carry On', Micky Stewart enquired of the rioters "Can't you just wait till we get these two wickets and knock off the runs?" Stewart was told that this wouldn't be possible so the team headed for their dressing-room from where they could hear gunshots ringing out. After a couple of hours they were whisked by military vehicle to an army camp, as they drove away they could see several dead bodies lying on the road. From the army camp they were later escorted back to their hotel where they had the good fortune of running into an airline pilot who'd just flown into Dacca, and who offered to fly the team out of the country. It was a surreal experience for Robin and his team-mates.

> We stayed in a hotel with bullet holes all through it and this plane just appeared from nowhere, it landed and the captain appeared at our hotel. Joe Lister, the tour manager, and Micky Stewart said we've got to get out of here and he said "What? I'm taking that plane off in about an hour, we're going back to Karachi."
>
> We got into an armoured vehicle with our cricket bags and headed for the airport but when we got there we couldn't get in so they cut a great big hole out of the wire fence and drove in. We got onto the plane and there were people already sitting in the aisles so we stood. There were people smoking pipes of peace at the back of this plane, there's f***ing fumes coming out of everywhere and the plane took off with no lights, there were no airport lights, it took off in the dark.
>
> The plane wasn't allowed to cross Indian airspace, they had to fly all around India, 9 ½ bloody hours and we stood all the way, the whole team with the cricket bags in the plane. That was an unbelievable tour; there were bullets flying around as we were taking off from the ground in Dacca. It was part of the excitement, you never really knew what you were going to get in Pakistan.

There was some humour to help lighten the mood during the tour. The night before the last of the three matches against the BCCP XI in Lahore, Micky Stewart had his drink spiked by some of his team-mates and was feeling the after-effects the following morning. His subsequent innings was short and not particularly sweet as he was caught behind for 12 off the bowling of a young Imran Khan. As he returned to the pavilion, Stewart was greeted by Robin who cheekily remarked, "I have to say, captain, that's the worst first-class innings I've ever seen." Stewart accepted Robin's ribbing in good nature, "He was a terrific guy as captain," recalls Robin, "we were all senior players and he took it in good heart, we still talk about it whenever we see each other."

Journalist Nigel Fuller worked for the *Southend Evening Echo* for over 20 years, covering his first Essex matches during the 1970 season. The newspaper wouldn't pay hotel expenses so Robin would take it in turns with the other Essex players to let him sleep in his hotel room on away trips. Tonker's face was a picture as the journalist joined the team for his free breakfast in the morning. Being so close to the team allowed Nigel to appreciate the camaraderie of the Essex team and to experience what they got up to off the field.

He recalls an occasion in July 1971 when Essex were playing Worcestershire away in a three-day Championship match with a John Player League game sandwiched in between on the Sunday. Tonker imposed a curfew and ordered that all the players had to be in the hotel by 10pm on Saturday night without exception. Deciding that he needed a senior pro to assist, Tonker instructed Robin to sit with him in the hotel foyer and count all the players in. Robin insisted that Nigel should keep him and Tonker company as the trio diligently checked all the players in. As the last one arrived back Tonker checked his watch, "My lads," he proudly remarked to Robin and Nigel, "they're disciplined, they know how to behave themselves. Job done, we can turn in now." "OK, night Tonker" said Robin, stretching his arms and letting out a yawn, "see you in the morning." As the captain headed contentedly upstairs to bed, Robin turned to Nigel: "Right, come on, we're off" and sneaking off to the rear of the hotel they, along with the rest of the Essex players, disappeared out of the back door and headed off to an all-night party they'd been in invited to in Worcester. "We were there until about four o'clock in the morning" says Fuller "and Essex got hammered on the Sunday by eight wickets but I don't think poor old Tonker ever found out."

A quick snooze, Essex v Surrey at The Oval, May 1971. Standing: Brian Ward, John Lever, Bruce Francis, Stuart Turner, David Acfield, Graham Saville. Sitting: Ray East, Keith Boyce, Brian Taylor, Keith Fletcher, Robin Hobbs.

Robin had a decent season in 1971 and topped the Essex averages with

61 Championship wickets at 20.47. Included in that number was the wicket of Geoffrey Boycott – but not before the Yorkshire opener had scored a double-hundred against Essex at the Garrison Ground in Colchester. The season before, at the same venue, Boycott had scored 260 not out. Robin remembers the dismissal well.

I got him out seven times in my career, two of which the umpires were fed up with him and gave him out. Sam Cook, who used to be a left-arm spinner for Gloucestershire, was one of the umpires in that game and I always bowled at Sam's end because you knew he'd look after you with a few lbw's. Boycott had scored 233 and I hit him on the pads; he ran down the wicket to take a leg bye so I shouted "Howzat?" and Sam put his finger up quick as you like and said "That's out." Boycott came down protesting; "Sam, you can't do that, it was never out." As he passed Sam said "We've seen enough of you Geoffrey." That's what they did though in those days, they caught up with some of these guys. Some of the umpiring decisions were dreadful.

Boycott didn't forget the dismissal either as Robin recalls an encounter between the pair many years later.

There used to be a very good independent bookshop in Chelmsford and Geoffrey was there signing his autobiography so I went along to get copies for a couple of guys I knew who wanted them. I went up to the first floor and there he was sat at a table about thirty yards from me and I called out "Geoffrey!" He stood up in front of this queue of people waiting with their books to be signed and said "Eh! There he is, that bloke over there, he cheated me out lbw in 1971 he did."

The deftest of late cuts eludes
Peter Parfitt, Lord's, August 1971.

Despite thinking that he wasn't bowling particularly well that season Robin still found that his name was back in the England frame and the possibility of a first Test match appearance for two years; closer to three-and-a-half if one discounts the abandoned match in Karachi in 1969.

Pakistan and India were the touring sides and both had improved significantly since Robin had played against them in 1967. In the first Test at Edgbaston, the Pakistan batsmen dominated the English bowling in reaching 608-7 declared. Having been invited to follow on, England avoided defeat largely thanks to the batting of Alan Knott, Brian Luckhurst and Basil D'Oliveira and poor weather on the final day.

Rain had spoilt the prospect of a result at Lord's in the second Test and so it was all to play for in the final Test of the three-match series at Headingley in July. Much to his surprise Robin found himself named in the 13-man squad but instead of being excited at the prospect of relaunching his Test career, he was anxious at the thought of being selected for the team.

I dreaded it. I don't know why for one minute I ever got picked. I went up to Headingley in the wrong frame of mind. I set off from home knowing I didn't want to go, hoping that I wasn't going to be picked to play. I drove up there the day before, we had a net and I said to John Price, the Middlesex quick bowler who was also in the 13 and a good friend of mine, "Christ, have you had a look at the Test pitch, I hope I don't play tomorrow" and he said "I think you'll find that you playing but you're going to need all the luck in the world on that pitch." "What?" I went in with a bad attitude, I didn't want to play. It was a dreadful bloody pitch, it was slow and low. I think I'd been sold down the river personally, still think to this day I'd been sold down the river.

Ray Illingworth was captain and officially informed Robin at the pre-match dinner, the evening before the first day of the Test, that he would be playing.

That's when I had a bloody great row with Illingworth.. I didn't like the man at all, he didn't like me. I had high respect for him as captain but I didn't like him. I said to him I shouldn't be playing.
"Well we've picked you haven't we, you're playing!"
"The wicket does nothing for me". It was a crazy decision.
He said "you're playing" and that was it.

When the squad had been announced days earlier, Clive Taylor of *The Sun* questioned whether Illingworth wanted Robin in for the game. According to

Taylor, the presence of Robin and the absence of John Snow from the squad was evidence that Illingworth was no longer the 'virtual overlord of the England side' that he had been on the Ashes tour and was now just another vote-carrying member of the selection committee. Taylor suggested that it was hard to reconcile Illingworth's known views with those two items of selectorial reasoning.

> 'Snow is an Illingworth man. He is out because he is still not succeeding in county matches, although that has not been much of a consideration in the past.
>
> Hobbs, whose way to Australia as a replacement was blocked, mainly by Illingworth, on two counts – he spun too little and was too vulnerable if he tossed the ball high – returns to Test cricket for the first time in three years.
>
> The fact that Hobbs has been picked to bowl on an English pitch, when he could not get the trip against an Australian side who considered the conditions encouraging enough to include at times both O'Keefe and Jenner, may have extra significance. It may mean that Illingworth has lost some of the power to sway selection meetings that he once had.'

Robin and Illingworth had very little in common but it would appear that they both agreed on one thing, neither were happy with the leg-spinner's inclusion in the team.

Writing in *The Times,* John Woodcock declared the pitch as being 'like plasticine' and was of the opinion that it would be a slow turner, well suited to a Pakistan side containing some top batsmen. Having won the toss, England chose to bat. Umpire David Constant, officiating in the first of his 36 matches at Test level, remembers the very first ball of the match from Asif Masood bouncing twice before it reached the 'keeper: "Crikey, the pitch wasn't the fastest", he says. England scored 316 in their first innings thanks largely to 112 from Boycott and 74 from D'Oliveira. Batting at number nine Robin was out for six, caught behind off Asif Iqbal by Wasim Bari, one of his eight catches in the match.

Robin went wicketless in Pakistan's first innings as they scored 350 to gain a 34-run advantage. According to John Woodcock, 'When Hobbs took Gifford's place at 100 for 2 he could not find line nor length. In ten overs he conceded 33 runs which would have been more but for some spectacular work at extra-cover by Lever.' Wicket-keeper Alan Knott had possibly the best view on the field as Robin struggled to make an impact. "The wicket was so ridiculously low in bounce," Knott recalls, "it was amazing, some deliveries practically ran along the ground; it was an impossible wicket for a leg spinner to bowl on." In desperation Robin switched to bowling round the wicket which surprised Knott, the tactic, according to him, was "not done really in those days" and he was unsure if it was Robin's decision or Illingworth's to try it. "It was totally my idea to bowl round the wicket at Leeds," says Robin, "I thought the only chance of getting a wicket was pitching in to the little rough on and around leg stump." In fairness Robin didn't bowl badly in the first innings and could have had a couple of wickets but finished with nought for 48 from 20 overs. He was effective as ever in the field and did well to reach a catch at mid-on to dismiss Intikhab Alam for 17 off D'Oliveira's bowling.

In their second innings England were bowled out for 264, the major contributions being 72 from D'Oliveira and 56 from Dennis Amiss – his first half-century for England. Robin was out for nought, bowled by the right-arm medium pacer Saleem Altaf and Pakistan were left with a target of 231 to win both the match and the series. The innings got off to a fairly steady start as Pakistan closed day four on 25-0 but England made the breakthrough they were looking for early on the final day with just five minutes play on the clock. Aftab Gul, advancing down the wicket in an attempt to hit Illingworth over the top, didn't connect cleanly and only succeeded in picking out Robin at mid-wicket who caught the ball smartly just below waist height. "I hated taking that catch", he says, such was the level of antipathy towards his captain. If this sounds like an over-reaction there is ample proof of its veracity on YouTube. Pakistan were four wickets down still needing around 130 runs to win when Illingworth decided to throw the ball to Robin.

> *"Right, have a bowl", said Illingworth.*
> *"What now?" I said.*
> *"Yeah," he replied: "Have a bowl."*
> *I turned round and saw Intikhab Alam, the captain of Pakistan, standing on the pavilion stairs and he was swinging his bat round which meant "F***ing hit him out of sight." – I thought, that's nice! And I bowled a load of junk, the biggest rubbish you've ever seen.*

Back in Test cricket and having gone wicketless in the first innings, Robin was under pressure. He felt he had to get a wicket or two straightaway otherwise he'd lose the Test for England or his place in the side, possibly both. In the words of John Woodcock in *The Times*, Robin 'had four disastrous overs at the end of the morning' and was removed from the attack having conceded 22 runs. Having only recently seen footage of the game Robin has had the opportunity to reflect on what did prove to be his final bowling spell in Test cricket.

> *You can see from the clip, my run-up and the pace I was bowling, I was rushing at the pitch, trying too hard and bowled badly under pressure, I couldn't take it. Instead of being composed, running up and bowling it where I wanted it, the ball*

went all over the place.

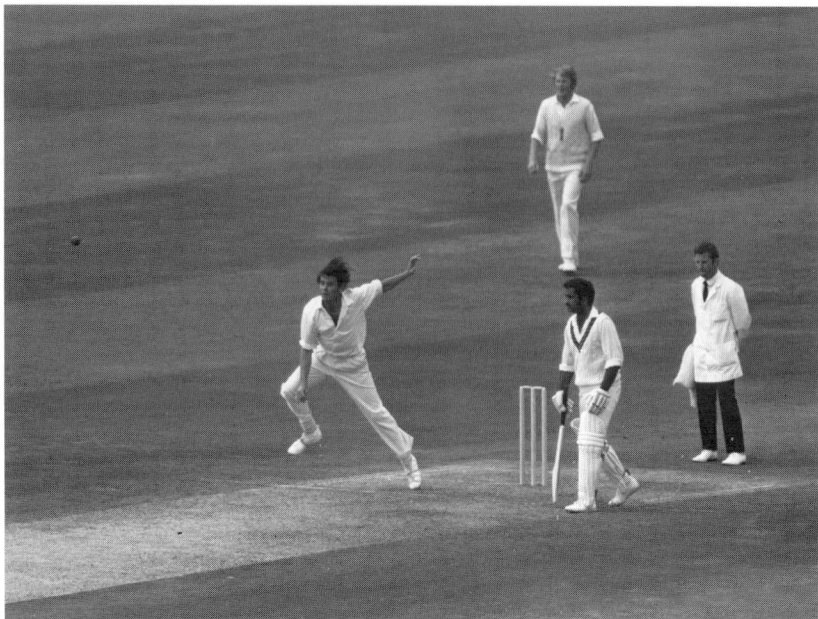

"I knew that was going to be my last Test", Headingley, July 1971. The umpire is David Constant, Peter Lever at mid-on and Mushtaq Mohammad the non-striker.

It was a close run thing but aided greatly by Peter Lever's three wickets in four balls, England held their nerve. Pakistan collapsed from a dominant position at 160-4 to 205 all out to hand the home side a win by 25 runs. Clutching a souvenir stump, Illingworth led his team off having won the series 1-0 but Robin wasn't planning on hanging around to celebrate and within minutes had left the ground.

I went up to the changing-room to get my bag and said goodbye to the lads. I didn't change, I went down in my whites jumped in my red mini and drove home to Ingatestone. I'd been decorating the house and I was so angry that I got a tin of red paint and I wrote 'F*** Illingworth' all round the walls in my lounge. Later on David Acfield helped me paint over it; it took ten coats to get rid of it.

It had been a poor spell of bowling but not necessarily one which should have signalled the end of his Test career although Robin had seemingly made his mind up.

I knew it was the end of the road. I went into the game in a bad frame of mind knowing I shouldn't have played on a pitch that didn't suit my bowling and a captain that didn't suit me. I'd bowled alright in the first innings but second innings I lost the plot, I bowled like a drain, just didn't pitch it properly. I knew that was going to be my last Test, I just got on with it and thought f*** it, I'm not going to play anymore.

Dennis Amiss remembers Robin's unhappy experience at Headingley and him saying that he wouldn't play Test match cricket again. 'He was a bit unlucky,' Amiss recalls, 'the wicket didn't suit him at all, it was more of a seamers' wicket.'

A few days after the game Robin received a letter from Colin Cowdrey who, like Amiss, felt the conditions had been far from ideal for the leg spinner. 'I cannot tell you how pleased I am that you are doing so well and are playing for England. I was sorry that the wicket was so hopeless for you to bowl on and I now hope that you will get some more opportunities.'

At the time Robin was seething, in his mind the wicket was dead, he'd been bowled at the wrong end, he'd been "sold down the river" by Illingworth, No longer an angry young man, Robin can look back at that spell with a sense of detachment.

I had to bowl in the second innings at some stage. I'm probably doing Illingworth a disservice, it wasn't his fault, he had to bring me on and I let him down through being temperamental, thinking to myself at the time why are you bringing me on when you've got them tied down or perhaps that he'd brought me on as a sacrificial lamb to have a few runs hit off me before reverting back to himself and Norman Gifford or whoever. That's what I thought at the time. Maybe he thought I had a chance of getting a wicket, perhaps I'm doing him down a bit.

One thing is certain though, Robin arrived at Headingley short on confidence and, in contrast to when he'd played under Brian Close in 1967, never enjoyed the full backing of Illingworth. Intikhab Alam, who captained Pakistan in the 1971 series, certainly had some sympathy for Robin in this respect.

'I always felt throughout my cricketing career that leg-spin bowling was fascinating art and you needed a very good captain who understood the psychology of a leg spinner and used the leg spinner at the right time and built confidence in him. Robin was a good leg spinner but I don't think he was used properly and intelligently, otherwise he would have done much better in the Test matches he played.'

Brian Close had been instrumental in making Robin feel at ease in making his

Test debut at Headingley in 1967, a stark contrast to what would prove to be his final Test, ironically at the same ground.

> *If it had been Closey it would have been a different ball game, he'd have come up to me and said "Hey Hobbsy, have a bowl", I'd have said – because I'd have had the confidence to do so – "Brian, it's the wrong time" and he would have said "OK, we'll leave it for a couple of overs.*

John Murray agrees with Robin. 'Closey and Illingworth were two very different people that's for sure. I can imagine Closey doing what Robin said but not Illy.'

Although they were both spinners, Robin and Illingworth had little else in common, Robin was very much a cavalier and played his cricket in a carefree way compared to roundhead Illingworth's puritanical, win-at-any-cost, take on the game. It was the wrong chemistry for Robin and did little for his confidence.

> *Ray Illingworth was a bloody good cricketer but as a captain he was selfish, most of the top sportsmen are. I've got nothing against him that way, I just didn't like him that much and the feeling was mutual.*

It was a sad way for Robin to end his Test career and on that day in July 1971, once he got into his red mini still in his cricket whites, he knew that was it and he never had another thought of playing for England again.

Chapter Twelve

I'm proud of being the last leg spinner to get 1000 first-class wickets in county cricket. It won't happen again, sad isn't it?

NINETEEN SEVENTY-TWO marked the beginning of the end of Brian Taylor's time as captain of Essex. He missed the match against Kent at Maidstone in early July and in his absence Keith Fletcher led the team for the first time. It was the first Championship game Taylor had missed since regaining his place in the Essex side in May 1961. In that time he'd made a record 301 consecutive appearances in County Championship matches. In his last full season with the club, Taylor continued to make his presence known to team-mates and opponents alike as Robin relives a Sunday League match in May 1972.

Tonker, taking no prisoners, runs out Peter Sainsbury at Harlow. Robin seems disbelieving.

We had a game against Northants, and Tonker was never short of a few words. We'd played them at Northampton the game before and David Steele was caught in the gully off his glove but given not out. The following Sunday we were playing down at Chelmsford in a Sunday league match and Brian Crump, a cousin of David Steele, hit the ball to Stuart Turner at mid-wicket off the bowling of John Lever. Stuart Turner caught it and Crump started to walk off and there was Acfield, myself and Lever standing in the covers saying "I don't think he caught that, do you?" He got 10 yards from the wicket and that put doubt in his mind 'Did he catch it?' and he started to go back to the crease. Everybody in the ground knew he'd been caught cleanly. Tonker turned round to see Crump heading back and bellowed "We had enough bloody trouble with your cousin last week; piss off."

Robin was always happy to play a game of cricket whatever the standard; on 5 June he ended up playing in three on the same day. Essex's Benson and Hedges fixture against Middlesex at Lord's on the Saturday was rain-interrupted meaning the match had to be concluded on the Monday. Essex were 80-6 chasing 233, it was a hopeless position and having already committed an Essex team to playing Barclays Bank at Chelmsford starting at 2pm Tonker decided there was no point all of the team going up to Lord's, just Graham Saville and Robin – the not out batsmen – along with Ray East, John Lever and David Acfield who had yet to bat. "I drove the Essex van," says Robin, "and we arrived at Lord's with the guys sitting in deck chairs in the back. We got to the gate and the attendant enquired "Who are you?" "Essex" I replied, "Essex! Is that how you travel?" Robin scored 40 in a partnership of 91 with Graham Saville but they never threatened Middlesex who won comfortably by 51 runs. As soon as it was over, Robin and the others zoomed back to Chelmsford for the game against Barclays where he picked up six wickets before playing an evening match at Writtle where he got a further five. Three games, 40 runs at Lord's and 11 wickets. It was a most enjoyable day, in stark contrast to the moderate season he was having with the ball in first-class cricket but as Essex were still operating with a small squad he was able to retain his place even if his form was slightly off.

Leading up to the match against Glamorgan at Swansea in mid-August, he had only managed to take a handful of Championship wickets. His luck didn't improve as Glamorgan chose to bat first.

I'd been in the side all year and I'd only got 14 wickets, that wouldn't happen nowadays, I'd be in the second team. One of the umpires in that game was Buddy Oldfield who had a real spate of blinking. In the first innings I got Roy Fredericks caught bat-pad but Buddy Oldfield was having a blink and gave him not out.

Fredericks went on to score 119 as Glamorgan declared on 338-9 and Robin was left with bowling figures of none for 56 from 12 overs in the first innings. At this point of the season, his 14 Championship wickets had cost 967 runs at an average of 69.07. He was a desperate man.

I had some mates at Glamorgan, I got on well with Peter Walker and Tony Lewis and the boys drinking-wise and going out in the evenings. I knew on the last day that they were going to go on a run chase to set a target so I went in their dressing room an hour before the start of play and sat with the Glamorgan boys and said "Look, I'm in a hell of a mess, I've got 14 wickets at nearly 70 a piece, I can't get a wicket" and they said "Don't worry Hobbsy, we'll go for you today." I got seven for 118 – they smacked it all over the place, but I still got seven for 118 so I went from 14 wickets at 69 to 21 wickets at about 52. A lot of them were given to me because they were in a run chase – caught on the boundary, caught at third-man, but I got wickets again, I'd gained my confidence. I don't care a monkeys if someone says "Shit, he got out to a rank long-hop", it doesn't matter. It's far better to get them with a genuine leg break, but if somebody holes out at mid-wicket it's still a wicket – getting wickets breeds confidence.

Essex went on to win the match by two wickets but, having finally got his season back on track to some extent, Robin would probably have preferred not to be faced with the prospect of bowling to Geoffrey Boycott in the following match. Despite having scored 260* and 233 on his previous two visits to Essex, Boycott was still aggrieved at being given out lbw by umpire Sam Cook who, along with the crowd at Colchester, had seen enough of him the previous year. Watching from the boundary just before play started, Nigel Fuller was puzzled to see Robin heading for long-leg rather than his customary position in the covers. "What are you doing down here?" he called out, "Tonker has got this plan," whispered Robin, "Boycie's going to bounce Boycott third ball, he's a sucker to the hook. I'm down here to catch it" he said, rolling his eyes, as he took up position.

Right on cue, Keith Boyce bounced Boycott third ball of the first over and in attempting the hook the Yorkshire opener gave Essex the early chance they so desperately craved but instead of top-edging the ball down to Robin as Tonker had envisaged, Boycott nicked it straight behind and the Essex captain dropped it. "Did he hit it?" Tonker enquired as the ball gently trickled to Keith Fletcher at first slip. Robin rolled his eyes again and turned to the Press Tent, "Well, that's got rid of the main weapon," he dryly remarked, "that's our first strategy out of the window." Essex did however succeed in preventing Boycott from scoring a double-century, out for just 121 runs on this occasion.

In the following match against Northamptonshire at Chelmsford Robin took eight wickets including five for 85 in the first innings. He'd managed to salvage his season to an extent and finished with 31 Championship wickets at an average of 40.58, his 10 in the match against Oxford University at the start of the season helped to give him a far more respectable average of 44 wickets at 34.86 in all first-class matches.

His final wicket that season came as he played for Tom Pearce's XI at Scarborough against the touring Australians. Robin was caught and bowled by his county colleague Bruce Francis for four in the first innings but was able to go one better having Francis stumped by Brian Taylor for just three in the Australian's first innings.

No longer in the reckoning for MCC tours, Robin was invited to visit South Africa in January 1973 with the Derrick Robins XI. These were great social trips, John Lever was in the party too, remembering them as 'absolutely world-class times', and could understand why his Essex team-mate wanted to get on as many tours as he could.

The first match ended in defeat against Eastern Province and it was here that Robin first came face to face with the 20-year-old batsman Ken McEwan. Robin dismissed him – caught by Roger Knight for 25 – and would meet up with him next time as a team-mate, when McEwan joined Essex in 1974. McEwan would go on to play for Essex until 1985, during which time he became a firm favourite.

> He wasn't a bludgeoner of the ball he was a graceful player, a lovely stroke-maker. You wouldn't see him trying to hit sixes, he was a classic player, very much in the mould of Tom Graveney. Ken was such a pleasant person, he was a very quiet South African who just enjoyed his cricket. He had a lovely laugh, was great company to be with and was a great team-mate. But for the apartheid ban he would have played for South Africa for 10 years, there's no question about that. Essex were very lucky to have him, he was everybody's favourite down there.

As well as getting his future team-mate McEwan out, Robin also had the pleasure of dismissing a former team-mate twice in the following tour match against Transvaal by having his good friend Lee Irvine caught by Clive Radley in both innings. "One of them was the most diabolical ball I've ever bowled," remembers Robin, "it nearly bounced twice and Lee hit it down straight down long-leg's throat. I got him out second time with a good ball but that first ball to get him out was a shocker, we still talk about it whenever we meet up."

Robin was delighted to see Irvine again but the same couldn't be said for his friend's captain, Ali Bacher. Robin had last encountered Bacher in 1965 when the South African hadn't 'walked' in the tour game at Colchester. The bad blood continued, when, at a cocktail party at the Wanderers club the night before the start of the match, Robin spotted Bacher on the other side of the room. He made a beeline for Bacher and without any pleasantries asked bluntly "Do you sleep well at night?" Almost eight years after the incident Robin was still smarting.

> *I was a fairly good drinker at those kind of functions; that probably gave me courage to go and approach Bacher. I had a row with him and called him a bloody great cheat. We've made up since and we get on alright. It's one of those things, forgive and forget, in the end life's too short but at the time I didn't like people cheating. I never cheated at cricket, if I hit it I walked and it was not in my nature to see somebody hit the cover off it and stay there. But as he admitted in his book he was so desperate for runs he was just going to stay at the crease.*

The match ended as a draw but Bacher would have the last laugh on this occasion, going on to score 147 in Transvaal's first innings.

Brian Taylor's appointment as a Test selector in 1973 limited his appearances in what would be his final season. With Taylor unavailable for half the matches the responsibility for leading the side fell to vice-captain Keith Fletcher but, having established himself as a Test player, he was unavailable for a number of matches as he was playing for England: three matches against New Zealand and three against West Indies. Robin ended up captaining Essex in seven County Championship matches that summer, more than twice as many as Fletcher, and it was an experience the leg spinner thoroughly enjoyed.

> *I took to it like a duck to water, we didn't lose many matches while I captained Essex; they were a bloody good side to play with. I enjoyed skippering the county, it was a highlight of my cricketing career, it gave me a real taste for it and that's probably what took me to Glamorgan a few years later.*

With Taylor and Fletcher both unavailable for so many games it was clear that Essex would need to strengthen the side, the batting in particular. Bruce Francis returned as the overseas player for a second and final season before retiring rather prematurely from the first-class game at the age of 25. Francis never touched alcohol or tea and, according to Robin, lived on coca cola and bread – eccentricities to perhaps only rival those of Jack Russell. "He was a lovely guy," says Robin, "his nickname was "the mule", he was a good player but he desperately hated fielding." During a match at Ilford Robin recalls that Francis was kicking his heels down at third-man. It was a steaming hot day and having spotted Nigel Fuller near the boundary, the Australian headed over to ask the journalist if he'd do him a favour and get him an ice-cream cornet. Fuller happily obliged but before Francis could tuck in the ball was hit down to him. "Poor Bruce," laughs Robin, "he didn't know what to do, he had this cornet in his hand and there he was running for the ball, he ended up missing the ball and the ice-cream went all over the place." Tonker was not impressed and Francis was moved to mid-on, away from the temptation of the ice-cream van and where the captain could keep an eye on him. The next morning, spotting Nigel before the start of play Tonker marched down to the Press Tent for a quiet word. "I want to see you." he bellowed, "What have I done" thought Fuller, "what have I written in the paper to upset him?" "What's the matter Tonk?" he innocently enquired, "Your job is to report on the cricket," barked Tonker, "not to buy f***ing ice-cream for the Aussie!"

In addition to Francis, Essex signed the trio of Brian Hardie, Neil Smith and Bob Cooke in 1973. The development of younger, more promising prospects like Graham Gooch and Keith Pont led to fewer opportunities for Cooke who was eventually released when his contract expired at the end of the 1975 season but Hardie and Smith were both astute signings, providing great service to Essex over the following years.

Gooch made his debut in 1973 playing in one Championship match before establishing himself in the side the following year. He did however make a number of Sunday League appearances in 1973 and remembers Brian Taylor regularly selecting Robin for the side but generally not for his bowling.

'He really rated Robin Hobbs. He would even play Robin in Sunday League games, in which he'd bat at nine or 10 and wouldn't get a bowl. "First on my list, first on my list," snapped Tonker. "Hobbs plays for his fielding." He was right there. Robin, a lovely man and good cricketer, was a brilliant fielder. In my first season at Leyton Robin made a brilliant stop at cover-point, diving to hold the ball like a goalie going for the bottom corner, and then doing a flamboyant gymnast's tumble-roll to celebrate the fact. Then he got up and just lobbed the ball to extra-cover to pass on to the bowler.'

Robin played in 93 Sunday League matches during his career with Essex, batting 64 times and ending with a respectable average, for a tail-ender, of 13.74 and a top score of 54 not out against Yorkshire at Colchester in 1970. He also took 31 catches and saved plenty of runs with his athletic fielding – vindication of Taylor's reason for playing him. Incredibly, in those 93 games, Robin only bowled 84.4 overs, taking 22 wickets at an average of 21.36. In those early days of limited-overs cricket a leg-spinner's lot was not a happy one. Despite this, Robin felt that he was fortunate to play in so many matches:

Most of the time I batted nine, 10 or 11 and hardly bowled a ball, you wouldn't have that now – you can't have a bloke as a fielder batting nine or 10 but we had a small playing staff then. I did open the batting on a couple of occasions and I certainly got some runs against Kent at Ilford in a John Player match. I did get to bowl against Hampshire at Harlow mainly because Hampshire were 180-1. Tonker turned to Fletcher and said "What are we going to do?" Fletcher replied "Well why don't you give Hobbsy a bleedin' bowl, he ain't bowled for a month and a half, you might as well give him a bowl." Of course it was the end of the innings and they all smacked it up in the air and I got six for 22, very chuffed I was.

"Why don't you give Hobbsy a bleedin' bowl?" After a rare Sunday League bowl and figures of 6-22. Harlow, June 1973.

Despite his pleasure, Robin considers that those were false figures, those six wickets were taken in one game and if those were taken out of his overall figures for Sunday League matches then his stats wouldn't look so good. He didn't really bowl much and Robin agrees with Gooch's observation that he was played mainly for his fielding, saving probably around 10 runs in the field and for scoring a quick 15 or 20 down the order. "Tonker used to have me in the side, that blue-eyed boy thing again wasn't it."

On reflection it appears odd to relate how few overs Robin bowled in one-day cricket when one considers the value of spinners in the modern-day limited-overs game. In John Lever's opinion the whole mental attitude towards spinners has changed.

'I was down at Chelmsford when they started to trial 20/20 games and all the press and everybody else we're saying we'll get eleven blacksmiths to go out there and smash the ball to all parts and we thought that's what would happen. We thought seamers would bowl the ball quite well and spinners would get smashed out of the park; there'd be no place for them. And it wasn't until the game got underway that people started to think a little bit more; spinners had a place, you could set a field for a spinner. The bowlers started to have a little bit more of a repertoire with back-of-the-hand slower balls and everything else that went with it but the spinners in the IPL were doing as well as the best left-arm-over bowlers which were also quite a revelation in one-day cricket.

I suppose we shouldn't have been surprised because to stop yourself being spanked as a spinner you've got to have a repertoire, you've got to have an inbuilt feeling that that batsman is going to come after you so you've got to get the ball right up there underneath him to stop it going out of the ground or, if he's going to come running at you you've got to have that feeling when he's going to come and of all those things I think the best spinners all had it, they just knew, they read the batsman. I can remember fielding at mid-off and Hobbsy walking back to his mark and he'd look at me and wink and the next ball has gone up a long way. He just had that feeling that this was the ball he was going to come down the wicket to and sometimes he did and sometimes they spanked him. He was always prepared to take that chance.'

The 1973 Championship season ended well with a nine-wicket victory over Nottinghamshire at Chelmsford in what would be Brian Taylor's final first-class appearance.

In November Robin went out to Pakistan to take part in two charity matches to raise funds for those affected by the terrible floods which had hit the country. Unfortunately his flight was delayed by 24 hours and both he, and his travel companion, Trinidadian left-arm spinner Inshan Ali, missed the first day's play as a Pakistan XI took on a Rest of the World XI in the first match at Karachi. The Rest of the World team was captained by Clive Lloyd and included Robin's Essex colleague Keith Boyce and Mike Brearley who had captained the successful MCC under-25 tour to Pakistan in 1967. Pakistan won both matches and £40,000 was raised for the flood-relief fund.

Following Brian Taylor's retirement, Essex officially appointed Keith Fletcher as his successor for the 1974 season with Robin as vice-captain. As far as Robin was concerned the club had made the right decision.

I think Keith Fletcher was the ideal choice, I think batsmen make better captains than bowlers. He proved over many years that he had a tactically acute brain. He was also lucky that he inherited a very good side which makes a lot of difference. I think it was the right decision for Essex and I was only too happy to be his vice-captain.

Essex 1974. Standing: Bob Cooke, David Acfield, Neil Smith, Stuart Turner, Keith Pont, Barry Lock, Graham Gooch, John Lever, Brian Hardie, Ken McEwan. Sitting: Ray East, Robin Hobbs, Keith Fletcher, Brian Edmeades, Keith Boyce.

Looking ahead to the season in the *Essex Journal*, Fletcher mentioned that if he was lucky enough to be selected for Test matches he was confident that in his absence Robin would ensure a degree of continuity. 'We almost invariably agree on policy and the tactics of any situation and I am looking forward to working with him immensely.' Fletcher continued, stating that Robin 'will have the extra duties of vice-captain but I'm sure it will make no difference to his performances.'

Fletcher was selected for the Test series that summer against India and Pakistan and was only able to play in seven out of 20 Championship matches for Essex. To make matters worse, when he was playing he had a poor time with the bat averaging only 18.76. Robin led Essex in 1974 in almost twice as many games as Fletcher, 13 in total. Vice-chairman, Doug Insole, summed up the situation in his review of the season stating that 'Robin Hobbs had the unenviable task of being an understudy who was on stage rather more than the principal boy.' It was not an ideal way for Fletcher to begin his reign at Essex according to Robin.

The only drawback was that Keith was away so much playing for England. I think if you take over the captaincy, as he did, you want to be there most of the time. Possibly there was a thought in my mind that the powers that be at Essex – knowing that he was going to be away for most of the summer for the next couple of years – could have said "OK Hobbsy, Fletcher is our preference for captain in a couple of years' time but will you take the helm now?" Which would have been fine with me, but no, it worked out OK, no animosity.

Doug Insole was also of the opinion that Essex did not look like a balanced side that season. They were a team in transition and weren't helped by injuries to Boyce, which restricted his appearances, and Lever, who struggled on through the season but lacked his usual form. It was a mediocre season for the team which finished in 12th place although they only lost three matches with 12 draws and one tied match.

Despite this, Robin had many qualities as captain according to John Lever.

'As a youngster I didn't feel as though I was bowling at the wrong time, I think he, as captain, put people on to bowl at the right time and took them off at the right time. He wanted to play entertaining cricket, he certainly wanted a changing-room that was enjoyed by all, you can only play your best cricket if you're enjoying the game. I think he captained the side better than Tonker, certainly not as good as Fletch, but Fletch was somebody who remembered the intricacies of how people played. As soon as a batsman walked to the wicket he'd say "Well you're going to need more on that side, you're going to need more on the leg side, we'll get him out here and that's how you should bowl to him." I don't think Hobbsy was quite in that vein but he certainly knew the batters that he could tempt to get out. That sort of ingrained knowledge as a leg spinner that if he tossed it up the person would have a go at him. He had plenty of spinners in his side to use but we were sort of middle of the table at that time, we were a young side that was growing into a side that ended up doing quite well but without Hobbsy's nurture, without Tonker's nurture – and then with Fletcher's drive

– we wouldn't have ended up the side that did so well.'

It was unfortunate that all of this coincided with Robin's benefit year. In 1974 his salary was about £1000 a year and in those days having a benefit was like a pension, a cricketer like Robin could expect to make around £10,000 or more tax free, which was a lot of money, but the added pressure of captaining the side and running a benefit affected his form as he readily admits.

It was a bit of a strain in my benefit year, I worked extremely hard as you did in those days. I had a small committee, I was out every single night during the summer and winter which didn't help my cricket, coming home at 11 o'clock having been to a function. I don't think I had a night in but it was the one time when you could actually make some proper tax-free money and I was going to make the most of it.

Benefit matches were played in July against West Ham United at Ford's ground in Dagenham and then a fortnight later against a combined team of West Ham United and Tottenham Hotspur at Theydon Bois. World Cup winners Bobby Moore and Geoff Hurst were keen cricketers and always turned up to play in matches if they could, along with fellow footballers Alan Sealey, Brian Dear and Ronnie Boyce. Robin was only too pleased that club sides like Broomfield and Tollesbury were able to host some of the other benefit matches in September. They were long days with lots of guests to entertain and items to be autographed and if, at the end of it, Robin had raised another £100 for his benefit fund then it was a decent result. It was all go and as well as the day job and benefit matches Robin also had work to do in the evenings and was rarely at home.

I had these pontoon boxes which I used to place behind the bars of pubs. The publican got a certain percentage and I got a certain percentage once the box was sold, I think the tickets in there were something in the region of £30 worth. I put these boxes round in most of the pubs I knew or even didn't know, I'd just walk in and say "I'm Robin Hobbs, Essex cricketer, I've got a benefit would you put a box of these behind the bar?" I spent so much time going round to these pubs, seeing how they were doing and chatting to the landlord, having a beer or a shandy and going on and doing six or seven pubs in a night and getting home at 11 o'clock and going straight to bed and then getting up. It was stressful in a nice way, there were several functions that I did very well at but the pontoon boxes were a way of life which kept me going. Even if I was in for an evening I'd still go out to a couple of pubs. There was a pub called the Red Lion at Boreham, they sold over £400 worth of pontoon tickets which was a lot of boxes but there were other pubs which never sold more than £10 worth and so I just took the boxes out.

Being for the benefit of Mr Hobbs. Marconi v Essex
at the Marconi Sports Ground in Chelmsford,
September 1974.

In August, Essex, under Robin's captaincy, enjoyed a win by an innings and 19 runs against Yorkshire at Leyton but there was little time to celebrate; the team were headed for Wellingborough where they'd be playing Northamptonshire in a three-day match starting the next day. On arrival the Essex players were split into two groups, half of them were staying in a hotel while the others were accommodated in an annex nearby. The next morning all hell let loose; channelling Basil Fawlty, the proprietor of the hotel asked to see acting captain Robin. "He was absolutely livid with me and the team. I told him I had no idea what he was talking about" "Oh really!" replied the hotelier, "Well, when I went up to the annexe this morning and knocked on Mr Pont's door with tea for one he called out "Tea for two, what about my friend?" The 'friend' was a full suit of armour which the Essex players had removed from the wall of the annex and put in the spare bed in Keith Pont's room. "This guy was absolutely fuming and I was reported to the club for not having control over the players" says Robin, sporting a twinkle in his eye as he recounts the story.

Following the end of the first-class season, Robin had a string of benefit matches to play in which ran until the first week in October. Unfortunately two 40-over matches against Worcestershire and Leicestershire had to be cancelled due to rain which made quite a difference to what Robin ended up with financially. Other events included a stag evening at Lord's – where Robin was supported by speakers including EW Swanton and Jim Laker – plus race nights and a ladies night. It was a hectic year but at the end of it Robin's efforts had managed to raise £14,000, a pretty hefty amount in 1974, which allowed him and Isabel to buy their first house for £6100.

The benefit, although a success, had proved to be a distraction for Robin affecting his form and the games in which he captained the county.

I was taking the field with my mind not 100 per cent focussed on the game. You're thinking 'Oh well where have I got to go tonight....Oh crumbs it's a bowling change, I've got to make a bowling change and I'm thinking of other things, where I've got to go tonight, what function I've got to attend' so it did affect my cricket, my mind wasn't totally on the game.

Despite the mediocre season there were some positives for Essex and bright signs for the future. Brian Hardie became a regular opening batsman and Ken McEwan proved to be a shrewd signing as an overseas player. It was also the year in which Graham Gooch began to establish himself and gave glimpses of what Essex could look forward to over the next 20 years.

He was a very quiet lad and in those days he kept himself very much to himself but you could see in the way that he played that he had vast potential. It wasn't long after that that he got into the England side. Talk about rapid progress, mine was fairly rapid from 1961 to 1967, his was even quicker, within two years he was playing for England. He was something special as a player. Nowadays the England players have to rest because the ECB says so but not Goochie, all he wanted to do, and quite rightly so, was bat. He wouldn't miss a game for anything, he'd want to be out every game playing, and he's right, when you're in form you want to make the most of it.

During the winter of 1974/75, Keith Fletcher was part of the England side which had been bruised and battered by the Australians and had lost the Ashes series 4-1. He came back shell-shocked by the experience but determined to put all his efforts into winning something with Essex.

Fletcher had felt that his absences while on Test duty hampered Essex throughout 1974. It wasn't so much his playing ability that was missed but the presence and authority of a resident captain. He felt that the team had drifted and his frustration was that he knew it was happening but that he was helpless to do anything about it. Fletcher felt that Essex had never developed a winning habit and he was determined to change that. The thought of captaining Essex to their first honour now motivated him more than the prospect of playing for England. He was only selected for two Tests in the summer of 1975 and was available to captain most of Essex's first-class matches. It was now that he could begin to mould the side to his design.

Essex did improve their standing in the Championship in 1975, finishing in seventh spot. They actually lost more matches but were able to win three more than they had in 1974. Having lost the season's opener against Hampshire at Bournemouth and drawn the next against Leicestershire, Essex travelled to Worcestershire to play the reigning county champions. Robin went into the match with 994 first-class wickets to his name and the possibility of reaching 1000 in the match was a tantalising prospect. On winning the toss, Keith Fletcher chose to bat but wickets fell easily and cheaply and by the time last man, John Lever, joined Robin out in the middle the score stood at 159-9. A fine stand of 63 brought some degree of respectability to the score before Robin was the last man to fall for 41. Essex managed to restrict Worcestershire to a lead of just 14 on first innings thanks to Lever and East, backed up by Robin who bowled 21 overs for just 29 runs, taking two wickets.

Essex started their second innings badly and were never able to settle. Wickets fell regularly and they were soon dismissed for just 164 off 54.4 overs with Brian Brain finishing with career-best figures of eight for 55 including Robin for a duck. It seemed a formality for Worcestershire to knock off the runs required for victory and at close of play on day two they were 14-1 only needing to score a further 137 runs with a full day's play left.

On 27 May, the Essex players took to the field followed by the overnight not out batsman, Joe Ormrod and night-watchman Howard Wilcock. The pair hit 40 off the first five overs and any slim hope Essex had of pulling off a win appeared to have disappeared. Despite the narrow margin of runs, Fletcher set attacking fields – slips, short-leg – all in close and ready to pounce as the ball invited the edge of the bat. Basil D'Oliveira, a batsman who always relished a challenge, fell cheaply edging a ball from East which Fletcher couldn't hold but Stuart Turner, at second slip, took, diving, about an inch off the ground. Fletcher employed spin from both ends most of the time but brought on Lever, Turner and Edmeades for occasional spells. Alan Gibson, writing in *The Times*, felt that spin would win or lose the match for Essex and he appeared almost a touch irritated by the interruptions of the seamers. For Gibson it was a sign of Fletcher's natural preference to turn to seamers: 'He is one of many captains who always look a little guilty unless the seam bowlers are on.'

On a dusty pitch, and with the ball turning, Robin was at his best. He bowled Wilcock for 33, had Tom Yardley caught in the slips by Fletcher, and Ivan Johnson, also edging a leg break, was caught behind the stumps by Neil Smith. Worcestershire, eight wickets down, needed another 50 runs to win. Essex needed two wickets, and Robin – in his 15th year as first-class cricketer – needed just one more to achieve the feat of 1000 wickets in first-class cricket. New batsmen, Norman Gifford and John Inchmore, edged the score along to 110 but shortly after lunch Robin, in his distinctive bowling style – stooping as he started his run to the crease, then flinging his arms and legs wide as he delivered the ball – bowled Inchmore and in doing so reached the milestone.

John Lever cleaned up last man Brain to seal the win. From 53-1 Worcester had collapsed to 121 all out to give Essex their first County Championship win of the season by 29 runs. Robin had been at his best, taking four for 21 from 15 overs, but it could have been even better according to Alan Gibson: 'I think Essex would have won more easily if Hobbs and East had been allowed to get on with the job uninterrupted from the start.'

Robin considers that Gibson had made a fair point about Fletcher's preference for seamers but that it seems to be the prevailing philosophy among captains.

Keith Fletcher was a believer in spin bowlers but it was very difficult, especially after I left the club, for people like David Acfield and Ray East. They could go two or three weeks before having a decent bowl and when they got on a turning wicket they were expected to bowl the side out. Nobody worries about the seamers. They can have a bad day on a green wicket and they'll come in at lunchtime and the captain will say "Well bowled lads, bad luck, you nearly got a few wickets." On a green wicket they should be getting wickets, spinners were expected to bowl sides out having not bowled for two weeks. To get a captain that understands spin bowling is so difficult because they are brought up on putting the seamers on: we'll stop the scoring by putting the seamers on, it doesn't work out that way. There are very few captains who understand spinners and Fletcher preferred seamers bowling, maybe because he was such a good player of spinners himself.

Taking his 1000th wicket that day was a highlight for Robin, the pinnacle of his career. It was something he'd dreamt about and, reflecting back on it more than 40 years later, to have achieved it as a leg spinner is even more special.

Looking back on it, it's not unique but it's something I treasure, I really do. It was a lot of hard grind. In those days it was quite commonplace for seamers to get a 1000 wickets in their career but there's no chance of a leg spinner nowadays doing it, they don't play enough games. I'm proud of being the last leg spinner to get a 1000 first-class wickets in county cricket. It won't happen again, sad isn't it?

Bowling well in a win for his beloved Essex against the reigning county champions had made the occasion that much sweeter. In his report for The Times the following day, Alan Gibson gave due respect to Robin's remarkable achievement and made a prescient point – 'That takes some doing by anybody nowadays. For a true leg-spin bowler to do it, with such limited opportunities, sometimes even dropped by his own county, nears the miraculous. No other leg spinner, I am afraid, will do it again.'

Stuart Turner was in the Essex side that day and gives due credit to Robin's achievement.

'To get a thousand wickets as a leg spinner was pretty special. He was a master of his craft and was immaculate in line and length. Purveying a very difficult art, control with leg spin is much more difficult than finger spin, you haven't got a great deal of margin of error but as I remember Hobbsy didn't bowl too many really rank bad balls. You see a lot of leg spinners these days, in between bowling absolute jaffas they bowl a lot of crap.

He could keep it tight as well. He wasn't the biggest leg spinner I've ever seen, not in the Warne category, but he had variation of flight and length and he had a googly. People used to take the mickey out of him a little bit, they reckoned they could spot his googly because it was so obvious but that was a bit unkind. Some leg-spinner's googlies are a bit obvious but I don't think Hobbsy's was.'

Robin himself was no great fan of the googly and tended to use it sparingly.

I probably started bowling googlies in about 1969/70 but generally to left handers, I wasn't a great bowler of the googly but I got a few wickets bowling to left-handers but it wasn't a ball that I could control that well and I think that when you bowl a googly, certainly with me, the little finger tends to stand up and the batsmen noticed that. Mine wasn't a well-concealed googly and I was never a great believer in it. I never overdid it, I found it difficult to bowl but when I did bowl it I tended to bowl it against left-handers and I got quite a few out stumped or caught at slip. There were great bowlers of it like Bruce Dooland but I think my decision was right, it was hard enough in those days trying to bowl economically without being smacked for a couple of long-hop fours.

If proof were needed that certain wrist spinners don't need to over-complicate their repertoire then it comes in the form of the greatest exponent ever to mark a run.

He was so different, he'd walk up to bowl the ball, he was so strong in the shoulder and in the fingers and he got such revs on the ball, he didn't need a run up. I needed a run up to get some momentum but he just kind of walked up and ripped it. He was an exception, I've seen a few other leg spinners bowl – Dooland, Peter Smith, Roly Jenkins and Salisbury, we all needed to have a run up to gain some momentum. In 2005 he got all his wickets with leg breaks and top spinners, at the top level he proved he didn't need the googly, he did without it but he's an exception, there'll never be a better leg spinner than Warne.

Despite the achievement of reaching 1000 wickets, being dropped from the Essex side was becoming more common and later in the season, the day after scoring his whirlwind 100 against the Australians, Robin wasn't selected for the Championship fixture against Northamptonshire at Chelmsford. With Fletcher moulding the side to his design it was unrealistic to expect to see all of Essex's three spinners in the side together. Ray East recalls the county being praised for their adventure in fielding all three at times but in those desperate days of the late sixties there was no choice, they had to play. Essex were now moving on and something had to give. Robin missed two further matches but was included in the side for the last match of the season against Yorkshire at Middleborough. Yorkshire won by 59 runs on the final day's play. David Acfield took seven wickets in the match, Robin went wicketless.

I could see the way the wind was blowing, I wasn't a fool. I knew what was going on, especially when I got left out of the side after the Australia game. I had a year left on my contract and the opportunity of captaining the second team but that really wasn't a step forward for me, I knew I had to get a proper full-time job. I didn't want to be an umpire, I wouldn't have fancied that: I didn't really have any ambition to stay in cricket coaching and I didn't want to captain the second team, I'd been there and done that.

Robin had spent a couple of winter's working for Barclays and there had been a certain amount of pressure being put on him, he couldn't expect to keep having six months off in the summer to play cricket and to keep his winter job. Barclays rated him as an employee and had made the offer of a permanent full-time job. It was time for him to weigh up his options: stay at Essex for another year or take the offer of the job, which – in the uncertain economic times of the mid-seventies – was not to be sniffed at.

Unorthodox batting. Cutting the uncuttable.

When the opportunity came up to have a full-time job it was something you grabbed with both hands. It didn't really secure my future because I only worked for them for 19 years but it was a permanent job. The time had come where I could see what was happening in the Essex set-up, that I was going to be carrying the drinks more than playing and having had a fairly successful career I wasn't prepared to do that, I wanted security. I weighed it up and thought I'm not going to play second-team cricket and eight games a year without a job in the winter. Barclays wouldn't have let me carry on being part-time, working in the winter only, so I thought 'bollocks to this, if they're going to offer me a permanent job it's time to go: I've sodded around now and enjoyed myself until 1975 I'd better take it'.

Robin's decision to jump before he was pushed came as a relief to Keith Fletcher, as he revealed in his autobiography.

'There had been a small inheritance of problems when I took over the side, the thorniest of which was that we had three capped spinners on the staff, none of whom could bat. That is not intended to be unkind, because both Robin Hobbs and Ray East had made valuable runs for the team even if David Acfield was a self-confessed rabbit; but not one of the three had any pretensions to be considered on their merits with the bat and there did not seem the slightest chance that we could keep them all happily employed. I envisaged this becoming a tricky situation, as they were all fine bowlers in their own right, but one of them clearly had to go. My own view was, and still is, that orthodox finger spinners, either right- or left-arm, will win more games in English conditions than a leg-spinner, and although 'Hobbsy' was the best of a dying breed in this country, it was something of a relief to me when he solved the problem by telling me he intended to retire at the end of the 1975 season.'

Robin could see how the situation was running, that he was the odd man out but he wasn't bitter about it. He had grown up and played in the same side as Fletcher since the early sixties. He readily agrees with Fletcher's opinion that the two best types of spin bowlers to have in county cricket are an off spinner and a left-arm spinner. If there's a leg spinner in the squad he's likely to be third choice.

I just thought that's the way it is. I didn't have any problems with it mainly because the two best and economical bowlers out of the three of us were East and Acfield without a doubt. I'd get you wickets but they would get you wickets at far less a cost than I would. Ray should have played for England and in any other era without Gifford, Underwood and Edmonds around he would have done. There weren't many better off spinners in the country than David, he was a terrible batsman and fielder but a bloody good bowler. It was a much better combination having those two in the team than me, they were the best pairing as far as Essex were concerned. I needed a proper job so I made the right decision there and then and packed up.

In spite of the preference for finger spin over the wrist version, the Essex records of the three bowlers don't confirm its superiority. Acfield's 855 wickets for Essex came at an average of 27.49 and 69 balls were needed for each one. East averaged 25.54 for his 1010 wickets at 64 balls per wicket. Robin's 763 came in off averages of 57 balls and 26.00.

Robin had been a big character at the club, in the changing-room and on the field and his presence would be missed by his team-mates. John Lever, initially wary of Robin in his early years at Essex, still fondly recalls some of the wildly exaggerated stories of cricketing feats which the senior pro' used to come out with. 'You'd have to go and check somewhere to see if it was true,' Lever laughs, 'he'd come out with these statements with a straight face and we're going

"Is he telling us the truth here, what's going on?"' Robin would observe with relish as those gullible enough to be taken in discovered the truth.

In spite of the fun still being had at times, Lever could understand why Robin had made the decision to leave.

'Before 1973/74 he was almost guaranteed a place in the side, and then when Fletcher took over the captaincy he looked for a balanced side and I think Hobbsy realised that he was going to be playing a bit part because of the number of spinners. He'd be in most one-day games because of his fielding – that would get him into a lot of games – but I think he got disillusioned by it. He couldn't see his name being first on the team sheet all the time and for Hobbsy playing was all important, it really was and I can understand that. I think I would give up the game if I was in that situation because it's playing that's all important and playing decent games of cricket, not just playing for the sake of getting wickets or getting runs, playing in games of cricket that mean something.'

Essex, led by Fletcher, would go on to win the County Championship for the first time in their history in 1979 and the side was still very much composed of the guys Robin had played with. 'It's sad that he was not around when we finally broke the back of winning something,' says Stuart Turner, 'it was just a shame that he wasn't involved then.' If East hadn't come along when he did or if Acfield hadn't matured so quickly into the fine bowler he was then Robin would likely have carried on for a few more seasons but time doesn't stand still for any cricketer. He'd seen a number of spinners go in his time at Essex – Peter Lindsey, Bill Greensmith, Terry Kent, Alan Hurd and Paddy Phelan – and he'd had a good run in the team for 14 years but now it was his turn to go too, time to pack up and prepare for a life outside of professional cricket.

Chapter Thirteen

They were magic days.

ROBIN WAS WORKING full-time for Barclays and after retiring from the first-class game he'd decided to stay away from going to watch Essex.

> *I made it a strict condition that when I packed up in 1975 I wouldn't actually go to Chelmsford for two years. It's difficult, people don't want to see you straight after you've retired. I used to drive across the bridge at Chelmsford and see them playing down there and think I wouldn't mind being there, I was working for the bank and it was a bit boring but I never felt envious or jealous because I wouldn't have been part of it anyway. By the time they started winning I would have been told to go and get my cards anyway.*

He was, however, too much of a cricket nut not to be playing the game at some level. There was still club cricket on Saturdays with Chingford and not long after announcing that he was leaving Essex he was approached by Suffolk with an offer to become their professional for the 1976 season. For years most minor counties had acquired an ex-professional cricketer for their side; a trend Suffolk had tried to resist, preferring to stick with home-bred Suffolk players. Things had reached the stage though where the county were struggling to compete in the two-day Minor Counties Championship without a senior professional of their own. Getting the right one was tough and for Suffolk captain, Bob Cunnell, the challenge was to get a special player; not just an ordinary professional, but somebody who could do something unusual, somebody with the capacity to pull out a performance and win a game for them.

Suffolk were fortunate that their desire to obtain such a player coincided with Robin retiring from Essex. Cunnell had known Robin from playing against him previously and wasted no time in approaching Tony Garnett, the Suffolk Secretary, stating that Robin was exactly the sort of player the county needed; if they were going to get anybody as a professional it should be him. 'We realised he'd be a very popular choice,' Cunnell recalls:

> 'We had to move quickly and within a couple of days we'd seen him, we'd had meals, even been greyhound racing with him and basically we'd done everything we could to persuade him that he'd have a good time with us. Other counties were

trying to get hold of him as well, but really the turning point was when we were having a meal at a hotel near Ingatestone and Robin turned to me and asked "How do you play your cricket?" I replied quite simply "Win or lose" and he said "None of these dull old draws?" I said "No, not likely, that's not me", to which he said "I'm in" and that was it.'

The arrival of Robin at Suffolk was, according to Garnett, 'a terrific boost'. The county played an attractive brand of cricket under Cunnell's captaincy and Robin was a perfect fit.

I enjoyed playing minor counties cricket, it was great stuff, we had good captains in those days and always got a result. If one side was doing well and it was their turn to win the Championship the opposition would make sure you got a good declaration. The cricket was bloody hard but if one side was going to win the Championship and the other was bottom of the table they didn't really bother.

Robin's first season went well, he became the workhorse of the Suffolk attack, bowling almost 300 overs in eight matches and taking 46 wickets at a very healthy average of 17.28.

Suffolk CCC. Standing: David Knights, Steve Long, Robin Hobbs,
Richard Robinson, Colin Rutterford, Simon Clements, Tony Warrington.
Sitting: Peter Jones, Stuart Westley, Bob Cunnell (captain), Roger Howlett.

He was really enjoying his cricket and, unsurprisingly, having only recently left the first-class game, was a key player in the team, regularly chipping in with important wickets and at times taking them in droves. At the Lakenham ground in Norwich in August 1976, he took 10 wickets in the match – 5 for 19 in the first innings, and 5 for 112 in the second – as Suffolk beat Norfolk by seven wickets. During Robin's time with Suffolk they regularly had the upper-hand over their local rivals and he was never on the losing side.

Former Norfolk bowler Ted Wright believes that Robin was well suited to the format of the minor counties game.

'We only played for two days at that time with 55 over first innings, he bowled very tightly during this time with economy being important. In the second innings his main object was to take wickets to win the match – run saving was not so important.'

Left-handed batsman John Barrett played 40 matches for Norfolk, six of them against Suffolk between 1976 and 1978. Norfolk lost five of these matches to their local rivals, the fact they didn't lose all six was due to the game at Mildenhall in August 1977 being abandoned after only 86 minutes because of rain. Barrett recalls a game at Felixstowe in August 1976, when Norfolk, batting first on a green pitch, were reduced to 80 for 6. Suffolk's opening bowler, Richard Robinson, had removed three of Norfolk's top four in a spell of sharp bowling that had left Barrett's thighs various shades of black and blue. Robin came on to bowl and, having seen off the hostile quicks, Barrett felt some relief at facing spin: 'Facing Robin Hobbs was almost a pleasure even though I had never met anybody with his spinning skills in club cricket.' Despite a first innings deficit of 34 runs Suffolk went on to win the match by seven wickets.

Robin had had a great first season with Suffolk. The county were delighted with his performances and his 46 wickets, particularly as the Ipswich builders Pennock, Haste and Howarth had pledged a £5 donation to Suffolk for every wicket he took, raising £230 in total.

Robin's second season would turn out to be a vintage year for Suffolk. Under the adventurous captaincy of Cunnell they proceeded to win the Championship for the first time since 1946 and Robin was an integral part of the side. A man-of-the-match performance in the first fixture against Hertfordshire helped Suffolk to a 103-run victory as Robin weighed in with seven wickets in the match. The spectators were also treated to some of Robin's tail-end big hitting as he and Stuart Westley put on 41 for the ninth wicket before Suffolk declared at 192-9 in their 55 overs. Robin scored 28 before he was run out but not before he'd smashed two sixes, one of which sailed high over the Ransomes Sports Club pavilion. Cameos like this were few and far between, his batting for

Suffolk was very rarely needed but the fact that it was seldom required didn't stop him making pacts with the opposition's fast bowlers so that if he did come out to bat he'd get one off the mark and he'd do the same in return when he was bowling: 'He had tricks of the trade' laughs Cunnell.

Robin's excellent early season form in the summer of 1977 continued, recording match figures of 11 for 87 as Suffolk beat Buckinghamshire by eight wickets at Ipswich followed by a 64-run win against Norfolk at Lakenham. In the away match against Buckinghamshire at Chesham in early August no play was possible on the first day due to rain. The following morning it was still drizzling and by all accounts the game could easily have been abandoned without a ball being bowled but with Suffolk and Buckinghamshire both eager for points in the race for the Championship the match went ahead as a one-innings-per-side contest. Having won the toss, Suffolk chose to field and despite the damp conditions, Robin disproved the theory that you need a dry ball to bowl leg breaks as he manipulated what felt like a bar of soap. Robin's figures of seven for 48 from 28.2 overs – his best bowling analysis in Minor Counties Championship matches – helped restrict the opposition to 184-9 and Suffolk went on to win the match by three wickets. It was a near-perfect performance from Robin in very trying conditions; those who were there witnessed a leg spinner at the top of his craft:

> The ball was slippery, it was hard to hold. If you look at the side we played against that day there were some very good players in there. I just got into some sort of rhythm, bowled well and landed it in the right place. That was the best I ever bowled without any question, it was the highlight of my three years at Suffolk bowling in that game.

For Bob Cunnell that particular performance summed up Robin's value to the team and vindicated his judgement and persistence in securing Robin as Suffolk's professional. It was also an example of Cunnell's bold captaincy; 99 times out of 100 the accepted orthodoxy would have been to rely on the seamers with the spinners unable to grip the ball, but Cunnell sensed that Robin had the skill and experience to suit the occasion and entrusted the leg spinner to bowl throughout the majority of Buckinghamshire's innings. It was in this kind of positive environment that Robin thrived. 'There were occasions when his figures looked better,' says Cunnell,

> 'But when you know the situation and you know how hard he tried; there were other events with Robin's bowling but that one I'll never forget. That's the sort of person he was, he wasn't prepared to say "Oh, somebody else can bowl" – and

a lot of the ex-pros would do, that's the sort of example he set and it just spread through the side. He was quite happy to let his bowling suit the occasion, he would willingly for example – and this is where he was also different from a lot of other ex-pros – give a few runs away off his own bowling to create a tight finish, whereas other pros would think, "Oh, I mustn't spoil my figures, I must have three for 10 not three for 50" – but that wasn't Robin's case. When it came to it and we needed his expertise and skill as a bowler then he was only too glad to apply it.'

Former Norfolk captain Quorn Handley similarly admires Robin's expertise and recalls a match against Suffolk at Mildenhall where he went wicketless and didn't turn a single ball in the first innings. 'We all said "Well, he can't bowl" but in the second innings he really ripped it.' Robin's figures of three for 92 helped Suffolk to a 40-run win and Handley is convinced that the wily leg spinner purposely didn't turn a ball in the first innings to fox Norfolk.

In their penultimate league match of 1977, Suffolk beat Hertfordshire by 30 runs in an exciting finish at Bishop's Stortford. In the fourth innings Hertfordshire were set the tough task of scoring 192 to win in an hour plus 20 overs and to their credit they never gave up the chase but Suffolk managed to snatch victory with just 12 balls remaining. The win saw Suffolk to the top of the table a position they maintained after overwhelming Bedfordshire by eight wickets in the final league match of the season.

At the time it was the best-ever season in Suffolk's history but there was still the small matter of the Championship title which, in those days, was decided by a three-day challenge match. Suffolk's opponents would be the reigning champions Durham and, having led the table, Suffolk would have the advantage of playing the match on their home ground at Ipswich. Durham won the toss and chose to field but they must have regretted the decision as Suffolk, with an outstanding 124 from wicket-keeper Westley, ran up a total of 461 from 170 overs. Having lost the initiative, Durham were bowled out for 296 on the third day and Suffolk, with the Championship in their grasp, closed off the match with the score at 42-1 in their second innings.

After nearly 20 years as a professional cricketer, Robin joked at the time that it was the only thing he had ever helped to win in his career. He'd had had another great season with Suffolk and the county had received excellent value for the 45 wickets he'd taken for them at an average of just 15.17. After being selected for the MCC tour of South Africa in 1964/65, Robin ranked winning the Minor Counties Championship as his second happiest moment in cricket and credits a great deal of the success to Bob Cunnell, whose company he so enjoyed.

Bob and I got on very well, we played cricket in the same way. In the two-day games he was such a good captain and was well respected. In that last match when we had to draw against Durham at Ipswich we played on the flattest wicket and it was a thing between me and Bob that I'd never been hit for a hundred in an innings.

Personal pride ensured that the closer Robin got towards conceding 100 runs the tighter he bowled. 'He knew what I was at,' Cunnell recalls with a smile, 'and I knew what he was at. When he perhaps had 92 off his bowling he'd suddenly find himself down at third-man in between overs because he didn't want to get the hundred up.' The pair had become close and now, with the Championship in their grasp, could engage in some friendly fun.

Bob made sure I was hit for a hundred, he loved it! 52 overs, two for 105 and I knew what he was thinking and I said "I'm not going to go for a hundred" and he said "You f***ing are today Hobbsy."

Robin had also been playing Birmingham League cricket for Duport in 1977 and would leave his home in Ingatestone early on Saturday morning to head for the Midlands. Having replaced Worcester in the first division, Duport were looking to strengthen their side and Peter Jones, who'd played with Robin for Suffolk, asked if he'd be prepared to go and play for them. "It was the best club cricket I've ever played in," says Robin.

It was a really strong league. We'd recruited a couple of other guys by then and I was their professional, I didn't bowl badly for them, we finished ninth but at the end of the season the travelling had got me down a bit and Keith Jones, who played for Middlesex, replaced me as the professional. There were some super players in that league – the likes of Dougie Slade and Ron Headley – it was hard club cricket, the hardest I've ever played.

Suffolk found it difficult to follow up their Championship winning success the following season but were still in with a shout right up until the final match against Bedfordshire at Felixstowe when, in front of their largest crowd of the season, they gave their poorest display and could only manage a draw. In spite of this they still finished third in the table and qualified for a place in the Gillette Cup for the second year in succession.

The season had started well with a 47-run victory against Cambridgeshire at Fenners in July. Robin took eight wickets in the match, a feat matched by the former Middlesex and Nottinghamshire leg-spinner Harry Latchman, who, like Robin, also enjoyed a spell in minor counties cricket after retiring from the first-class game. Also playing was Alan Ponder, a left-handed batsman who made 152 Minor Counties Championship appearances for Cambridgeshire. Ponder recalls that Suffolk were a very good side in those days and that Robin was a more than useful member of the team.

'They were well-balanced and benefited from being able to field a regular side. In fact one season I believe they played all nine games and only used 13 players, quite remarkable, although players tend to be more available when you are successful. Robin was an excellent attacking bowler who I am sure won them many games. He was a wicket-taker with lots of variations, not frightened to "throw" the ball up and be hit, he would sooner or later get his man. He was an ideal pro at that time when the game was played over two days and as a batsman you had to get on with it. When I first played for Cambs we had Johnny Wardle who was even more successful but again someone who was prepared to give the ball a bit of "flight", which nowadays spinners do not seem to be encouraged to do. Robin was a really likeable opponent and person, he seemed to really enjoy the game and was a pleasure to play against and chat to after in the bar; he didn't seem to take things too seriously.'

Robin performed admirably throughout the season and was never afraid to toss the ball up and buy wickets when the occasion demanded it. Tony Garnett recalls one such incident when Suffolk were playing Hertfordshire at Cheshunt. Requiring only one wicket to win, but with time running out on the final day, Robin lobbed up a gentle ball outside the leg stump inviting tailender Brian Collins to hit for six which he duly did to bring Hertfordshire back into the game. Robin then produced another, almost identical delivery, and Collins, having accepted the bait, tried again to hit it out of the ground but only succeeded in picking out Stephen Long on the boundary and Suffolk won by 21 runs. 'He never worried about averages' recalls Garnett, 'he played it like that, that's why we wanted him. If we lost we lost.' A further five wickets followed in the home match at Mildenhall against Cambridgeshire and Robin finished the 1978 season with 41 wickets at 21.20.

Having achieved a top five position in the table the previous season, Suffolk had qualified for the 1978 Gillette Cup and had been drawn away against Sussex in the first round. Robin only managed to score four before being adjudged lbw to John Spencer as Suffolk were bowled out for 101 after Sussex had won the toss and chosen to field. Sussex won comfortably by six wickets but Robin bowled accurately for nine overs, conceding just 18 runs and taking the wicket of Paul Parker. He had shown that he could still do it against first-class opposition despite three years out of the professional game.

In that time he'd been the perfect minor counties professional, his team-mates had thoroughly enjoyed both his company and his attitude to the game. Robin was certainly enjoying his time with the county.

> *The great thing about it in those three years was that I was totally accepted by the team. They were a great bunch of lads, they knew I was a pro, there were only one or two players who knew what I was getting paid but they never moaned. There was a great team spirit, I had good fun with them. They were magic days playing for Suffolk.*

Robin's sense of fun and the opportunity for a laugh was never far away, even in a tight match situation. Cunnell recalls a game at Mildenhall when, as it got towards the final over, the opposition batsman cut the ball past Robin, who was fielding at squarish-cover, over the boundary and it into the groundsman's hut. Robin went to retrieve the ball and for several seconds there was no sign of him. Players, umpires and spectators were staring in the direction of the hut when he suddenly reappeared with a hosepipe coiled around his neck like a snake, calling for help. Quite simply, according to Bob Cunnell, Robin brought with him to Suffolk the pleasure of playing cricket; win or lose, he wanted to enjoy the game:

> 'His major influence was not so much his individual performances, which of course were good, but the influence he had on everybody in the nicest possible way, I don't think anybody would have known that Robin Hobbs ex-England cricketer was playing for the county, he was just another Suffolk player. He would do exactly the same that I wanted from my youngest player, he wouldn't consider himself above anybody else. I would have had him in my side anytime; batsman, bowler or fielder, just for his personality because he dragged everybody along with him.'

As a professional, Robin was paid £100 a game, which he received at the end of the season. The arrangement, as Bob Cunnell and Tony Garnett hoped, had worked well for both him and Suffolk. All of the games were played in the Eastern region so there was never far to travel and the match fees he received were a useful supplement to his salary from Barclays. In the course of three seasons he'd taken 132 wickets at an average of 17.78. He was comfortably the bowler who bowled the highest number of overs each season, on average bowling 37 overs per game and regularly bowling one end. Suffolk certainly got their money's worth and, feeling like he'd earned it, Robin was happy to take his £800 at the end of the season without any guilt though ultimately for him it wasn't about the money, it was about the joy of playing the game.

Robin's bowling for Suffolk over the three seasons had been good, possibly too good at times. He'd been successful in most of the games and there was a nagging thought that perhaps he'd packed in the first-class game too early. The opportunity to find out for sure would soon present itself.

Chapter Fourteen

I should never really have signed for them, they were the only county I ever did well against.

'HOBBS FOR GLAMORGAN' announced Peter Jackson in *The Daily Mail* as he broke the story in January 1979 that Robin would be launching a new career as captain of the Welsh county. Jackson revealed that Robin would be taking over from Alan Jones and would be tasked with the challenge of reviving the side which had been stricken by one of the most traumatic periods in their history. In the three preceding seasons they hadn't finished higher than 13th in the table, winning only eight Championship matches out of 64.

Glamorgan had given Alan Jones the captaincy in August 1976 in succession to Majid Khan, who later claimed that he'd been driven out by a conspiracy between senior players and certain members of the committee. Majid had adopted a very laid back approach to captaincy which met with criticism from certain factions and he'd found it difficult to communicate with the young Welsh players. Things came to a head in 1976 with the team enduring a poor season and finishing at the bottom of the table for the first time since 1929. Majid also lost form and in the middle of the season quit the club.

Jones had done a reasonable job and had the support of his team, but after an indifferent season in 1978 the Glamorgan committee decided that change was required. Jones, halfway through a coaching stint in South Africa, had heard rumours circulating before he left that the county were actively searching for a new captain but he'd put it down to idle gossip. It wasn't until he was 4000 miles away in South Africa that the decision was made to replace him.

At the time, Robin became only the second Englishman to skipper the Welsh county, the first being Ossie Wheatley who was now chairman of the club. Completing a triumvirate of Englishmen was Tom Cartwright who'd joined Glamorgan as coach from Somerset two years earlier. The general consensus among the players was one of surprise when they heard of Robin's appointment, mainly because he hadn't played first-class cricket for some time as former player Alan Wilkins recalls.

'No-one doubted his record as a Test cricketer, or as a wicket-taking leg spinner who had been prolific in the County Championship for many years but I guess it was a surprise to have someone at a struggling county like Glamorgan who had been out of the game for four years. No-one really knew what we were going to get in Hobbsy, how effective a bowler he'd be, would he be as good as he was when he was at his peak with Essex? In this respect, there was a certain feeling of doubt that he could replicate those halcyon years with Essex, but the general feeling at Glamorgan was to give him his chance.'

'It was a little bit of a shock to the camp really,' remembers Malcolm Nash when they heard that Robin would be joining them as captain. But Nash was aware that the club was in a downward trend and had been struggling since the mid-seventies:

Glamorgan CCC, 1979. Standing: John Derrick, Michael Thornton, Geoff Holmes, Jeremy Newman, Andy Mack, Neil Perry, Mark Davies, Arthur Francis, Alan Jones. Sitting: Rodney Ontong, Michael Llewellyn, Peter Swart, Robin Hobbs, Tony Cordle, John Hopkins, Gwyn Richards.

'We started to lose personnel; Peter Walker, Roger Davies and Tony Lewis all finished playing and we were not getting that wealth of experience coming in replacing them. Alan Jones was captain and we were doing alright but we lacked real good experience. It's easy to point fingers and say well we could have done this and we could have done that but there was no consultation with players. Committees make these decisions and they go ahead whether they're right or wrong and certainly players were never consulted about whether it would have been the right choice or whether we all appreciated Hobbsy coming or not. At the time I felt hey, this wasn't too bad a move, he plays cricket the right way, he hasn't played for a few seasons but the game hasn't changed too much from the time when he finished playing with Essex to when he came to us so I was quite happy for him to be there.'

Robin was under no illusion that it would be a tough job; he'd be inheriting a struggling team and one which seemed to have entered into a period of depression under Majid Khan's captaincy and still hadn't shaken it off. The gloom Glamorgan were experiencing was in complete contrast to the three happy summers he'd spent at Suffolk: "The best three years of my cricketing life," he recalls, "the players all had to take time off from work and they made sure it was fun."

It was a gamble for a man in his late thirties but made easier by the understanding nature of Barclaycard and Robin wouldn't have taken the plunge had they not been so accommodating. He'd consulted with Barclays as soon as Glamorgan first approached him in October 1978, and they generously allowed him to have the summers off, a job during the winter months plus the promise of a full-time job again at the end of his spell with Glamorgan. He agonized for several weeks but decided it was worth a punt and signed a three-year contract.

Commenting in the press at the time of his appointment, Robin remarked that he had no worries about his bowling form; he'd been playing, and bowling, a lot for Chingford and Suffolk since he'd left Essex. Throughout his career he was never overly concerned if he went for a few runs and indicated that this might even be his chosen role at times in the Glamorgan bowling attack. He also lamented the sorry state of leg spin in the first-class game.

I shall bowl a lot and hopefully get about 60 wickets, although they may cost me a bit. When we are bowling for a declaration and the flog is on, I shall make sure that I get it and not the young spinners. It's my job to take that. I've got past the stage of worrying about figures of 0 for 80 or 0 for 90.

Everything is against the leg spinner these days. All the competitions, including the Championship, are now played with an over limitation. Captains naturally think defensively, and who would risk a leg spinner? If I was 18 again I wouldn't want to bowl leg breaks. Unless I could bat a bit, I would be struggling.

John Lever took it as a compliment that Glamorgan had appointed his former Essex team-mate.

'I thought it was a great tribute to the Essex attitude when Robin Hobbs, who had retired in 1975, made a comeback four years later as captain of Glamorgan. Tony Lewis said that the reason why they had appointed him was that while they had some good cricketers in Glamorgan they did not seem to be getting anywhere so they wanted somebody in charge who would at least help them to enjoy their cricket. I do not know whether it worked. But it was nice to think that they had looked around and found somebody from our changing-room to do that for them.'

The Glamorgan committee were taking a big gamble, they had opted more for a personality captain than a technical one, with the hope that Robin's enthusiasm would be infectious. His task was simple; make the players enjoy the game again. Robin too was looking for the enjoyment which he knew the game gave him; his decision to return to county cricket was very much to do with his life outside cricket.

I'd had three reasonable seasons out of the game with Suffolk and got quite a lot of wickets and thought I was still quite a good cricketer in those days and Glamorgan were looking for an outsider to go down and add a bit of enthusiasm to their game and to their cricket. Tom Cartwright, who was a good friend of mine, and Ossie Wheatley approached me and I was pretty bored at the time working for Barclaycard. It wasn't a great job in those days because all you did was go round the merchants; we had our share of the merchants and Access had theirs. It was a monopoly, there was no competition. If you took credit cards you had to have either Barclaycard or Access. I found it got a bit boring and it gave me an opportunity to get back into cricket.

There was also the nagging thought that he could still do it; maybe he'd packed it in too early at Essex, maybe he could still cut it at first-class level.

Robin stated before the start of the season that he'd be disappointed if Glamorgan didn't win six matches: they didn't, they didn't win any. It was a disastrous summer, Glamorgan finished bottom of the table and became only the second county in 41 years to fail to win a single match in the County Championship since Northants' three-year winless run from 1936-38.

If things could go wrong they did; badly. A visit to Ilford in May 1979 set the tone for the rest of the season. The first two days of the County Championship fixture against Essex were washed out and on the third the game was reduced to a one innings contest. Glamorgan, having won the toss, batted for four hours and limped to 184-8 off 75 overs before declaring at tea. "It was horrendous," recalls Robin, "our two overseas players were fighting and there were screams of 'Declare Hobbs you turncoat' from the crowd so I thought I'd better give them some sort of token declaration." In the Essex reply Mike Denness fell cheaply but Gooch and McEwan, both in one-day mode, battered the Glamorgan attack and reached the winning total in just 27 overs with time to spare. "Well played Robin, lovely declaration", he remembers people wryly congratulating him after the game.

"We were a poor side," he says, "it was hard work playing a whole county season without winning a match although we very nearly won one." Glamorgan played Gloucestershire at Cardiff in early July. The visitors, led by Mike Procter, were a strong batting side with Pakistan batsmen Sadiq Mohammad and Zaheer Abbas as star turns. On the final day Glamorgan declared their second innings at 308 for five, setting Procter's side a target of 324 to win. When the ninth wicket fell with the score on 206, the Gloucestershire last man John Childs joined number eight, David Graveney out in the middle. With his side having dismissed world-class batsmen Sadiq, Zaheer and Procter, and with widely acknowledged rabbit Childs at the crease, Robin must have felt that his first win in the Championship was only a matter of moments away.

How we didn't win I'll never know. John Childs and I still laugh about it whenever we see each other; Graveney wasn't a bad player but John couldn't bat, he was worse than I was. I just couldn't get our bowlers to bowl quick enough at him, they wouldn't bounce him. I said to them "Bounce him, knock his f***ing head off." We had an hour to bowl against him, an hour, and we couldn't get him out. With half an hour to go I knew we wouldn't win, I just got that feeling, I thought the only way we're going to win this is if I go off the field and offer Procky a few quid. I saw him a few years later and he joked: "We had nothing to play for. If you'd have dropped me £50 you could have had it!"

If Robin's target for the team of winning six matches had been wildly optimistic then so was his personal one of 60 wickets for the season as he ended up with just 22 at an average of 36.59. It was a hugely disappointing return for, at the time, the last English leg spinner in county cricket. Towards the end of his playing career with Essex in 1975 Robin had likened himself to the white rhino for he was becoming an endangered species. Four years later things hadn't improved but the rare sight of a leg spinner plying his craft was an absolute pleasure for team-mate Alan Wilkins.

'It was quite a poignant sight to see Hobbsy take the ball and bowl, a throwback to bygone years in the game, but he bowled with menace, with great experience and thought, and he never looked out of his depth, given that he had not bowled at first-class cricketers for four years. Make no bones about it, Robin Hobbs was still, in 1979, a top-class leg-spin bowler.'

Despite Robin's modest haul of 22 wickets it was largely on a par with his colleagues: 38-year-old veteran seamer Tony Cordle was the exception with 58 wickets at 27.65, Rodney Ontong was the next highest taker and his tally was only 32. It didn't help that Malcolm Nash was unwell and only able to play in nine matches. Nash, one of the best new-ball bowlers in the country with a priceless habit of dismissing the best batsmen, took 16 wickets at an average of nearly 40 runs apiece. 'I battled through that season,' Nash says 'but I wasn't able to give 100 per cent, I was disappointed at not being fit for the whole of the summer. We lacked strength in depth with the bowling, not the fact that Robin was there as captain. It wasn't his fault that we didn't win any games; we just didn't have the personnel, that was the problem.'

It was a pretty miserable return to first-class cricket for Robin, even the odd bright moment seemed to be laced with pain, sometimes quite literally according to Alan Wilkins:

'We were playing in one of the early Benson & Hedges matches on a cold day in Cardiff against Worcestershire and Younis Ahmed smashed a swinging half-volley from me uppishly to Hobbsy at cover. I can still see him now, flying through the air like a grasshopper taking a magnificent one-handed catch. When we all gathered around to congratulate him on his effort, he turned to me and said: "You f***ing owe me for that." He made us all laugh but he was clearly in a lot of pain and in the process of making me look good, he had almost dislocated his right thumb. He went to hospital for X-rays which later showed that there was no break, but he had a problem gripping the ball and couldn't therefore contribute for a few weeks as a leg spinner. I know that the injury set him back more than he was prepared to admit at the time, but he just got on with the job. He probably didn't bowl as much as he could have for the rest of the season.'

Robin, an undemonstrative captain who only bowled infrequently and batted way down the order, puzzled many of the Glamorgan faithful as Pat Pocock discovered when playing for Surrey at Cardiff. The Surrey captain Roger Knight was putting in an all-round performance, picking up wickets and scoring stylish runs, and as Pocock was fielding near the boundary one of the Glamorgan members called out to him: "Percy, you're very lucky with your captain. He bats and he bowls. Our one does bugger-all."

Robin readily admits that he didn't bowl as much as he could have done that season but with the team consistently failing to score enough runs, particularly in the first innings, there were precious few opportunities for him to come on and bowl lengthy spells. In the 22 matches Glamorgan played in 1979, they only managed to post first-innings' scores of 300 or more five times. If they'd scored more runs Robin would undoubtedly have bowled more, as a leg spinner if he bowled two or three bad overs the game could quickly run away.

Robin had underestimated the pressure of returning to game, particularly as captain, after a four-year absence. David Acfield had warned him that the game had changed, the bowling was faster, batsmen were wearing helmets and being bounced regularly, it was a different game. "I lived in cloud cuckoo-land thinking it was going to be the same happy-go-lucky ride." admits Robin on reflection.

Even his fielding was beginning to suffer. Before the start of the season Robin stated that the captaincy didn't worry him but that he was worried about his fitness and reactions. He was right to be concerned.

I was 36, going on 37, and I'd always been a good fielder but time catches up with you. I could remember the catches I'd dropped in first-class cricket on one hand but I went through a period with Glamorgan where I dropped 12 on the trot. We won a Benson & Hedges match at Swansea against Gloucestershire who had an all-powerful side, and I dropped Mike Procter four times in an innings and we still won. Everywhere I went, Procter hit the f***ing ball. I kept dropping it but we won the game, God knows how.

It had an effect on me because I always felt I was a good fielder. When I was at Essex I always wanted the ball to come to me, every ball, because I knew 99 per cent of the time I was going to catch it. And then you go through a stage like that dreading the bloody thing coming towards you.

We played Gloucestershire at Cardiff in the Championship and David Graveney hit it in the air: this bloody ball went up many a mile and I was underneath it thinking "I'm never going to catch it", it goes through your mind – I've dropped 12 on the trot. I caught this thing: most relieved man ever! It wasn't a difficult catch but it felt like the hardest catch in the world at that stage.

Robin was a struggling player in a struggling side and there was a suspicion, although nothing was actually said in the dressing-room, that some of the home-grown players didn't want an Englishman captaining the county. For Robin, and Glamorgan, the season was a disaster. Towards the end of the summer he conducted an interview with the Western Mail and on local radio to convey the message publicly to the Glamorgan committee that unless new players – and new overseas players in particular – were signed, he wasn't prepared to captain the side.

In spite of this he was still a popular figure at the club and despite the poor record under his captaincy in 1979 he had many qualities according to Alan Wilkins.

'Hobbsy was a great character and an absolutely top bloke to have at the club. Everyone quickly warmed to him because he was such a genuine person. He called it as he saw it, pulled no punches, and was absolutely straight down the line with all of us. He knew the game intrinsically. Cricket is in his DNA. He was a natural at garnering morale and getting a good team spirit going, and we needed that, and we all pulled for him as our new captain. I have no doubt that at times he probably felt a little out of touch with certain players in opposition counties because he had not seen them play in the four years that he had been away from the first-class game. He would therefore rely on input from some of the senior players. That wasn't construed as a weakness on Robin's part, because he was always keen to get the views of other players in the side, but possibly some players within the squad felt that we needed a more demonstrative leadership. From a personal point of view, I enjoyed his captaincy, and he always had the knack of motivating me whether I had the new ball or whether I was first change. The essential theme was that we wanted to do it for him because he was such a great guy on the field and in the dressing-room.'

The pain of the 1979 season didn't end for Robin who had two cartilages taken out that winter in Carmarthen Hospital. It was clear that he wouldn't be fit enough to captain the side for the 1980 season and it was whilst Robin was in hospital recuperating that Malcolm Nash recalls receiving a phone call from chairman Ossie Wheatley asking if they could meet for a conversation. They met and Wheatley enquired if Nash would be interested in taking over the captaincy. Nash was shocked, particularly when he discovered that Robin was oblivious as to Glamorgan's intentions. Nash recalls telling Wheatley he wasn't happy conversing about the captaincy behind Robin's back. 'I got really upset about it,' he says,

'I found out which ward Robin was in and I called into the hospital to see him and asked if the club had spoken to him about next season.' He said "No, they haven't said a word." I've always shot straight from the hip; I've never beaten about the bush, so I told him I'd been approached by the chairman and asked whether or not I'd be interested in taking over the captaincy but had said that they needed to talk to him and find out what his thoughts were. I think that shocked him a little bit. I told him "Look if you're not going to be fit or you're not wanting to do it and you have an arrangement with the club and you're not going to captain next year I would then consider it if it's all done officially and properly." He thanked me for coming in to speak to him, I think he appreciated that. It was sad the way it ended for Robin as captain of the club, it upset me, I just didn't think it was the right way to treat people.'

Robin wasn't enjoying his return to county cricket and this, combined with the cartilage operation, meant he was only too happy to relinquish the captaincy while remaining keen to see out the playing aspect of the contract. It was a sorry end and Robin, still unable to drive, had to phone best friend Roger White who caught a train to Wales and drove Robin, his leg resting on the dashboard, home to Essex. Nash, who'd regained full fitness after his own injury problems, took on the captaincy and further changes saw Alan Wilkins leave to join Gloucestershire and Peter Swart opting not to seek a renewal of his contract. Glamorgan signed Ezra Moseley, a pace bowler from Barbados, and their batting was also strengthened by the addition of the brilliant Pakistan batsman Javed Miandad. 'He was a very interesting guy,' remembers Robin.

> *He was cricket mad. We were having a full-scale practice match at Neath and he turned up in his civvies with a couple of guys with him carrying his bags, and he said "I think I'll have a bat". So he came out in his civvies, put a pair of pads on and a box, and people played it properly and he got a hundred in 40 balls against proper bowling.*

Under Nash's captaincy the team made an excellent start to the season but the improvements were short-lived and the team finished in 12th place in the Championship. Whilst Nash made a full return to fitness and form, finishing with 74 wickets at 23.28, Robin struggled with both. He only played in seven matches and his eight wickets were taken at a cost of 51.75 apiece. A rare highlight of the season was taking Geoffrey Boycott's wicket in the match against Yorkshire at Park Avenue in Bradford.

Whilst in Bradford on that away trip Robin witnessed the reverence in which Miandad was held.

> *Javed had a sponsored car which he hated driving so I was driving this thing which had 'Javed Miandad' on the side. Wherever we went he knew somebody who had a curry house. So there we were in Bradford and we were lost so I drove up to this bus stop to get out to ask these people who were waiting where this place was. Next thing this bus came along and pulled up at the stop, the passengers all got off and Javed got out of the car and signed autographs for everyone. The whole thing came to a grinding halt. Tony Cordle and I were just standing by this bus stop while Javed*

was holding court amongst all these Pakistan and Indian cricket fans.

Robin played more second- than first-team cricket in 1980 but there was the consolation of helping them to win the 2nd XI Championship and he performed admirably as senior pro taking 16 wickets at a shade over 14 runs apiece. Despite a pretty miserable second summer Robin still had the prospect of another year at Glamorgan, having signed a three-year contract. He'd managed to escape the boredom of working for Barclaycard all year round and was in no rush to go back to working for them full-time.

I was happy not to have to go back to Barclaycard; Glamorgan were paying a wage which they'd committed themselves to and I did as well. They had agreed to pay me six grand a summer for the three seasons which, in that era, was quite a wage, and which I could never have earned at Barclaycard. Money didn't rule my world but I thought bollocks, I'm going to stay here for 18 grand for three years, like it or lump it, whether I'm in the first team or not. That's what I did, I probably shouldn't have done it but it was three years of playing cricket, or some of it. So there I was playing seven first-team games in 1980 getting six grand a year.

In spite of everything Robin had a pretty solid third year at Glamorgan and the introduction of covered wickets combined with the abolition of the 200-over limit for first innings led to him becoming a regular in the first team once more. He played in 15 of Glamorgan's 21 Championship matches taking 35 wickets at 32.88 as the county finished 14th in the table.

In the drawn match against Worcestershire at the Racecourse, Hereford in June 1981, Robin took eight wickets – including five for 67 in the first innings. His bowling was getting back to the standard he'd set in his prime at Essex and was good enough to draw praise from one of Pakistan's most stylish batsmen.

I was bowling against Gloucestershire at Bristol which was not my favourite ground because the ball didn't used to bounce. I'd bowled 30 odd overs and Zaheer Abbas got a hundred, I'd got him missed a couple of times but he actually came up to me after the game and said "You're one of the best leg spinners I've ever faced." I felt a million dollars because he was a great player, I thought to myself "You've still got life left in you at 38 – you can still bowl." That was nice that.

Robin was also contributing with the bat. In July at St Helen's in Swansea, he and Rodney Ontong put together an unbroken 10th-wicket partnership of 140 in the first innings of the match against Hampshire. Robin's share was 49 not out and at the time it was the highest unbroken last-wicket stand ever in county

Bowling for the final time in first-class cricket, 5-85 against Essex at Colchester, 1981. Roger White's sequence of photos captures Robin's action; still plenty of energy through the crease at the age of 39.

cricket, beating the previous record which had stood for 62 years.

Robin played his part in another significant unbroken stand that year, his share only being negligible on this occasion but it did allow his batting partner to reach a personal milestone. Glamorgan were 295-9 in their first innings against Somerset at Taunton as Robin, batting at number 11, walked out to join Miandad who needed another 30 runs to reach his double-century. As they met in the middle of the pitch Miandad set out the strategy for their partnership.

Javed said to me "Hobbsy, I will not let you face Garner, you just take Colin Dredge." He was a good as his word because I only faced two balls from the great West Indies fast bowler. He was a bloody good player, he was brought up in the back streets of Karachi with nothing, that's how some of the best players start out.

Backed-up well by Robin, Miandad manoeuvred the ball into the gaps and went on to reach a double-century, Robin's share of the 41-run partnership was three not out but he considered it a privilege to be at the other end and witness another of the great Pakistan batsman's hundreds. It was a record-breaking summer for Miandad; he was the first Glamorgan player to score 2000 runs in a season and hit eight centuries. As a self-confessed cricket anorak, Robin took great delight in Miandad's batting exploits in 1981 and the pair had become good friends off the field.

I roomed with him for the whole summer, we got on famously. On away trips he was welcomed at all the Indian restaurants, we never bought a curry. I admired him as one of the finest players I've ever seen in English conditions playing in a poor side on green wickets against good bowling attacks.

Another great overseas star playing in that match at Taunton in 1981 was Viv Richards, who, like Robin, would also go on to play for Glamorgan in the twilight of his career. Robin had previously encountered the 'Master Blaster' during Richards' first season in county cricket in 1974. Essex were playing Somerset at Taunton and Robin was captaining the side in place of Keith Fletcher. Having just dismissed opener Mervyn Kitchen, Robin watched as Richards made his way out to the middle to face his bowling. Even early on in his county career, Richards' swagger was unmistakeable.

Viv came in, strutting to the wicket in his normal way. He took guard and to the first four balls he played beautiful shots straight to fielders. The fifth ball I bowled was an over-spun leg break, Viv played back and it hit him in front of middle and off. I appealed to the umpire and he was given out. As he walked past me he simply said "Well bowled."

Robin hadn't bowled at Richards since that occasion but the opportunity now presented itself again as Glamorgan set Somerset a target of 322 to win with four hours play remaining on the final day. Richards had a long memory, as Robin was about to discover.

I was bowling and Viv strutted to the wicket, he hadn't forgotten because as he walked past me he said "Hobbs, the day of reckoning has come!" I was nearly 40 years old then and I thought "Christ almighty". He smashed some quick runs but then lo and behold it started to rain and the game was abandoned, thank God, otherwise I think I might have been on for a right hiding.

Robin felt privileged see all of Miandad's hundreds that summer and was present at Colchester for what Graham Gooch described as 'probably the most brilliant innings I have ever witnessed' on 1 September 1981.

Glamorgan had been set 325 to win in the fourth innings of their Championship match against Essex but collapsed to 44 for four on a pitch that was turning square for spinners East and Acfield, and also offering plenty for the left-arm pace of John Lever. 'They had no chance,' remembers Ray East, 'batting on it was impossible.'

Wickets continued to fall at the other end and by the time Robin joined Miandad, Glamorgan were 227 for seven. As with the game against Somerset in July, Miandad expertly shielded his partner and minimised the number of balls Robin had to face on the minefield of a pitch. It was a batting master class admired by all. The Pakistan batsman wristily manoeuvred the ball around the field and, after waiting for the field to come up for the fifth delivery of each over, would loft the ball over the top of the infield for six or four. Essex strived to cut off the single off the last ball of each over but Miandad excelled at stealing singles and Robin did his bit by backing up far down the wicket and responding to Miandad's calling.

John Lever recalls the sense of frustration among the Essex players as time and again there were denied the opportunity to get their old county colleague on strike.

'There were these long gaps in his knock where he didn't face a ball and it seemed like forever, so if Javed got a single or three off the last ball of the over we thought "Christ, we're never going to bowl at Hobbsy" and we were sort of trying to hold back the person we wanted to bowl at him so that we could shove him on if he got to face the beginning of an over, we were trying to get our quickest bowler to run in and bowl at him.'

The pair batted together for 37 minutes before Robin's luck ran out. His old friend David Acfield bounded in and Robin edged an off break which was caught by Keith Fletcher at forward short-leg. The partnership for the eighth wicket was worth 42 runs, Robin's contribution had been nought from 20 balls. With the game unexpectedly heading right down to the wire Essex had the jitters but, agonizingly for Glamorgan, last man Simon Daniels fell lbw to John Lever and they lost by 13 runs. Miandad was still there unbeaten on 200 not out, the rest of the team had only managed to score 89 between them. It was a remarkable innings, one of the best on a bad wicket which Robin, and the players on both sides that day, had ever seen.

Taking on old friends. Caught Fletcher, bowled Acfield. Javed Miandad looks on from the non-striker's end.

When we were four down for forty, everyone was saying we'll be all out for a hundred. There were great big pieces out of the wicket but Javed was a master of playing spin and the bowlers were starting to get a bit tired. Javed was a fantastic player of balls for two's and one's, he'd chip it over mid-on on purpose for two and you never thought you'd get run-out by him because he was such a good judge of a run. He was a world-class player and I had total confidence in him. It was a terrible track, a dustbowl, big bits of it were flying out and he was just playing it like it was a table top. He never looked like getting out in that innings.

Earlier in the match Essex had been bowled out for 187 in their first innings and when Glamorgan gained a slim, but useful, first-innings lead of 87 they were confident of a win. That was until Gooch and Hardie proceeded to put on 169 for the first wicket in the second innings and Essex went on to declare on 411-9. As the Essex players went in search of quick runs to set the declaration, Robin became the main beneficiary among the Glamorgan bowlers. Ray East was caught and bowled and John Lever stumped as Robin finished with five for 85. It was his 50th five-wicket return in first-class cricket and would be his last. Against his old county Robin fittingly played his last first-class game of cricket and ended his career with 1099 wickets.

The Welsh adventure hadn't gone well, but in fairness Glamorgan had gone through a tough few years before Robin joined and, under a variety of captains, things still wouldn't improve for a few years to come. During his captaincy Robin had been hampered not only with injury but the lack of a top-quality overseas player before Glamorgan managed to strike it lucky with their signings for the 1980 season.

> For the two years after I was captain we had terrific overseas players in Javed Miandad and Ezra Moseley. Well, if you've got a world-class bowler and a world-class batsman you're going to win a few games. They didn't win many but they won more than nought. In the season when I was skipper they won none, f***ing none.

Robin had had a lot of success against Glamorgan as a player for Essex and that, combined with his ebullience, had made him such a tempting proposition but unfortunately the gamble hadn't paid off. "I did get quite a lot of success against them," he recalls, "and they thought I could be as successful against other counties – it didn't work out like that. I should never have really signed for them," he jokes, "they were the only county I ever did well against."

Glamorgan decided not to retain Robin at the end of the 1981 season and despite interest from Surrey he decided to call time on his first-class career a second time; this time for good.

> I was approached towards the end of my career by Surrey, they wanted me to go there for a year after Glamorgan but I decided no, I couldn't go on for another bloody year, I'd had enough by then. I had a commitment to a certain extent with Barclays Bank as well. They let me off three summers to play and had me back which was good of them. They let me have a car for three summers which I drove

into the ground. I made more money out of expenses than I did with the salary. I used to take it everywhere. Glamorgan offered me a brand new Volvo with 'Robin Hobbs – Glamorgan and England' on the side. I didn't want it, not after the season I had, so I gave it to Alan Jones, I said "You better have that, I'll keep the Morris Marina."

Robin's decision to join Glamorgan had placed a strain on his marriage. At the time he'd wanted to get away from the boredom of working for Barclaycard and felt that he could still do it at first-class level but, as warned, the game was quicker and it had changed. Robin and Isabel never came close to divorce but looking back he considers it a selfish thing to do.

On reflection it was probably the worst thing I ever did because Glamorgan were a pretty insular side at the time and it certainly put an unfair burden on Isabel leaving her at home in Essex for most of the summer. I used to come back as much as I could, it still wasn't the best decision but it wasn't made on the spur of the moment. Isabel was against it but I was all for it and being a chap who wanted to have his own way and do his own thing I made the decision and you live with it. It was pretty unfair on Isabel. I did get home as much as I could but it still weren't the right thing.

Isabel had stood by him for three summers while he was enjoying himself in Wales but she was now pregnant and it was time for Robin to settle down to a life outside professional cricket.

Chapter Fifteen

Some players when they finish playing hardly ever go and watch matches, but I love it.

NICK HOBBS WAS born in January 1982, it was a bitter winter and Robin made several trips through the snow to St John's Hospital in Chelmsford before Nick finally arrived. Isabel took maternity leave from her teaching job and once she'd returned to work Nick was looked after by a childminder during the day and Robin would pick him up after work. Despite his new responsibilities as a father, Robin still found some time to play cricket and that summer he returned to play for Suffolk. In the three seasons he'd spent with them in the 1970s he'd been highly successful and once they became aware that he was leaving Glamorgan they approached him with an offer to be their professional again. The attraction for both parties was too good to resist but unfortunately the magic of those glorious summers of his first spell with the county wasn't reproduced. Bob Cunnell was no longer captain and although Robin got on OK with the new skipper, Colin Rutterford, they didn't really see eye-to-eye on the field. He had to take annual leave from Barclays to play and he ended up only appearing in half of Suffolk's matches that season.

The match against Cambridgeshire at Bury St Edmunds in August 1982 turned out to be Robin's last minor counties appearance for Suffolk; he bowled nine wicketless overs and was run out for five in the second innings. By his standards his performances and figures weren't good enough and he finished the season with just 12 wickets at an average of 35.33 from 121 overs.

I was poor, piss poor. I had one good game and I felt guilty taking the money. I don't feel guilty taking the money if I've performed well but I do if I haven't. I'd come to the end of the road, I was 40 and I didn't think I was up-to-the-mark. Whether they would have paid me for another year I don't know but I wasn't prepared to do it. If I couldn't give as good as I could do it was taking money under false pretences and I wasn't prepared to do that so I finished with them although I think they would have finished with me, and quite rightly so.

Robin was content to pack it in then and having played cricket full time for over 20 years, it was time to put that behind him and focus on family life and his job with Barclays which he'd fitted into well. He found it to be a relatively easy job in the early days as there was little competition in the credit-card industry beyond Barclaycard and Access. As an area rep one of the shops he'd call into was Mike Norris Sports in Billericay where Neil Burns, who'd been so captivated as a nine-year-old by his batting against the Australians, had a winter job. The teenage Burns was now on the staff at Essex and enjoyed Robin's occasional visits to the shop and their chats about cricket. Burns still possesses his first ever pair of wicket-keeping gloves which Rod Marsh signed for him at Chelmsford in 1975 and by the early 1980s had his sights set on a career as a professional cricketer.

Having represented Essex at youth level, Burns was making strides in achieving his goal but cites the importance of having belief instilled in him by senior players such as Ray East, Graham Saville and Robin. Although Robin's professional career had ended by this stage, Burns found it a thrill to keep to the former Test match bowler in the occasional Essex Club & Ground matches they played together. Burns had experience in the Essex youth set-up of keeping to Nasser Hussain – at one stage rated as the best schoolboy leg spinner in the country – but keeping to Robin allowed him to witness the master spinner's full repertoire.

> 'The difference keeping to Hobbsy in those games was the pace at which he bowled, the variation of delivery and also his use of the crease. There was a lot of trickery to his bowling and it helped open my eyes to the fact there that there was so much more to the game than I had previously considered.'

Robin's passion and enthusiasm for the game was undimmed; he'd still prowl the infield and Burns was able to appreciate at first-hand the accuracy of Robin's throws as the young 'keeper took the veteran's powerful returns over the stumps just as Tonker had done years earlier.

Learning wasn't restricted to the playing field; Burns refers to Robin's sharp cricket brain and the quality of conversation about the game whilst waiting to bat being an education in itself. This experience gave Burns an insight into what it took to excel at sport and he firmly believes the encouragement offered by Robin, along with East and Saville, helped in making his transition to professional cricket easier than it might otherwise have been.

Neil Burns eventually had to move from Essex to Somerset to further his career and his efforts, both behind the stumps and with the bat, in a 15-run defeat against Middlesex in a Benson and Hedges Cup match at Lord's in May 1987 drew praise in a speech afterwards from the Gold Award adjudicator – Robin Hobbs. He picked out Wilf Slack as the player of the match – the opener's century was the difference with his side winning by 15 runs – but Robin cheerfully admitted to Burns later in the Long Room that he'd been desperate to give him the award, "If you'd managed to get another 16 runs and won the game I'd have been able to!"

Although professional cricket had been left behind, links were still firmly in place and Robin was able to enjoy the camaraderie and renew acquaintances from the first-class game by playing for the Whitbread Wanderers, a team of former England players. He'd received an invitation from Tom Cartwright and ended up playing about 10 games a year with them on Sundays. It was good, fun cricket, playing with the likes of Jim Parks, Alan Oakman, David Allen, Basil D'Oliveira, Brian Luckhurst, Roger Tolchard, Geoff Humpage, John Lever, Derek Randall, Pat Pocock and Derek Underwood.

We were brought up of an age, myself, Pat and Derek who I've known all my life, it was great to see them on a Sunday, I looked forward to every game I played. The hospitality was always lovely, the lunches were always nice and we generally had good crowds, all in all it was just a lovely relaxed atmosphere to meet guys that you've played with all your life.

Old England XI. Front: Robin Hobbs, Roger Tolchard, Brian Luckhurst, John Lever, Jim Parks, David Allen, Pat Pocock, Derek Underwood. Geoff Humpage. Tom Cartwright. Alan Oakman and John Jameson are in the back row.

He never missed a game when selected, or dropped out because of the distances involved. Charity games were played all over the country and Robin recalls doing many miles on the road, sometimes as far as Plymouth in a day, travelling down early in the morning, getting home the other side of midnight and then up for work at Barclays just a few hours later. In spite of the long days and travelling, Robin was as keen as he'd been as a youngster playing for Chingford.

In some ways it was a throwback to the Scarborough Festival days and the many fun times he, and the big crowds, had enjoyed at the North Marine Road ground. The cricket wasn't too serious and it was very entertaining; Robin was hit for many sixes on many grounds but it never bothered him, he was able to smile it off in the same old way he'd always done throughout his career. "It was good for the team we were playing against," he says, "although I didn't want to get smashed round the park every game." Robin continued playing until he was 68. The players were all getting older and there weren't enough 'youngsters' in their thirties, forties and fifties coming through. It gradually died a death but it had been fun while it lasted. He also kept an involvement in the game through occasional hospitality work at Lord's Test matches and he enjoyed entertaining guests with various stories from his career and the many characters he'd played with, and against.

There were also fun times in 1985 as Robin headed for the Cayman Islands on tour with the Fred Trueman International XI in the company of old friends Colin Milburn, Brian Close and Trevor Bailey. It was a two-week trip with some gentle social cricket but was almost more notable for the various cricket bats and assorted memorabilia which Trueman had taken out with him, raffled and kept the proceeds of, at great expense to the Cayman Islanders who seemed happy enough to continue handing over their dollars. The trip also provided the unexpected pleasure of Colin Milburn rolling back the years as he treated guests at an official welcome to the Cayman Islands reception to an impromptu rendition of Green Green Grass of Home, reviving for Robin happy memories of England tours with Ollie in the 1960s. It was a good trip but would be his last one playing abroad.

It wasn't until the late 1980s that Robin was drawn back into playing club cricket when his friend Roger White talked him into playing for the village side near Colchester which he captained. Robin felt quite at home playing for Copford in lovely surroundings on a ground with a tree only a few yards off the main square and he'd often take Nick with him who'd spend many hours cycling around the ground on his bike.

It was at Copford that Robin had his only experience of the yips, the dreaded condition that can afflict bowlers resulting in them losing their ability to bowl line or length; sometimes both. "I was very lucky, I never had the yips when I was a professional," he says.

I never had what Phil Edmonds, Fred Swarbrook and Keith Medlycott got, where they couldn't bowl. I got the yips when I was 58 at Elmstead Market playing village cricket for Copford! I'd just got 70 runs in our innings and went on to bowl. I got the ball, went back to my mark and I said to our skipper, Roger White, "I can't bowl"; he said "What's wrong with you?" and I replied "I can't bowl, I don't know how to run up!" I was 58 and I could not bowl, I couldn't work out how to run up. I got it back to some extent but I couldn't bowl properly. Bowling comes naturally, you run up and bowl but if you think "How do I do that?" it can mess you up.

Fortunately Robin's brush with the yips was only temporary; he had five fabulous years at Copford and still retains a great deal of affection for what he describes as "a terrific little club."

Ever since his trip to East Africa in 1963 Robin had wanderlust and family holidays inevitably involved travel to warmer climes. He had been a big fan of the Beatles in the 1960s and got to know their former producer George Martin after they met on a family holiday to the Greek island of Lefkas. Robin and Isabel had decided to go on a holiday organised by The Cricketer magazine and ended up in the same accommodation as Martin, his wife Judy and son Giles. Nick was only a toddler at the time and the Martin family would occasionally babysit allowing Robin and Isabel some time to share a meal or do some sight-seeing together. "I didn't even know at that time that he was involved with the Beatles," says Robin, "he didn't talk about them, he was just George." Martin may not have mentioned the small matter of being the 'fifth Beatle' but there was a connection – he also loved cricket. Coincidentally, in the week in which Robin made his Essex debut in 1961 Martin also had a notable achievement; his first No. 1 as a record producer with *You're Driving Me Crazy* by The Temperance Seven.

Martin had a home and studio on the island of Montserrat and following the devastating volcanic eruptions in the 1990s he organised a charity concert at the Royal Albert Hall to raise funds for a new community centre and cricket field. Judy made an appeal for cricket kit and Robin helped out by obtaining quite a collection of bats, pads and gloves which he delivered to their home for them to take over to the Caribbean. Robin had enjoyed his visits to the region and been only too happy to help. On the 1968 tour of the West Indies he'd only played one Test but had got onto the field many times as a substitute fielder and had effected the run-out of Basil Butcher in the third Test with a superb piece of work. A family holiday to the Caribbean in the late 1980s gave him the opportunity to reminisce with Isabel and Nick.

We were on a cruise to Barbados and went to the cricket ground in Bridgetown, I said this is where I fielded it and this is how I ran Butcher out and I showed them exactly where I threw the ball from. "This is where I was fielding, note that Nick" and his expression was like: 'This is really boring dad, what are we doing here?'

There were many happy times for the family but tragically things changed forever on Saturday 22 February 1997. Robin had gone to bed early, tired after a busy few days, and was suddenly awoken by a panic-stricken Nick who'd come running upstairs to tell him that Isabel had collapsed in the kitchen. By the time Robin reached her she was unconscious, an ambulance was called but she sadly died by the time help arrived. Unbeknown to Robin and Nick at the time, a piece of food she'd swallowed had become trapped in her larynx and she had asphyxiated. Isabel was 54 and had been due to retire from her teaching post at Brentwood School the following month.

Robin and Nick, 15 years old and studying for his GCSE's, struggled to cope – they were hard, dark times for the pair. Robin is proud of his son and how he coped with losing his mum at such a young age. After finishing his A-levels, Nick spent a winter playing cricket for Cambelltown in Sydney which, according to Robin, was the making of him as a person. Nick went on to study at the University of Brighton and worked as a teacher before more recently launching Blackmore Apparel, an online cycle-wear company, born out of his passion for cycling. The pair are close and although Nick may not have inherited Robin's almost geek-like love for the game – he's never picked up a Wisden – he's certainly inherited his father's sense of fun and, like him, is a sharp exponent of friendly banter.

Robin had cherished the times he'd been able to play in the same Chingford side as his dad Reg and likewise he enjoyed the occasions when he was able to play alongside his son. Nick was playing club cricket for Hutton in 1999 when Robin was roped in and asked if he would captain the third team that season. Nick was mostly playing in the second team with some games in the firsts too but when it came down to the last game of the season, with Hutton thirds needing a win against Saffron Walden to clinch promotion, he was drafted in to play for them. Robin remembers that Nick wasn't too impressed that he'd been dropped from the second team to play for the thirds.

The crunch game was played at Wendens Ambo, a tiny ground with an even tinier boundary according to Robin, "From the stumps to the boundary was no more than 22 yards." Hutton had batted first and posted a score of over 200 and Saffron Walden were on course to reach the victory target. They also desperately needed the win to stay in the division and had brought in a couple of players with first-team experience. Both were well set when Robin decided to bring himself on but was hit for five fours on a mercilessly short ground which left little margin of error, even for a bowler of his experience.

I took myself off and just said to Nick "Well you've got to do something." He came on and got five for 20 and we won the game and got promoted. It was an incredible match. That was the last proper time I played with him but it was great to be able to play a few games together.

When Nick went to university in Brighton, Robin got in touch with Peter Graves who was on the coaching staff at Sussex and asked which club he should play for in the area. Graves mentioned Preston Nomads and Nick went on to the play for them for several seasons, picking up a healthy haul of wickets with his left-arm seamers although it helped, according to Robin, having overseas player Carl Simon bowling at the other end. "He was a bit quicker than Nick," says Robin, "so they used to try and get the runs at Nick's end because that was a bit easier and he ended up getting quite a lot of wickets."

Robin retired from Barclays in 1995 and since then has shared his time between looking after the home and working part-time doing odd jobs. In 1997, however, he was given a new lease of life in cricket when he was approached by Alan Lilley from Essex and asked if he'd be interested in coaching the county's under-12 side. He accepted the offer gladly and worked with that age group for a couple of years before moving up and looking after the under-15s. It kept him involved at his beloved Essex and he enjoyed the opportunity of working with the boys in a similar way to how Basil Dowling had encouraged him at Raine's school in the 1950s.

We had some really good cricketers during that time, many of whom are still playing club cricket in Essex. The Prowting brothers were two very good cricketers but so different in character, Nick was a most stylish batsman who found the game so easy while his brother Chris, a fine wicket-keeper, worked so hard at both batting and keeping.

The late David Randall of Maldon C.C. was a lovely quiet guy who amassed hundreds of runs at youth level but appeared to lose interest in the game when he went to Cardiff University to concentrate on his musical talents. Tom Yallop was a fine batsman at youth level but hampered by a serious injury and Ollie Allen was another great prospect but decided to concentrate on football.

Of all the players Chris Swainland was the one I thought would make a professional career at the game. The best wicket-keeper I saw in my years as a coach and a pugnacious batsman. I'm still not sure why he didn't make it – perhaps like so many he wasn't around at the right time; luck is so important.

Current Essex players Ravi Bopara and Varun Chopra were also in the youth set-up when Robin was coaching and he's proud of their achievements.

> *Ravi always had something about him but I never thought Chopra would make a good county cricketer, he couldn't hit it off the square but he's a bloody good cricketer now. I still speak to them at the ground and they say "we had some terrific years with you Hobbsy", it's nice.*

Although he enjoyed the involvement, Robin wouldn't describe himself as a great coach but then he'd never been a great believer in coaching throughout his career. He found that having two-way conversations with the under-15s he worked with was the most effective way of developing them as players, discussions about field placings, quick singles and where slip should stand on a slow wicket, rather than coaching per se.

> *I'm not a great believer in trying to change things in players. If a guy's got natural batting ability and he hits the ball across the line so be it, or if a guy's got a natural bowling action and it's a peculiar action just let him bowl. I'm not a great one for altering anybody. I think it's been proved at Loughborough that so many people have had their actions changed and it can ruin them, it really can.*

When Terry Jenner was appointed to mastermind the search for an English leg-break bowler Robin was called in to help. The results were, however, very disappointing.

> *When you think of the money they've spent through the Brian Johnston Trust by getting counties to recommend leg spinners. I went on one in Guildford for two winters with these guys from all over the area to come and have nets with myself and Wasim Raja. They were very enjoyable, these lads used to come along, a group of about 18 who'd been recommended from Surrey to Hampshire. They spent quite a lot of money, this was all under the guidance of Terry Jenner who organised it because he was going to find the next leg spinner to play for England. A lot of investment was made and the top two were picked out at the end of each winter to go to Jenner's camp in Adelaide. But did Jenner find a leg spinner to play for England?*

Perhaps it was the simplicity of Robin's approach that made him something of a hand's-off coach. Having developed his own method he was cautious of trying to change that of others. He had respect for how others went about their business without wanting to emulate them.

I never styled myself on anyone particularly, I've always had my own action, I've never copied anybody, I think each leg spinner is unique in their action, everybody's different.

I had basically a good solid action which I could revert back to if I got smacked for two or three fours. I used to think I could have a stock ball and bowl it; 'Right, I've been hit for two or three fours and I've varied my flight, but the time's come now subconsciously, let's get back to what we were doing, bowl three of four balls fairly quickly on middle stump just to get some control back.

Pat Pocock used to bowl six different balls an over. Ray Illingworth was a guy who just bowled off spinners on the spot all the time and an arm ball, that's all he did, he tied them down, he never varied it much, he just bowled and bowled waiting for the batsman to make a mistake, he didn't vary it at all.

Robin continued coaching until 2003 and he's pleased that this son Nick is now involved in the Essex youth system. "He's got a great manner with the kids, far better than I probably had," says Robin, "he's a lot younger than I was but he works hard down there, gets on with all the kids and he thoroughly enjoys it. He continues doing something that I got a lot of enjoyment from and I'm delighted for him."

Retirement from Barclays gave Robin the chance to start watching County Championship matches regularly again as a fan, something he'd enjoyed so much in his youth when he'd head off to Ilford or Brentwood to watch his boyhood heroes. It had been over 20 years since he'd finished playing for Essex but there were still reminders on the field, just about, with Graham Gooch, the last of Robin's former colleagues, playing on until his retirement in 1997.

I enjoy watching Essex, I just enjoy the atmosphere. I know that some players when they finish playing hardly ever go and watch matches, but I love it. I'll go and watch any type of cricket, youth cricket, county cricket, I've always enjoyed it, I'm a cricket nut, a lot of the other ex-players enjoy golf but my main interest in the summer is watching cricket.

Robin is happy to sit at Chelmsford watching the day's play and hoping there's some good cricket on show, whether it's Essex or the opposition. "I'm not critical when I'm watching, there's a lot more pressure these days," he says reflecting on the 1960s when the county only had 12 paid players on the staff at one stage.

There was less pressure in those days mainly because you played so much cricket and also because you knew that you were going to bowl quite a number of overs in each game whereas poor old Mason Crane, when he does get a game he's probably thinking "I haven't played in Hampshire's first three games of the season now they've given me a game in the fourth and they're playing me at Essex on a wicket that's green, what am I going to do? How am I going to keep in the side? How am I going to get wickets to keep in the side for the next game?"

We didn't have that pressure. We just went from game to game knowing we were in the team; I was playing against Notts and next week I'm playing at Swansea, my place was never in jeopardy. There wasn't any pressure, you had pressure during a game when I'm bowling to so and so thinking crikey how am I going to get him out but not about thinking "Christ, if I don't get five wickets in this game I'm out on my ear", but they do now, there's so much less cricket with only 14 County Championship games these days.

Like all Essex fans Robin had been impressed by the county's resurgence of late.

Paul Grayson did a reasonable job but I think that after a few years you run out of ideas as a cricket coach. Ronnie Irani has come in and done a good job and the best thing Essex did was to get Chris Silverwood in as coach with Anthony McGrath as his assistant. Nobody ever thought for one minute, me included, that they would win the Championship in 2017, I thought they'd get relegated but to win 10 games out of 14 was quite incredible.

They're a tight-knit side. Silverwood made some big decisions during the year – James Foster wasn't in the side in the early stages of the season. Foster is every member's favourite, he's a bloody good player and he's fought his way back in. Silverwood made those decisions which some people weren't very happy with but it's proved successful and I wouldn't be surprised if they win the title again next season even now Silverwood has moved on because they've got such a good, settled side.

Alastair Cook's availability for the first half of the summer was a bonus and Robin feels that his presence and influence in the dressing-room combined with his heavy run scoring was a cornerstone of Essex's success. More significantly perhaps was the contribution of the bowlers. With the retirement in 2016 of club stalwarts David Masters and Graham Napier, Robin worried where they were going to find wickets in 2017. He highlights the significant contribution of Jamie Porter and Simon Harmer who finished as the leading wicket takers in division one of the County Championship. As a fellow spin bowler he's particularly appreciated the efforts of the South African off spinner Harmer who has seemingly committed his long-term future to the county. "The signing of Harmer as a Kolpak player has been an outstanding success," enthuses Robin. "He's a bloody good bowler. He does two things really well; he attacks when it spins, and when he has to contain he's able to do that job very well too."

The contribution of seamer Jamie Porter – who seemed set to give up the game in 2014 – has also been a major factor. "Porter has bowled his heart out," says Robin, "they can't get the ball out of his hands, he took 75 wickets which was a brilliant achievement."

The fact that many of the Essex players are local boys and have come up through the Essex system is a source of major pride to Robin and he beams as he draws parallels with the old Essex sides of the past.

> It's great that two lads from my old club Chingford – Porter and Lawrence – have made such an impact this season. It's like the old days when we had guys like Lever, East, Fletcher, Acfield, Gooch and Pont. It creates a great deal more interest for local clubs because you'll get people from South Woodford cricket club come along to watch Nick Browne bat, more people come because they're local guys. Some counties have signed far too many Kolpak players and you really do wonder what they're doing with their academies; they want instant success but you don't get that. Essex's policy over the last 20 years has been first class and in the wings they've got some really talented youngsters at 17 and 18 years old who could get into that side now. I don't know where they're all going to go. Essex to me now look like Yorkshire of old where players might have to leave the county to play first-class cricket.

Robin had himself very nearly left the county before Trevor Bailey stepped in and signed him for Essex in 1960. Bailey very much took him under his wing and acted as his mentor and for that Robin says he owes him everything. Tragically, Bailey died at the age of 87 in a fire at his home in Westcliff in February 2011. A memorial service was held in May that year at Chelmsford Cathedral and Christopher Martin-Jenkins, a former BBC Test Match Special colleague, was among those who delivered eulogies in Bailey's honour. Robin, sitting amongst the many hundreds of people in the cathedral, felt a tingle as he recognised a familiar story which Martin-Jenkins began to recount about a meeting between the two former Essex players. "I was waiting in the car park before the service," he remembers, "and I was telling this story about Trevor to some people when CMJ came over having heard part of it so I told him the story although I never expected him to repeat it, especially not in front of hundreds of people just a few minutes later."

Martin-Jenkins revealed that the last time Robin had seen Bailey before he died was at Westcliff Cricket Club, Bailey's beloved ground just across the road from his house. Robin had gone there to watch his local club who were playing against Westcliff. When he arrived somebody from Essex radio told him that Trevor was upstairs in the pavilion and that he'd like to see him. He went up to the first floor and could see Trevor, immaculately dressed, sitting at the window and staring ahead at the game. He sat down next to him, said "Good afternoon" and Bailey returned the greeting, "Good afternoon old boy." There was an awkward silence. Robin, unsure what to say next brought up a subject he knew was dear to both their hearts and asked Bailey about the leg spinners he had encountered in his time. Robin was well aware that Bailey had been a pupil at Dulwich College, where his cricket coach had been Father Marriott who'd played one Test match for England in 1933 and taken 11 wickets with his leg-break bowling.

"I was at Dulwich and Father Marriott used to bowl at me for hours and hours in the nets, that's why I was such a good player of leg spin."

"Tell me about Bruce Dooland" asked Robin.

"He had a perfect action."

"Roly Jenkins, he was pretty good wasn't he?" enquired Robin.

"Good bowler Roly" said Bailey, who still hadn't realised that he was talking to his former county colleague and protégé.

Robin went through all the leg spinners he could think of, Eric Hollies and Doug Wright, before moving the conversation on to Essex bowlers.

"We've had a few good leg spinners at Essex haven't we?" said Robin.

"Oh yes, Peter Smith, he was a wonderful bowler, he could put it on the spot."

"Anybody else?" asked Robin, certain that at any moment Bailey would recognise him.

"Oh yes, a chap called Bill Greensmith."

"Did we have anyone after that?" said Robin knowing full well that he had succeeded Greensmith.

"No, we never had anybody else after that."

Martin-Jenkins' retelling of the story brought the house down. 'Christopher was so gifted as a speaker', says Robin, "he'd only heard the story a few minutes earlier but there he was telling it to a Cathedral full of people."

Sadly two other key figures from Robin's time at Essex, Brian Taylor and Doug Insole, passed away during the Championship winning summer of 2017; they would have enjoyed the county's triumph – the first since 1992 – as would Bailey whose work to secure a permanent home for the county helped put in place the foundations for success in later years.

Robin can be found on match days watching Essex at Chelmsford, the same cricket nut he was as a boy supporting the county in the 1950s. He's one of the few ex-players who goes regularly (not to the T20) and at the four-day matches he's very much part of the furniture at the ground and on any given day he'll get around half-a-dozen people greet him and remark how they enjoyed watching him bowl for the county.

There are quite a lot of people who still remember, which I am surprised about, but they're getting fewer and fewer obviously. A number of them still bring up the Australian match when I got the hundred, if there were that many people who saw me get it there must have been 20,000 in that day.

The hundred against the Australians in 1975 is understandably what many people remember Robin for and it was a fitting end to his time with Essex, entertaining the crowd in his last home appearance for the county. Robin however considers the highlight to be his career milestone. "I regard myself having been very lucky to be the last English leg-break bowler to get a thousand wickets. Ian Salisbury just missed out."

In his match report in *The Times* Alan Gibson had stated that 'No other leg-spinner, I am afraid, will do it again' – more than 40 years later his bold prediction is still standing firm. Ian Salisbury finished his career with 884 wickets and at the end of the 2017 season, Adil Rashid had 490. Rashid's decision to focus solely on white-ball cricket in 2018 makes the possibility even more remote. Robin appears destined to retain the honour aided by the reduction in the number of county games being played. Although heartened by what appears to be a renaissance of leg spin in the English first-class game, he remains sceptical about the long-term prospects.

I'm a little bit optimistic with players like Adil Rashid, Mason Crane and Matt Parkinson around but then you've got others like Max Waller at Somerset who mostly only plays in their T20 side and Will Beer of Sussex is another who's hardly played a dozen county games. I was lucky to be brought up in an era where we played 28 county games, the universities and the tourist games. Crane will be lucky if he bowls 200 overs in first-class cricket a season. The ECB sent him off to Australia in 2016/17 saying that's the only way he'll learn by bowling overseas because they don't play enough here. He didn't play in the first three matches of the 2017 season, and there are only 14 matches a season now, how's he going to learn if he isn't playing?

I think it's so hard to play county cricket as a young spinner these days, it's become virtually impossible unless you can bat and field well too. There has been a resurgence in leg-spin bowling but in my eyes not in the right way. They're getting wickets in T20 matches but I can't see any county persevering with a young leg spinner, playing every game as I was so lucky playing for Essex in those days. It's a different age now.

Robin feels that in spite of a number of leg spinners now playing the first-class game in England there are many more playing in youth and club cricket who aren't being nurtured.

The most important person a young leg spinner will have is their captain. Quite often the most economical bowlers in limited-overs cricket are the spinners, their run-rate is less than the seamers but you get the impression that if he's been hit for two fours in two balls, they'll take him off and put the seamers on and he's forgotten. There are exceptions and I think there are captains who take a gamble but the majority of them have blinkers on, that's the way they play, they have no idea of how to set fields for leg spin. You've got to have an understanding captain. At Essex, I've seen so many leg spinners come through the age groups and then they finish at 16 or 17, go and play for their clubs and what happens to them then? They either disappear from cricket or they give up leg spin, not many carry on. Very few guys that I knew, and I knew a lot, still bowl leg spin in club cricket.

Against the odds, Robin was able to make a career as a leg spinner in the professional game but considers that he was fortunate. When he broke into the Essex side in 1961 the wickets were always green; tailor-made for Trevor Bailey, Barry Knight and the other seamers. In those first few matches he didn't turn the ball very much, he tried to be as accurate as possible and bowled fairly flat with the aim of staying in the side. He had the lucky breaks of the East Africa and Cavaliers tours in 1963/64 which gave him the belief that he really could bowl and get in the Essex side which he did regularly after that and his confidence grew. He began to spin the ball more as he got older and more experienced; by the time he was 30 he modestly admits that he had become "a reasonable bowler." In the early days of his Essex career, Mike Brearley suggests that Robin was doing what he needed to do to survive in the professional game.

'Hobbs always claimed that his captain wanted him to bowl like a slow left armer. The result was that he lost his ability to spin the ball sharply and became exactly what his captain wanted; he even drifted the ball in, like the left armer. But this may, in fact, have been his best chance of building a career, and surviving in a form of county cricket which already included one-day matches. Possibly, too, Essex were never in his formative years powerful enough as a side to be able to afford a potential match-winner who was also quixotic and experimental.'

"He was a very tidy bowler," Brearley says, reflecting on his *The Art of Captaincy* quote, "I'm just not sure how good he could have been if he'd been encouraged to be a more attacking leg spinner." John Arlott held a similar view, lamenting that Robin 'often seemed to lack only a fraction more confidence to dominate instead of concentrating on accuracy.' Robin did build a career in the game, a successful one at that, going on to win seven England caps, although he wasn't able to fulfil the level of expectation heaped on his shoulders early in his career by the likes of Richie Benaud, Keith Miller and EW Swanton in what Brearley refers to as "a romanticization of the leg spinner." According to Robin, the "old school" had seen leg spinners all their lives and they wanted one in the side, "I was the only one around," he says, "so they plumped for me."

I had an ambition to play for England but never thought I was good enough to play Test cricket and when I did and had a run of four games on the trot I thought I was very lucky to have that quite honestly, I could just as easily been a one-Test wonder.

I don't think I was hard done-by by the England selectors, I was glad I was given a chance. Once Derek Underwood came on the scene, with him bowling on uncovered English wickets it was no contest as to who you'd pick. Off spinners came into it too like Pocock and the two established off spinners, Fred Titmus and David Allen, so I never had any pretensions of ever being a regular Test cricketer.

If you're playing the odd game – I know I had a bit of a run under Close in 1967 but other than that they were just one-offs – you don't feel really part of the team. You're not a regular, you're just thrown in. I think it's different nowadays, the side really picks itself with central contracts. It was a different era back then, you walked into the dressing rooms, and I knew most of the guys, Barrington, D'Oliveira, Boycott; everybody was there for one thing, to do well for themselves, you didn't have a manager as such to lay down the law about how you played, you just went out as an individual; it was a different ball game.

I always thought I'd go on tours because the wickets suited me better – they bounced more – and I'd be good enough to go as a 12th because I was a good fielder. I was a very popular tourist too mainly because I was a happy-go-lucky guy, I always enjoyed a drink and organising parties. I was quite happy being 12th man – looking after the lads with their salt tablets and their various whims, making sure that their gloves were dry or whatever.

Robin considers that he was lucky enough to be around at the right time and to go on the MCC tours that he did, he never really considered himself a Test-class player, simply a decent, average county cricketer. 'No, I'd disagree with that completely,' says John Lever without hesitation.

'I rated him a lot higher than that, he's a very modest man. He was a complete entertainer, one of the best cover fielders I've ever seen, he had a great pair of hands. He was a far better than average county cricketer, far better than that. I think he plays down the fact that he was a way better than average leg-spin bowler, he really was. I know it was a long time ago but I see some of the bowlers today and I think Hobbsy was as good, if not better, than some of those and I think had England picked him on the right trips he could have ended up with more Test wickets and more tours than he actually did. But they were very much a luxury, it wasn't really until Warne came along that we realised – the cricketing public realised – how much of a match-winner leg spinners can be.'

"Robin is very modest about having played for England, dismissing his achievement as mere luck, thoughts which could be referred to as imposter syndrome. It's so difficult to separate confidence and sheer ability," says Mike Brearley, "someone like Shane Warne strutted the cricket field, he owned it, Test cricket was his stage. He was a brilliant bowler of course but he was even better because of his confidence and his personality and I don't think Robin was like that, he was a bit self-effacing and self-questioning." Robin was undoubtedly a better player than he gave himself credit for but perhaps ultimately lacked the self-belief, desire and drive to succeed at Test level. His overall Test analysis of 12 wickets at 40.08 is disappointing at first glance; most of his bowling was against Indian and Pakistani players well used to facing spin, but he kept it tight and tidy throughout (except for Headingley 1971) with an economy rate of 2.23. There were also those crucial dropped catches.

I suppose in a lot of ways I was most happy getting picked for tours but I didn't really want to play in Test matches, I was quite happy to play up-country against the Windward Islands or Border or Griqualand West, and to be a tourist enjoying the good things of life knowing if I went on the field I'd be the best fielder on the team but as for actually bowling against the likes of Barlow and Pollock and all those I probably thought "Oh no, I don't fancy that at all", no, I was quite happy running around with salt tablets and towels and things.

I got some of the greats out at Scarborough but you can't count that, it was played in such a different spirit. I got some of the best players in the world out there, caught at mid-wicket, caught on the boundary or stumped, that wouldn't happen in a Test match. I didn't have any fear bowling against the best batsmen, it didn't worry me but I didn't think I was good enough. I always thought they were better players than I was a bowler.

Robin is as much in love with the game as he's ever been, the ground at Chelmsford is like a second home to him in the summer as it is for many of the other diehards who are always there. One thought has, however, always puzzled him. "The minute the season finishes where do they disappear to?" he says perplexed. "The same as me I guess, the end of the season is like 'Oh my God, draw the blinds, what the f*** am I going to do for six months?' They must feel the same way."

Occasionally Robin will manage to get away from the winter gloom and South Africa has always been a favoured destination. A recent visit in early 2017 resulted in him bumping into Geoffrey Boycott whom he hadn't seen for a few years. It gave him the opportunity to reminisce with his former England team-mate and to mischievously bring up the subject of Boycott being dropped by England in 1967 knowing full well that Doug Insole had also recently been in South Africa and had attended the same Test match against Sri Lanka at Newlands.

> *"We got chatting and I said to Geoffrey, 'Did you enjoy the Test match here earlier in the winter?'"*
>
> *"Aye, I really enjoyed it."*
>
> *"Did you enjoy Doug's company?" Robin innocently enquired.*
>
> *"Don't talk to me about Insole" Boycott replied tetchily "They should have spelt his name with an A, he dropped me for getting 246 not out at Headingley."*
>
> *"I know, I was there", replied Robin.*
>
> *"Did you play in that game?"*
>
> *"Yeah, you batted too slowly", said Robin, barely able to conceal a wicked smile.*
>
> *"I got two hundred and forty f***ing six and he dropped me!"*
>
> *"You should have got them a bit quicker Geoff", suggested Robin.*
>
> *"But I was playing for the side lad", pleaded the hard-done-by Yorkshireman, "I was playing for the side."*

It's not uncommon for Robin when he's at home in Essex during those long, dark winter months to reminisce about some of the games he played. Often he'll reach for an old copy of *Wisden*, prompted by the thought of someone he used to play with or against and look them up and some of the games they played in.

Some players struggle to recall games in which they scored a hundred but Robin can summon up virtually every match. He can pick up a *Wisden*, look up a game and remember whether he bowled well or not, irrespective of how many wickets he got.

At the Essex games he attends these days Robin will still get one or two people come up to him and ask for his autograph and he's still as accommodating as Martin Douglas remembered him to be back in his beloved Scarborough Festival days of the 1960s. For many Essex spectators though, unaware of who he is, he's just one of them, a fan, there to enjoy the summer game. One might never realise that this unassuming old boy had played so many games for the county; Essex never won anything at the time but they were fun to watch and he was one of the reasons why. Those who were lucky to play with, or against him, won't forget his effervescence in the field, his improvised batting or his skill with the ball; neither will those who had the pleasure of watching him. Colin Cowdrey said that Robin was successfully able to combine attacking cricket with a twinkle in his eye and it was this spirit which made him so popular. 'He was great crowd-pleaser,' according to Doug Insole, 'well-liked by friend and foe as any player in first-class cricket that I can remember, and when he shone, with the ball, bat or in the field he was dynamic.'

Cricket has been his life since he was a boy and it's been good to him. Twenty years of doing a job he loved so much, lifelong friends and travelling the world – usually at MCC's or someone else's expense. How would Robin like to be remembered? Simply as someone who really enjoyed the game. That much would be obvious to anyone who knew him; from team-mates he played with over the years, to the spectators he entertained at Scarborough, Chelmsford – and the many grounds which hosted the Essex circus – to Lahore, Cape Town and Kingston. For those fortunate enough to have been there at the time, it was never dull when Hobbsy was on the field.

Robin's Best Essex XI

Selection is based on players Robin played with during his career with Essex. Total first class records for Essex CCC are included.

Graham Gooch
Played: 1973-1997. First class matches: 391. Runs: 30701. HS: 275. Av: 51.77. Centuries: 94. Fifties: 143. Wickets: 200. Av: 32.70. BB: 7-14. 5wi: 3. Ct: 386.
One of the finest batsman Essex have ever had, somebody who was always way above everybody else. When I first met him he looked as if he was going to be one of the great players of Essex cricket and England and it turned out to be so.

Brian Edmeades
Played: 1961-1976. First class matches: 335. Runs: 12593. HS: 163. Av: 25.91. Centuries: 14. Fifties: 61. Wickets: 374. Av: 25.90. BB: 7-37. 5wi: 10. 10wi: 1. Ct: 105.
People often forget him but he was a fine all-rounder, he was a bit lazy about bowling. I thought he could have played for England at one stage but he was one of those laid back guys but he made himself into a very good opening batsman.

Keith Fletcher (captain)
Played: 1962-1988. First class matches: 574. Runs: 29434. HS: 228*. Av: 36.88. Centuries: 45. Fifties: 176. Wickets: 29. Av: 43.72. BB: 5-41. 5wi: 1. Ct: 519.
Led Essex to so many trophies, a fine player of spin bowling. A legend in Essex cricket and my choice as captain.

Lee Irvine
Played: 1968-1969. First class matches: 54. Runs: 2674. HS: 109. Av: 34.72. Centuries: 1. Fifties: 15. Wickets: 1. Av: 70.00. BB: 1-39. Ct: 40.
He was with Essex for two years. A tremendous talent, if South Africa hadn't been banned from Test cricket he would easily have played for them for ten years or so with the likes of Barry Richards and Mike Procter. Lee was a great competitor, a tremendous lad to be around with. A great number four and a bloody good 'keeper.

Ken McEwan
Played: 1974-1985. First class matches: 282. Runs: 18088. HS: 218. Av: 43.37. Centuries: 52. Fifties: 82. Wickets: 4. Av: 75.25. BB: 1-0. Ct: 197.
I didn't see a great deal of Ken, I retired just after he joined the staff but he was an undoubted talent, one of the most graceful batsmen Essex have ever had. He was one of those guys who if he got a nought or a hundred he was still the same if

he got out, he'd come into the dressing room, put his bat down and he'd light up a cigarette. A very quiet South African, there's not many of those about!

Barry Knight
Played: 1955-1966. First class matches: 239. Runs: 8798. HS: 165. Av: 24.64. Centuries: 8. Fifties: 46. Wickets: 761. Av: 22.55. BB: 8-69. 5wi: 39. 10wi: 8. Ct: 171.
A terrific all-rounder who left us unfortunately to go to Leicestershire. He was a very fine player of most bowling except quick stuff, he didn't fancy quick bowlers too much but he was a bloody good bowler.

Keith Boyce
Played: 1966-1977. First class matches: 211. Runs: 6848. HS: 147. Av: 22.75. Centuries: 3. Fifties: 37. Wickets: 662. Av: 23.72. BB: 9-61. 5wi: 30. 10wi: 6. Ct: 181.*
Without doubt one of the best allrounders I've ever seen, a tremendous bowler, hit the ball remarkably hard and was a fantastic fielder anywhere that he was placed. He had a great physique and would have made so much money playing IPL cricket were he around today.

Brian Taylor (wicket-keeper)
Played: 1949-1973. First class matches: 539. Runs: 18240. HS: 135. Av: 21.92. Centuries: 9. Fifties: 78. Wickets: 1. Av: 21.00. BB: 1-16. Ct: 1040. St: 191.
One of the nicest guys you could ever wish to meet, he led from the front and he expected all the players to wear their blazers at all times at lunch and tea time, he did have his priorities right in that respect.

Trevor Bailey
Played: 1946-1967. First class matches: 482. Runs: 21460. HS: 205. Av: 34.50. Centuries: 22. Fifties: 119. Wickets: 1593. Av: 21.99. BB: 10-90. 5wi: 91. 10wi: 10. Ct: 320.
There nothing much more I can say about him other than he was a wonderful allrounder for Essex and England. I owe a lot to him for my progress through the years he was captaining the county side.

Ray East
Played: 1965-1984. First class matches: 405. Runs: 7103. HS: 113. Av: 17.66. Centuries: 1. Fifties: 22. Wickets: 1010. Av: 25.54. BB: 8-30. 5wi: 49. 10wi: 10. Ct: 251.
Best left arm spinner not to play for England in my opinion, a country boy from the

start, came into Essex cricket virtually from playing village cricket for East Bergholt and made the place his own for many, many years. A tremendous comedian.

John Lever
Played: 1967-1989. First class matches: 443. Runs: 2830. HS: 91. Av: 10.17. Wickets: 1473. Av: 23.53. BB: 8-37. 5wi: 77. 10wi: 11. Ct: 160.
Played a lot of cricket through his life carrying injuries but he always played and gave it his best shot. A tremendous swing bowler with a wonderful record for Essex and England.

Twelfth man – Robin Hobbs
Played: 1961-1975. First class matches: 325. Runs: 4069. HS: 100. Av: 12.44. Centuries: 2. Fifties: 2. Wickets: 763. Av: 26.00. BB: 8-63. 5wi: 32. 10wi: 5. Ct: 222.
I'd be quite happy to come on to the field for a bit which I loved doing!

A Life in Cricket in Numbers

BOWLING

Season	Country	Overs	M	Runs	Wkts	Ave	5w/10w	Best
1961	England	239.2	58	659	23	28.65	-	3-6
1963	England	470.2	117	1365	32	42.65	-	3-59
1963-64	Uganda	7	4	14	1	14.00	-	1-4
1963-64	West Indies	102.2	12	381	16	23.81	1/-	5-69
1964	England	760.3	148	2342	81	28.91	4/2	6-73
1964-65	Sth Africa	316	103	796	27	29.48	-	3-24
1965	England	692.3	199	1752	75	23.36	4/1	6-30
1966	England	752.4	177	2268	88	25.77	7/2	8-63
1966-67	Pakistan	254	62	693	27	25.66	1/-	6-39
1967	England	922.4	268	2401	101	23.77	5/1	6-50
1967-68	West Indies	107.4	21	333	19	17.52	1/-	5-50
1968	England	757.5	194	1988	83	23.95	4/1	7-73
1968-69	Pakistan	20	3	71	2	35.50	-	2-71
1969	England	708.5	226	1760	73	24.10	2/-	5-52
1969-70	West Indies	77.3	17	269	15	17.93	1/-	6-82
1970	England	736	178	2183	102	21.40	5/-	7-59
1970-71	Pakistan	92.2	16	333	9	37.00	-	3-69
1971	England	604.4	131	1702	78	21.82	5/-	5-38
1972	England	483.5	114	1534	44	34.86	3/1	7-118
1972-73	Sth Africa	98.2	18	325	10	32.50	-	4-55
1973	England	464.3	112	1409	47	29.97	3/-	5-34
1973-74	Pakistan	80	8	339	4	84.75	-	2-110
1974	England	368.1	98	1061	34	31.20	1/-	5-73
1975	England	508.4	109	1428	43	33.20	1/-	5-108
1979	England	269.3	78	805	22	36.59	-	3-21
1980	England	113.3	27	414	8	51.75	-	2-58
1981	England	390.3	99	1151	35	32.88	2/-	5-67
	Total:	**10,399.1**	**2597**	**29,776**	**1099**	**27.09**	**50/8**	**8-63**

BATTING AND FIELDING

M	I	NO	Runs	HS	Ave	100	50	Ct
440	547	139	4942	100	12.11	2	2	295

TEST RECORD

Bowling:

Year	O	M	R	W	5w	10w	Best	Ave	SR	ER
1967	163.1	59	333	10	0	0	3-25	33.30	97.90	2.04
1968	28	3	78	2	0	0	1-34	39.00	84.00	2.79
1971	24	5	70	0	0	0	0-22	-	-	2.92
Overall	215.1	67	481	12	0	0	3-25	40.08	107.58	2.23

Batting:

Year	M	I	NO	Runs	HS	Ave	Ct
1967	4	5	3	26	15*	13.00	5
1968	1	1	0	2	2	2.00	1
1969	1	-	-	-	-	-	-
1971	1	2	0	6	6	3.00	2
Overall	7	8	3	34	15*	6.80	8

Acknowledgements

This book would not have been possible without the many hours Robin Hobbs spent with me recalling his life. It has been a privilege getting to know Hobbsy, record his memories and capture his story; I hope I've done him justice.

I'm indebted to a number of people who played with, or against Robin, as well as others who watched him from the boundary or the press box. It was an absolute pleasure to communicate with the following either in person, on the telephone or by email: David Acfield, Intikhab Alam, Dennis Amiss, John Barrett, Mike Brearley, David Brown, Neil Burns, David Constant, Bob Cunnell, Martin Douglas, Nigel Fuller, Tony Garnett, Quorn Handley, Brian Hardie, Alan Knott, John Lever, Andy Mack, Javed Miandad, John Murray, Malcolm Nash, Peter Parfitt, Pat Pocock, Alan Ponder, Brian Scovell, Peter Smart, Stuart Turner, Roger White, Alan Wilkins, John Woodcock and Ted Wright. I would also like to thank Graham Gooch for very kindly providing the foreword.

Most of the photographs used in this book are from Robin's personal collection but I would also like to acknowledge the help I've received from Roger White, Tony Garnett, and Tony Debenham, they have all been so kind in allowing me to use photographs from their personal collections. I'm also grateful to Dr Andrew Hignell at Glamorgan CCC who has provided help in tracking down photographs of Robin during his time with the county. The staff at Essex Record Office were very helpful and efficient in supplying reproductions of Essex CCC scoresheets for my research. I'd like to thank Colin Panter at The Press Association for his assistance and Peter Perchard and Ben Thornton for their help in supplying the Walter Lawrence Trophy photo. A thank you is also due to Tony Story who worked his magic to restore a number of photographs to their former glory.

I'm grateful to John Parke for help with obtaining material and memories from the late Doug Insole; Mike Davage, Tim Hardwicke, the late Ralph Dellor, Hugh Turbervill and Neil Robinson at the MCC Library have also all kindly lent their time, support, and, in the case of Abigail Saltmarsh, her digital voice recorder, thanks Abby!

As a first-time writer I have been very lucky to receive invaluable help, advice and support from Stephen Chalke. Thanks also to the following for taking the time to read through various drafts and provide much appreciated feedback and suggestions: Karen Kelly, Caitlin Kelly, Paddy Kelly, Grahame Lloyd, Simon Woodhead, Peter Smart, Martin Douglas, Duncan Sears, Nick Hobbs, James Mettyear, Mark Taylor and Hannah Prince. A special thank you to Patrick Ferriday for taking the book on and knocking it into shape, I feel honoured to have become part of the Von Krumm stable.

I'd like to thank my parents - Chris and Val Kelly, Liz Gwyther, Gill Leeder, Fran Cox, Leanne Kendrick and friends at Horsford Cricket Club who have all offered ideas and support along the way.

Finally, thank you to Karen, Caitlin and Paddy for all the encouragement; I couldn't have done it without you.

Bibliography

Amiss, D. and Carey, M. (1976). *In Search of Runs: An Autobiography*. London: Stanley Paul.

Bailey, T., ed. (1976). *John Player Cricket Yearbook 1976*. London: Queen Anne Press.

Bailey, T. and Trueman, F. (1988). *The Spinners' Web*. London: Willow Books.

Barker, J.S. (1969). *In the Main: West Indies v M.C.C. 1968*. London: Sportsmans Book Club.

Bateman, C. (1993). *If the Cap Fits*. London: Tony Williams Publications.

Boycott, G. (1987). *Boycott: the Autobiography*. London: Macmillan.

Brearley, M. (1985). *The Art of Captaincy*. London: Hodder and Stoughton.

Brooke, R. (1991). *A History of the County Cricket Championship*. Enfield: Guinness Publishing.

Butt, Q. (1968). *The Oval Memories: Pakistan Team's Tour of England 1967*. Rawalpindi: Qamaruddin Butt.

Chalke, S. (1999). *Caught in the Memory: County Cricket in the 1960s*. Bath: Fairfield Books.

Chalke, S. (2012). *Micky Stewart and the Changing Face of Cricket*. Bath: Fairfield Books.

Chalke, S. (2015). *Summer's Crown: the Story of Cricket's County Championship*. Bath: Fairfield Books.

Close, B. (1968). *The M.C.C. Tour of West Indies, 1968*. London: Stanley Paul.

Cowdrey, C. (1976). *M.C.C. The Autobiography of a Cricketer*. London: Hodder and Stoughton.

Debenham, T., Hiscock, P. and Lansdowne, G. (2010). *60 Classic Essex Matches*. M Press (Media) Ltd.

D'Oliveira, B. (1980). *Time to Declare: An Autobiography*. London: J.M. Dent & Sons Ltd.

East, R. and Dellor, R. A Funny Turn: *Confessions of a Cricketing Clown*. London: George Allen & Unwin.

Fletcher, K. (1983). *Captain's Innings: an Autobiography*. London: Stanley Paul.

Fortune, C. (1965). *M.C.C. in South Africa, 1964-5*. London: Robert Hale.

Frindall, B., ed. (1985). *The Wisden Book of Test Cricket 1877-1984*. London: Queen Anne Press.

Frith, D. (1984). *The Slow Men*. London: George Allen & Unwin.

Gooch, G. and Keating, F. (1995). *Gooch: My Autobiography*. London: CollinsWillow.

Hartman, R. (2004). *Ali: The Life of Ali Bacher*. Johannesburg: Penguin.

Hayes, D. (1991). *Famous Cricketers of Essex*. Tunbridge Wells: Spellmount.

Hignell, A. (1992). *A Who's Who of Glamorgan County Cricket Club, 1888-1999*. Derby: Breedon Books.

Hignell, A. (1988). *The History of Glamorgan County Cricket Club*. London: Christopher Helm.

Hignell, A. (2005). *Summer of '64: a Season in English Cricket*. Stroud: Tempus Publishing.

Hill, A. (2003). *Brian Close: Cricket's Lionheart*. London: Methuen.

Hill, A. (2012). *The Valiant Cricketer: The Biography of Trevor Bailey*. Durrington: Pitch Publishing.

Jones, A. and Stevens, T. (1984). *Hooked on Opening*. Llandysul: Gomer Press.

Knott, A. (1985). *It's Knott Cricket: The Autobiography of Alan Knott*. London: Macmillan.

Lemmon, D. and Marshall, M. (1987). *Essex County Cricket Club: the Official History*. London: Kingswood Press.

Lemmon, D. (1994). *The Book of Essex Cricketers*. Derby: Breedon Books.

Lemmon, D. (1982). *'Tich' Freeman and the Decline of the Leg-Break Bowler*. London: George Allen & Unwin.

Lever, J.K. and Gibson, P. *J.K. Lever: a Cricketer's Cricketer*. London: Unwin Hyman.

McKinstry, L. (2005). *Geoff Boycott: a Cricketing Hero*. London: CollinsWillow

Milburn, C. (1968). *Largely Cricket: An Autobiography*. London: Stanley Paul.

Miller, D. (2004). *Born to Bowl: the Life and Times of Don Shepherd*. Bath: Fairfield Books.

Oborne, P. (2014). *Wounded Tiger: a History of Cricket in Pakistan*. London: Simon & Schuster.

Parkinson, J. (2015). *The Strange Death of English Leg Spin: How Cricket's Finest Art was Given Away*. Durrington: Pitch Publishing.

Peel, M. (1998). *Cricketing Falstaff: a Biography of Colin Milburn*. London: Andre Deutsch

Pocock, P. (1987). *Percy: the Perspicacious Memoirs of a Cricketing Man*. London: Clifford Frost Publications.

Powell, W. (2002). *Essex County Cricket Club*. Stroud: Sutton Publishing.

Quelch, T. (2015). *Stumps & Runs & Rock N' Roll: Sixty Years Spent Beyond a Boundary*. Durrington: Pitch Publishing.

Shindler, C. (2015). *Bob Barber: the Professional Amateur*. Nantwich: Max Books.

Snow. J. (1976). *Cricket Rebel: An Autobiography*. London: Hamlyn.

Titmus, F. and Hildred, S. (2005). *Fred Titmus: My Life in Cricket*. London: John Blake Publishing.

Underwood, D. (1975). *Beating the Bat: An Autobiography*. London: Stanley Paul.

Westcott, C. (2000). *Class of '59: From Bailey to Wooller: The Golden Age of County Cricket*. Edinburgh: Mainstream Publishing.

Woolley, T. (2015). *Unnatural Selection: 50 Years of England Test Teams*. Hove: Von Krumm Publishing.

Other printed sources:
The Cricketer
Playfair Cricket Monthly
The Times, The Guardian, The Sun, The Daily Mirror, The Daily Mail, The Daily Express, Jamaica Gleaner, The Cape Times, The Daily Telegraph, The Sunday Times, The Evening Standard, The Walthamstow Guardian, The Chingford Gazette
Essex County Cricket Club Yearbooks
Essex Cricket magazine
Essex Supporter
Glamorgan County Cricket Club Yearbooks

Online sources:
Cricinfo.com
Cricketarchive.com
Howstat.com.au
Test-cricket-tours.co.uk
YouTube.com

Picture credits:
Most of the photographs in this book are from Robin Hobbs' personal collection, but some appear by kind permission as follows: PA Images for the front cover, inside lead photo, pages 97, 135 and 164; Essex CCC, page 6; Walter Lawrence Trophy Limited, page 9; Tony Debenham, pages 50, 160 and 175; Roger White, pages 178, 206 and 209; Tony Garnett, page 188; Glamorgan Cricket Archives, page 197.

Index

A

B